the foodies' guide to melbourne 09

THE AGE

the foodies' guide to melbourne 09

**Allan Campion
Michele Curtis**

More than 450 butchers, bakers, food stores and chocolate makers

Hardie Grant Books

Contents

Introduction	vi
Foodies' awards 2009	viii
How to use this book	1

Asian food	2
Bread and cakes	9
Butchers	23
Chocolate	34
Coffee and tea	43
Delicatessens	51
Farmers' markets	58
Fine food stores	62
Fish and seafood	66
Greengrocers	73
Ice-cream and gelato	78
Indian and Sri Lankan food	83
Italian food	88
Kitchen equipment	95
Markets	100
Middle Eastern food	107
Organic food	113
Takeaway/traiteurs	118
Wine and beer	124
World food	129

Food experiences

BREAKFAST	20
BURGERS	32
CAKE DECORATING	16

COOKING CLASSES	**40**
DINING IN MELBOURNE	**132**
FISH AND CHIPS	**70**
FOOD TOURS	**103**
LATE-NIGHT MUNCHIES	**123**

Out of town

Mornington Peninsula	137
Yarra Valley and Dandenongs	140
Daylesford and surrounds	143
Geelong and Bellarine Peninsula	148
Great Ocean Road	152
Further afield	157

Regional food experiences

BREWERIES	**139**
DAIRIES	**142**
FARM GATES	**146**
FARMERS' MARKETS	**154**
FISH AND CHIPS	**151**
PIES	**160**

Maps	161
Store index	173
Locality index	180

Introduction

Welcome to *The Foodies' Guide to Melbourne 2009*, our annual compilation of the finest food stores in Melbourne and regional Victoria.

Each year as we head out to visit suburbs near and far we wonder exactly what we'll be faced with. What we've come to find is a food community that is incredibly dynamic. It is one where change now happens in a flash, it seems. Invariably there are stores gone out of business, others changed hands and a few simply gone off the boil. Our task is to walk every high street and shopping strip, to poke around in food stores, bakeries, delis, fishmongers, Asian grocers and the like, to direct readers towards the establishments we consider to be the best places to shop for produce and ingredients.

We have no doubts whatsoever that Melbourne retains its crown as the culinary capital of Australia. Every day, across the city, food stores, greengrocers, butchers and produce merchants open their doors to eager customers. Bakers stock their shelves with warm breads and sweet treats, fresh seasonal fruit and vegetables are trucked into our produce markets in huge quantities, while butchers prepare sausages, slice steaks and debone legs of lamb for the home barbecue. Chocolatiers fill display cabinets with cocoa-dusted truffles, raspberry-filled shells and chocolate bars studded with roasted hazelnuts. Fishmongers fillet and trim fresh fish ready for the pan, open oysters and display the sea's bounty for seafood lovers. Then there are bustling Middle Eastern, Italian and Spanish food stores, plus the hundreds of cafés, bistros and restaurants presenting meals for keen customers. All this combines to make Melbourne one of the world's great food cities.

Recently we have seen an amazing boom in the rise of quality food providores – the new kids on the block. These are intrepid souls who have decided to open the door on a new venture to see what local food lovers make of it. Arno Backes has established a delicious store called Ganache Chocolate in South Yarra and Port Melbourne residents are enjoying their wonderful deli/café called Eurodore.

There have also been some serious renovations at Melbourne's fresh produce markets. Queen Victoria Market now has a state-of-the-art fish and meat hall, while South Melbourne Market boasts a brand new food shopping aisle, which rivals the best food halls.

We also note a terrific resurgence in the French food scene around town. It's never been better with wonderful places such as Filou's, Le Croissant, La Tropezienne and Le Petit Gateau for stunning patisserie, La Parisienne Pates for smallgoods and Monsieur Truffe for wonderful chocolate bars and flavoured truffles.

Finally we hope you enjoy exploring this wonderful food-obsessed city – with a copy of *The Foodies' Guide to Melbourne 2009* firmly in hand.

Allan Campion and **Michele Curtis**

Foodies' awards 2009

Each year we carefully choose retailers who we believe are worthy of extra recognition. This year we have highlighted a mix of people who have been in the food game for many years alongside some exciting newcomers. They are passionate food lovers who day after day open their stores and help make Melbourne the wonderful foodie capital that it is. Here are our award winners.

Damian Pike, Wild Mushroom Specialist, page 75

For over two decades Damien Pike has been providing his Prahran Market customers with the very best in specialist ingredients, including everything from baby Roma tomatoes to stunning asparagus and baby beans, not forgetting the wild mushrooms every autumn.

Ganache Chocolate, page 37

Ganache is a chocolate store and café all rolled into one delicious mouthful. Display cabinets are packed with oriental spice chocolates, peppermint-filled mint leaves and impressive patisserie. It's a terrific addition to the chocolate stores of Melbourne.

Hausfrau, page 13

Lucky Yarraville residents get to enjoy Hausfrau as their local bakery. From the mini lemon cheesecakes to the iced gingerbread hearts, this place is style and quality all the way. If only all suburbs could be blessed with a bakery as gorgeous as this one.

Il Dolce Freddo, page 80

The gelati here are the real McCoy, fresh seasonal fruit is churned with great skill into two dozen or so daily flavours. Rich styles such as rocher, chocolate and Snickers sit alongside fruit mango, passionfruit and coconut. What a decision to have to make!

John Cester Poultry & Game, page 28

When you want to choose from the best range of poultry and game in Melbourne, make a beeline for John Cester. It's all on offer here from the corn-fed drumettes and wings to the wild boar, emu, wild hare, rabbit and turkey.

Le Petit Gateau, page 17

This very glamorous addition to the CBD has so many good things on offer it's almost impossible to decide. Will it be the vanilla mille-feuille or the brownie and passionfruit chocolate gateau? Either way we can guarantee it'll be delicious.

Tartine, page 122

Jan Maskiell and her team still rule the roost of take-home food stores with beautifully prepared and presented dishes. It could be a Moroccan chicken tagine, Catalan chicken or a summer lasagne layered with mushrooms, mint, spinach and feta cheese. Yum!

OUT OF TOWN
Annie's Provedore, page 148

This place is enough to make anyone want a sea change with a relaxed beach vibe and terrific coffee and cakes. The range of food-to-go is extraordinary, perfect for those of us who may have had a hard day in the surf and need some help with dinner.

How to use this book

The Foodies' Guide to Melbourne is a list of food stores, wine stores and produce markets that we believe are the best in Melbourne. The chapters are arranged in alphabetical order and run from Asian food stores to world food stores, with butchers, delicatessens, Middle Eastern food stores and many, many others in between.

Maps can be found towards the end of the book that locate every store in metropolitan Melbourne. Each entry also has a Melway reference for when you need a little more detail. Two comprehensive indexes ensure ease of use, so you can search for the best food by store name, or by locality.

Although we double-check everything to the best of our ability, shops do inevitably close, move or change hands. Opening hours can change at the drop of a hat, so if you're thinking about visiting a store a little out of the way, it is best to phone ahead to make sure it'll be open when you get there.

In the Out of town chapter, we've also included a region-by-region pick of our state's best farmers' markets, bakeries, fruit farms and food stores.

Our biggest thanks go to the many dedicated foodies who own and operate fabulous food stores around Melbourne and regional Victoria. Without you there would be no *Foodies' Guide to Melbourne*.

Asian food

Asian food and cooking is a firmly entrenched part of the local food scene, as are the excellent food stores dotted across the city and suburbs where you can purchase every imaginable ingredient for whipping up all manner of Asian dishes. There are stores dedicated to specific cuisines such as Japanese, Korean and Indonesian as well as superstores with a huge array of ingredients that allow keen cooks to prepare Chinese, Thai, Vietnamese and Indonesian meals. These stores also offer amazing value for money with many items in bulk such as rice, noodles, soy sauce (don't miss the Kim Vee Wong brand soy), plus great brands way beyond the local supermarket offerings. In fact, a shopping trip to a good Asian grocer can set you up for weeks of terrific cooking.

AKK Supermarket

AKK really is a 'super' market in the best sense of the word. Situated in the cool confines of the Springvale Central Shopping Centre, it has a good array of ingredients and brands without offering aisle after aisle of choice. The staff always seem approachable too, so if you're heading in with a long list of ingredients don't hesitate to ask for advice. Fresh ingredients are at the front of the store – there's a huge selection of Asian greens and vegetables to add to stir-fries, plus herbs and tropical fruit including lychees and mangoes in season. Dried noodles, soy sauce, peanut oil and rice are on hand in quantities large and small. There is also tea from jasmin to green, plus exotic flavoured drinks such as sugar cane juice and winter melon.

SPRINGVALE
Shop 18–21, Springvale Central Shopping Centre, 268–274 Springvale Road
9540 3618
Daily 9am–6pm
Melway 79 K9
Map page 169

Emma's Seafood Yong Tofu

These stores are a treasure trove of ready-to-cook Asian foods. Shoppers have a choice of fresh or frozen yum cha – fresh to use within a day or two and frozen to stock up the freezer at home. Browse through the many different choices including pork, prawn and chicken wontons, curry puffs and dim sim in numerous flavours, not forgetting pork balls and fish balls, plus thickly sliced pork and beef. There are also spring rolls, dumplings, wontons and excellent buns that are steamed to serve. Shoppers can pick up frozen seafood, such as scallops and prawns. There are also Japanese nori snacks, interesting ice-creams, and even fruit spring rolls and red bean dumplings. **Also at:** 31 Leeds Street, Footscray, 9687 7011; 3A Windsor Avenue, Springvale, 9558 5981.

BOX HILL
576 Station Street
9890 0818
Mon–Sat 9.30am–6.30pm;
Sun 11am–5pm
Melway 47 D9
Map page 171

Great Eastern Food Centre

The Great Eastern Food Store is set on Russell Street and is perfectly located to offer city commuters a place to shop on the way home. It's well lit, well presented and filled with virtually everything you could need for Asian cooking. Wander the wide aisles and you come across all manner of good things: spices and spice blends for mild curries and stir-fries, noodles and rice of all varieties. There's chilli sauce from mild to extra hot, black bean, hoi sin and plum sauce to add flavour to home cooking, as well as a sizeable selection of fresh fruit and vegetables, fresh noodles and aromatic herbs. Great Eastern is also big on Asian snacks and cold drinks to service the needs of a large contingent of ex-pat students from RMIT and Melbourne University.

CITY
185 Russell Street
9663 3716
Daily 10am–11pm
Melway 1A Q4
Map page 162

Huy Huy Supermarket

Huy Huy offers a great opportunity to do a one-stop shop in Victoria Street, Richmond because it has a butcher shop, masses of fresh ingredients and aisles filled with Asian essentials. The meats range across the classic Chinese cuts of pork, beef and chicken – beef shin, pork belly and boiling chickens are strongly featured here. Browse the aisles to pick up essential kitchen condiments – coconut milk in a variety of brands and styles, fried and dried noodles, rice paper wrappers and bean curd in its many guises. The fresh produce is probably the best selection on Victoria Street. Browse through the excellent greens, fragrant herbs, tropical fruit and myriad vegetables – everything from wonga bok to bean sprouts and wing beans.

RICHMOND
Shop 11, 240 Victoria Street
9429 0221
Daily 8am–8pm
Melway 2G K1
Map page 166

Indomart Asian Grocers

If you need to stock up on your favourite Indonesian ingredients, look no further than Indomart Asian Grocers. From sauces and spice pastes, to noodles and pickles, the shelves are groaning with everything you may need for an Asian feast. The friendly staff are always ready to assist and offer their advice on the best products for your needs. Fresh ingredients also feature, with delicious Asian greens, a great variety of fruit and vegetables, and a nice selection of fragrant freshly cut herbs. Indomart also offers a fantastic range of products from Korea, Japan, the Philippines and China. There are noodles, soy bean pastes, tofu and delicious Asian treats. If it's rice you're after, then the window display here is sure to satisfy.

HAWTHORN
739 Glenferrie Road
9818 8507
Daily 10am–9pm
Melway 45 D9
Map page 167

KFL Supermarket

KFL is an extraordinary shopping experience – it's like mixing a modern local supermarket with a top Asian grocery. Shoppers can grab a trolley and wander aisles stocked with everyday ingredients and Asian ingredients. Sauces are assembled together – everything from chilli paste and char sui sauce to soy and tamari. The range continues across items such as salted duck egg, frozen durian, bamboo shoots, fresh watercress and dried mushrooms. Fresh meat includes pork, beef, chicken and goat. There are also cooking utensils on hand. The range of chilled, ready-to-cook foods is impressive too, with barbecue pork buns ready to heat and serve. As these stores begin to spread further afield, we will be able to enjoy even more Asian food.

FOOTSCRAY
176–180 Barkly Street
9687 4855
Mon–Sat 9am–7pm;
Sun 9am–6pm
Melway 2S F8
Map page 163

Korea Kimchi Grocery

Most of the Asian grocers around Melbourne stock a bit of this and a bit of that; they skip across cuisines picking out the most popular ingredients. Korea Kimchi Grocery is not one of those; instead, they focus on Korean ingredients with a smattering of Japanese food for good measure. That makes it a terrific place to shop for specialty foods such as spicy fermented cabbage (kim chi), which is served as side dish, hot pepper sauce, soybean sauces, sesame oil, spice mixes and dried vegetables. Alongside this are a host of different noodles (udon, rice noodles and vermicelli) and rice cakes. Tofu is big too, with soft, silken, firm, fried and spicy styles all on hand. You can even pick up cookware and dishes in which to serve your Korean-inspired feast.

FITZROY
161–163 Brunswick Street
9416 3438
Daily 10am–10pm
Melway 2C A9
Map page 164

Laguna Oriental and Indonesian Supermarket

Laguna offers a different shopping experience to the typical Asian grocery we might come across in Springvale, Footscray or Chinatown. Here the focus is on Asian snacks and drink with a selection of general foodstuff to supply the local student population with foods they're missing from home. The range is incredible: jellies in flavours such as mango, pineapple and coconut; shelf after shelf of peanut crisps, crispy fish, beef jerky, sesame snacks, rice crackers, wasabi peas and spicy peanuts, as well as Asian biscuits and crackers, sauces, chilli pastes and rice noodles. Instant meals such as two-minute noodles, instant curries and soup mixes all feature heavily, backed up with baby corn, bamboo, water chestnuts and tropical fruit.

HAWTHORN
772 Glenferrie Road
9818 5581
Daily 10am–9pm
Melway 45 D9
Map page 167

Maxim's Cakes

Maxim's bakery has long been one of Melbourne's foodie hot spots. We've been fans of this place for years – particularly if we time our visit just right to get an egg tart warm from the oven. They appear all through the day and their soft, sweet pastry combined with a just-set egg custard filling is hard to beat. There are lots of other sweet and savoury treats in store too. They do big business in snack foods throughout the day – the barbecue pork buns, curry puffs and chicken pies are all worth checking out. If you're after a sweet treat check out the red bean buns, walnut napoleon, macaroons and swiss rolls. Maxim's also does a roaring trade in special-occasion decorated cakes. This is a must visit place when you're in the CBD.

CITY
173 Little Bourke Street
9662 1980
Daily 9.30am–8.30pm
Melway 1B Q4
Map page 162

Minh Phat

There are two stores that carry the Minh Phat name – a small version alongside the Queen Victoria Market and a mega store off Victoria Street. No matter which one you choose you'll receive excellent service, advice and a top range of ingredients to choose from. Rice is available in many different varieties. Bottled sauces range from sweet chilli to soy, kejap manis, tamari and everyday tomato. Specialist products include palm vinegar, Chinese black vinegar and a good selection of Chinese cooking wines, palm sugar, tamarind, dried legumes and Japanese seasonings. Chilled and frozen foods extend from seafood and roti bread to noodles, gyoza and wonton wrappers. There is also a great selection of essential kitchen utensils. **Also at:** 2–8 Nicholson Street, Abbotsford, 9429 4028.

CITY
125–127 Therry Street
9328 3156
Daily 9am–4pm
Melway 2B C12
Map page 162

Nan Yang

Shopping at Nan Yang is a big experience. You don't just run in to grab a few things on the way home from work, its enormous size demands you walk the aisles and explore properly. There's plenty on offer for those who do just that, starting with woks, clay cooking pots, steamers, serving dishes and myriad kitchen utensils. Aisles are filled with exotic spices and spice blends: Sichuan pepper, cardamom pods, cinnamon sticks, cumin, coriander and dried chillies of varying intensity. There are masses of curry pastes too, ready for an instant dinner: Thai green and red, massaman and tandoori, as well as essentials such as chilli jam. There's also frozen seafood, fresh meat and poultry (even frozen crocodile meat), plus fruit, vegetables, herbs and greens to choose from.

SPRINGVALE
307–313 Springvale Road
9546 9756
Daily 8.30am–6pm
Melway 79 K9
Map page 169

O Mu Ro

This Church Street store is a combination of food-to-go as well as a top spot to pick up all the necessary ingredients for your Japanese cooking at home. There are good brands of soy and tamari on offer plus mirin and Japanese rice wine. If it's sushi you're keen to whip up then you'll be able to get your hands on sushi rice, nori sheets, wasabi, pickled ginger and even bamboo rolling mats. Pickled vegetables are offered alongside Japanese snack foods both sweet and savoury. The frozen-food section offers wafer-thin pork, beef and fish, as well as soy beans that are delicious steamed and served with a sprinkle of salt. If you really don't want to cook then order up big on gyoza dumplings, crunchy katsudon and sushi rolls.

BRIGHTON
9 Church Street
9591 0633
Tues–Fri 10am–7pm;
Sat 9am–5pm
Melway 67 D11
Map page 170

Suzuran Japan Foods

Suzuran is a welcoming and food-filled store just on the edge of bustling Camberwell. Two separate rooms are dedicated to Japanese food and cooking. The smaller is the ever popular kitchen where sushi lovers trek in day and night for their favourite selections. The larger space offers all you'll ever need to create Japanese food at home. Sushi rice is available in bags small and large, there's all manner of soy sauce brands, plus pickled ginger and wasabi. The extensive selection continues with rice wine vinegar, mirin and tofu. Fresh and frozen salmon and tuna are also here, along with ready-to-cook gyoza dumplings. You can even grab a few bottles of imported Kirin and Asahi beer to complete the meal. **Also at:** Shop 16/31 Chambers Street, South Yarra, 9804 7396.

CAMBERWELL
1025–1027 Burke Road
9882 2349
Tues–Thurs 9am–6pm;
Fri 9am–8pm;
Sat 9am–7pm;
Sun 10am–3.30pm
Melway 45 J10
Map page 167

Tokyo Deli

Elsternwick may not quite be the Japanese epicentre of Melbourne, but it sometimes feels like that at Tokyo Deli. The store always seems to be brimming with shoppers browsing the shelves, discussing ingredients with the helpful staff or picking up takeaway from the rear counter. It's had a renovation in recent times and is looking very smart indeed. There's all manner of soy sauces, vinegars, wasabi in powders and pastes, rice wine and pickled ginger in single serves and family packs. There are plenty of nori sheets and nori seasoning mixes, sushi rice and utensils for preparing sushi rolls at home. Japanese beer, plum wine and sake are also on hand. The takeaway counter is a local hot spot too with all the classic dishes available.

ELSTERNWICK
418 Glen Huntly Road
9523 6200
Mon–Sat 10am–7pm;
Sun 11am–4pm
Melway 67 G3
Map page 170

Highlight
ASIAN FOOD-STORE ESSENTIALS

A few essential ingredients to consider when you are next stocking up on Asian ingredients at one of the many food stores listed in this chapter.

Kara coconut milk or cream
This is an excellent-quality product and recently made widely available in a UHT pack. Use as much as you need, then freeze the rest.

Kim Vee Wong soy sauce
This has long been a favourite brand of ours. It's made with no preservatives, is 100 per cent brewed, and has a sweet and not too salty taste.

Fraternity brand rice paper wrappers
These are excellent-quality rice paper wrappers and Vietnamese made. Choose the large round wrappers as they are the easiest to use for beginners. Firm plastic containers protect them from breaking.

Maesri red curry paste
This beautiful paste is Thai made and can be recognised by the lady's face on the label. A beautiful mix of galangal, shallot, kaffir lime, dried red chilli, lemongrass and garlic, it creates the most fragrant, full-flavoured curries.

Amyson Chinese rice wine
Amyson comes in a dark glass bottle and has a very glam red label. Use it instead of water to add a little liquid to stir-fries.

E & C Japanese seasoned seaweed
Look for these twelve packs of long nori strips seasoned with soy sauce and spices. They're great for kids' lunchboxes.

Kinaee jasmine rice
This is a great value fragrant Thai brand of rice. It is available in 1 kg packs to 25 kg sacks.

Lungkow vermicelli noodles
Vermicelli noodles are essential parts of rice paper rolls and Asian salads. This brand's 50 g pack is a perfect size for home cooks. Simply place in boiling water to soften.

Tsukiji

Japanese food stores are often a combination of sushi shop, specialist supplier of ingredients and café all rolled into one. Tsukiji is all of this with a strong focus on fresh seafood. A chilled cabinet holds all kinds of prepared fish and seafood. Tuna, salmon, blue-eye, sea perch and king dory appear alongside ready-to-use foods such as sea urchin, salmon roe, oysters, crayfish and abalone. Besides fish there's also an excellent selection of ingredients such as sushi rice, wasabi, nori, pickled ginger, mirin and Japanese-flavoured ice-creams, plus sliced meats for sukiyaki and shabu-shabu. Customers can pick up prepared sushi packs and hand rolls ready to go or enjoy a quick bite to eat at the small café area at the rear of the store.

PRAHRAN
237 High Street
9510 2318
Tues–Fri midday–5pm;
Sat 10am–5pm
Melway 58 E6
Map page 166

Wing Cheong

Chinatown used to have many Asian grocers dotted around Little Bourke Street and the smaller lanes that run off it. Nowadays, this has been reduced to two main stores, the Great Eastern Food Centre (page 4) and Wing Cheong tucked away up Heffernan Lane. The range here is really terrific. Shoppers can pick up fresh pork, chicken and seafood, as well as all the Asian greens you could wish for. Fresh ingredients also extend across ginger, garlic, chillies and spring onions, as well as fresh vegetables and fruits. A select list of condiments covers soy, sesame oil, peanut oil, chilli sauce, fish sauce, soy bean paste and hoi sin. Noodles are extensive too with everything from mung bean vermicelli to flat rice noodles. Local Chinese language newspapers are also on hand.

CITY
2–4 Heffernan Lane
9663 1668
Daily 10am–9.30pm
Melway 1B Q4
Map page 162

Win Sam Groceries

The Kingsway shopping strip in Glen Waverley has become a terrific place to gather all the essential ingredients for Asian cooking. Win Sam is in fact a duo of stores – the second sells seafood and meat just up the street. The advice here is always topnotch, so don't be afraid to ask for help in finding ingredients. It's all on offer here with bean curd, fresh noodles and Asian greens – everything from bok choy and wonga bok to choy sum and tatsoi. Shoppers can also pick up fresh vegetables and Asian fruits, plus aromatic herbs. Shelves are packed with every imaginable sauce and paste to add flavour to your cooking – chilli, soy bean, lemon, hoi sin, black bean and so many more.

GLEN WAVERLEY
103–105 Kingsway
9561 0888
Mon–Sat 8am–9pm;
Sun 9am–7pm
Melway 71 C2
Map page 171

Bread and cakes

bread and cakes

Melbourne has a history of wonderful baking that stretches back to Paterson's opening its doors in Windsor in 1916, and later the arrival of continental cake shops such as Monarch, Le Bon and Europa in Acland Street, St Kilda. Today, this growth continues with a vast array of places to source top-quality bread, cakes and patisserie. There are so many in fact that this chapter is one of the biggest in this guide. Terrific sourdough bread is available from well-known places such as Baker D. Chirico, Dench, Phillippa's, Firebrand and Noisette to name just a few. If it's a beautiful cake you're seeking (and who isn't, really) then Hausfrau in Yarraville should be on your hit list, as should Aviv Cakes & Bagels, Let Them Eat Cake, Le Petit Gateau and Zimt Patisserie Bakery. Bakeries are also excellent spots to pick up a quick lunch when you're out and about around Melbourne.

Aviv Cakes & Bagels

Aviv Cakes & Bagels has long been a Foodies' Guide favourite. That's because we've never had a dud product over the years, the service is always excellent and the window display is always so good it'll entice you inside. There's a strong European heritage here and it's shown in the baked goods. Beautiful boiled bagels come in sizes from cocktail through to regular, plus there's a selection of bagels with a range of toppings. Still on the savoury side, don't miss the quiches and pies around lunchtime. For those with a sweet tooth, you're in the right place. Just try to choose between the delightful doughnuts, plum cakes and cherry tarts. There are also amazing baked cheesecakes, bubka ring cakes with a swirl of chocolate and one of the best vanilla slices in town.

ELSTERNWICK
412 Glen Huntly Road
9528 6627
Mon–Fri 7am–5.30pm;
Sat 7am– 2pm;
Sun 7am–1pm
Melway 67 G3
Map page 170

Babka Bakery Cafe

As the name suggests, Babka is a combo of bakery and café in one. This can make for a tight squeeze at rush hour, but the baked goodies on offer will make it worth the wait. Tall bakers' trolleys are filled with breads, so many it's hard to decide. Will it be the sunflower loaf, the vegetable bread or the much loved multigrain? The same applies to the sweet selection with beautiful things just dying to be enjoyed. There's gorgeous baked cheesecake, tall plum cake, ganache iced chocolate mud cake – plus the classic currant-filled, orange-flavoured shoo-fly buns. Decisions, decisions! Babka is also a great spot for lunch on the run with terrific pies and filled baguettes. Babka is a Brunswick Street classic. Long may it reign!

FITZROY
358 Brunswick Street
9416 0091
Tues–Sun 7am–7pm
Melway 2C B6
Map page 164

Baker D. Chirico

Daniel Chirico has created what many believe to be the perfect modern sourdough bakery. This means the breads are created in the true sourdough manner – hands on technique and long fermentation creating wonderful flavours and textures in each loaf. Customers can even get a good look through large windows at the bakery in action through the early morning and daytime. Favourite loaves include the wonderfully chewy, full-flavoured casalinga bianco, delicious rye loaf and the wholewheat with seeds. The fruit loaf is a beauty too, packed with apricots and dates, and the filled rolls each lunchtime are some of the best in town. If it's a sweet kick you need, then the fruit garibaldi could be just the thing, or the divine meringues, mini lemon tarts or vanilla custard doughnuts.

ST KILDA
Shop 3–4, 149 Fitzroy Street
9534 3777
Tues–Sun 7am–5pm
Melway 2P B4
Map page 170

Brioche

Brioche baker Philip Chiang made quite a name for himself at the Daimaru bakery not so many years ago. Now he rules the roost at his own place in Prahran. Brioche brings together a combination of French baking tradition and mixes it with Japanese baking. The results from this cross-cultural collaboration are here for all to see. The place has a terrific ready-to-eat sense about it with a large glass cabinet displaying treats such as chocolate brioche, cheese brioche and even black sesame brioche. There are also cheese scrolls, red bean buns and coffee glazed Danishes with flaked almonds sprinkled on top. Breads are offered too and include a dill, green chilli and garlic loaf, plus a multigrain bread made using wholemeal flour, rye, oats, brown rice and rice bran oil.

PRAHRAN
208 Commercial Road
9525 1966
Mon–Sat 8am–5.30pm;
Sun 8.30am–3.30pm
Melway 2L H9
Map page 166

Brunetti Cakes

It's hard to imagine Carlton without Brunetti's; it just feels as if it has always been there. The bustling store encompasses a large café area, gelaterias, bakery display room and coffee-central near the front windows. The daily pizzas and filled foccacias are excellent. The bakery display is always packed with stunning decorated celebration and wedding cakes, from black forest to baked ricotta cake. Smaller treats are always enticing too with mini custard-filled crostoli, coffee profiteroles, cinnamon dusted beignets and lemon tarts to name just a few. There's also the terrific City Square Brunetti's store, which has outdoor seating and an almost hidden dining space upstairs. One not to miss! **Also at:** City Square, 214 Flinders Lane, City, 9663 8085; 1/3 Prospect Hill Road, Camberwell, 9882 3100.

CARLTON
194–204 Faraday Street
9347 2801
Sun–Thurs 7am–11pm;
Fri–Sat 7am–midnight
Melway 2B G7
Map page 164

Daley at Chimmy's

Daley at Chimmy's is situated in a beautiful old building in Park Street, South Melbourne, and unlike many bakeries around town, space is not an issue here. This means customers can relax in-store and enjoy the great foods on offer. It might be a beautiful filled roll at lunchtime or perhaps a freshly made pie or a big pizza to share. Many of the breads here are made in the sourdough style, so you can be assured of great flavours, terrific crust and textures in the loaves. Choices include white, wholegrain and a particularly good 30 per cent rye loaf. Ciabatta is also available daily. Cakes and sweet treats are excellent here too and include sweet brioche, croissants, scrolls and mini lemon tarts with a beautifully zesty filling.

SOUTH MELBOURNE
276–278 Park Street
9696 7418
Mon–Fri 7am–5pm;
Sat 7am–4pm;
Sun 7am–3pm
Melway 2K A4
Map page 168

Highlight
BEAUTIFUL BREADS

Wholemeal, Baker D. Chirico, page 11
This stunning loaf is an absolute ripper. It has a nutty, moist and full-flavoured centre, and a terrific crispy crust. Try it as an open sandwich or to encase the best cheddar cheese you can fine in a toasty.

White casalinga, Irrewarra Sourdough, page 149
This is a classic pane casalinga-style loaf full of beautiful gutsy flavours and a superb crispy crust. It makes excellent open sandwiches and has good keeping qualities.

Pane francese rye, Phillippa's, page 21
What a wonderful loaf this is – earthy and beautifully textured with a moist centre and not too crisp crust. This is a loaf for all bread lovers.

Grain loaf, Dench Bakers, page 12
A beautiful loaf is a wondrous thing and this version is made with organic stone-ground wholemeal wheat flour, sunflower kernels, linseed and has a moorish nutty sesame seed crust.

Dench Bakers

Dench Bakers are based in the foodie pocket of Fitzroy North yet their loaves and reputation travel far and wide to selected retail outlets. Those lucky enough to get to the bakery will have the full range to choose from. Their breads have a depth of flavour, chewy texture and delicious crust, which can't be achieved without going down the sourdough route. The organic stone-ground spelt loaf is a great one for bread lovers to get their teeth into. The same goes for the house stone loaf and wonderfully nutty sesame seed coated grain loaf. The beautifully named raisin loaf makes the most delicious toast too. There's always a good selection of sweet things here too with brownies, bomboloni (doughnuts), blackberry frangipane tarts and old-fashioned hummingbird cakes.

FITZROY NORTH
109 Scotchmer Street
9486 3554
Daily 7am–5pm
Melway 30 B12
Map page 164

Fatto A Mano

It's a pretty big task to take over a popular bakery and to keep the regular customers coming back for more. Well husband-and-wife team Mario and Sandra Cucuzza have done just that at Fatto A Mano. Regulars are still flocking in for the delicious focaccias. Favourite flavours include potato and olive plus egg and bacon. Their calzone also make a great a lunch on the run. Popular sourdough breads here include pumpkin loaf, multiseed, honey and walnut. Also worth checking out are the Saturday-only Italian doughnuts (bomboloni), sugar-coated, sultana-studded balls of goodness and a real treat for doughnut lovers. Other sweet treats worth checking out here are the almond biscotti, the chocolate caramel peanut balls and handmade panforte each Easter and Christmas.

FITZROY
226–228 Gertrude Street
9417 5998
Tues–Fri 8am–6pm;
Sat 8am–3pm
Melway 2C C11
Map page 164

Filou's

There's a certain charm that comes with a bakery like Filou's. It's partially the intimacy of the building with its classic corner store feel and rustic verandah. But it's also the fact that the beautiful French foods on display have been made in the kitchen alongside the counter. Their baguettes, long crusty ones, are calling out to be filled with camembert and rocket. Golden croissants, raisin-filled escargot pastries, gorgeous mini white iced custard-filled éclairs and warm pan au chocolate are also essentials here. Food options through the day range from the beef and burgundy pies to quiche Lorraine. Sweet items are also here in abundance – classic treats such as tangy lemon tarts, orange and pistachio cakes, flourless chocolate cakes and scrumptious mini strawberry tarts.

CARLTON NORTH
cnr Lygon and Fenwick Streets
9347 4029
Tues–Fri 7am–6pm;
Sat 7am–5pm;
Sun 7am–3pm
Melway 2B H1
Map page 164

Firebrand Sourdough Bakery

Firebrand Bakery are one of the sourdough pioneers of the local baking scene. All the breads here are hand-shaped and baked in a wood-fired oven, which all adds to the resulting flavour. The bakery opens its doors at midday and breads begin appearing from the oven immediately. Wonderful breads on offer include the much-loved pane casalinga, sprouted wheat, light rye and the delicious white high top. There are a number of specialty breads made on specific days too. Check out the walnut bread each Wednesday and the crusty Parisian sourdough that appears on Fridays. Other special treats include pizza by the slice – the tomato, salami, basil and rocket version is especially good. There are also berry muffins, flourless orange cake and crunchy granola.

RIPPONLEA
69 Glen Eira Road
9523 0061
Mon–Thurs midday–6pm;
Fri midday–6.30pm;
Sat 9am–1.30pm
Melway 67 E1
Map page 170

Frank's Elsternwick Bakery

In times when glam bakeries are fitted out at huge expense, it's great to see Frank's sticking to a style that has seen them through three decades of great baking. It's just a simple counter here with racks of bread and the ovens from where it came at the rear. No more and no less. This simple approach hasn't stopped those who love Eastern European–style breads from patiently queuing for their turn. At the counter it's a choice between a classic rye loaf with the optional extras such as sunflower, caraway or sesame seeds. Don't miss the yeasty fruit buns and apple scrolls either, they're beauties. Frank's Bavarian pretzels and onion rolls are also worth a serious look. There are also pies, sausage rolls and pasties available each lunchtime.

ELSTERNWICK
291 Glen Huntly Road
9528 2380
Mon–Fri 6am–4pm;
Sat–Sun 6am–2pm
Melway 67 F3
Map page 170

Hausfrau

How lucky are Yarraville residents to have Hausfrau as their local bakery? It's beautifully decked out with huge floral lightshades, communal or individual tables, and comfy pale-blue banquettes. The extensive bakery selection ranges from delightful corn muffins and kranksy-filled sausage rolls to amazing sweet treats. There are ginger puddings with butterscotch sauce and mini lemon cheesecakes, fruit mince slice and iced gingerbread hearts. The display cabinet also features lemon meringue pie, hummingbird cake and a delicious black forest roulade filled with fresh cream and black cherries. Freshly baked breads are on offer too from Noisette and you can even grab a cone of Jock's ice-cream. If only all suburbs could be blessed with a bakery as gorgeous and delectable as this one.

YARRAVILLE
32A Ballarat Street
9687 8364
Tues–Fri 9am–5pm;
Sat–Sun 9am–4pm
Melway 42 A9
Map page 163

Hootsen's Bakery Conditorei

This long-running Malvern bakery has a great local following. Step inside the doorway here and you'll soon see why – the colourful array of chocolates, cakes, biscuits and breads on offer. As is often the case, the classic truffles are the biggest sellers from the chocolate display. Other lines include pralines and the wonderfully named nipples of Venus. There are lots of other sweet treats too, including Hootsen's own nougat, Turkish delight, strawberry tarts, vanilla slice, French apple flans and the delicious coffee éclairs. Gingerbread makes an appearance with mini iced cakes and gingerbread biscuits. There's also a good selection of shortbread, fruit scones, slices and muffins. Bread baked on-site includes wholemeal, salty-topped bagels and lots of different bread rolls.

MALVERN
179 Glenferrie Road
9509 1418
Mon–Fri 7am–6pm;
Sat 7am–3pm
Melway 59 B8
Map page 167

Il Fornaio

This much loved St Kilda institution looks more café than bakery after a refit, but it still has that semi-lit modern industrial concrete and metal interior we've come to know. Bread and cake lovers know to make their way up the steps to the food-filled counters. Here the impressive display can include crispy baguettes, pull-apart ficelli, sourdough loaves and filled rolls. Sweet treats are well presented too with chocolate cakes, raspberry cakes and a classic lemon tart. The lemon meringue pies and fruit-topped Danish pastries are worth a try too. A selection of fresh and frozen ready meals includes soups, casseroles, pastas, mousses and ice-cream. **Also at:** Shop 11, 459 Toorak Road, Toorak, 9827 2727.

ST KILDA
2 Acland Street
9534 2922
Mon 7am–6pm;
Tues–Sat 7am–10pm;
Sun 8am–6pm
Melway 2N K6
Map page 170

Il Migliore

This Hawthorn location is the production centre of Il Migliore with a retail store fronting onto the main kitchen. They are in the business of producing some excellent sweet and savoury food for delis and food stores far and wide. The benefit of coming directly to Il Migliore is the enormous range on offer. Absolute favourites include the dried apple sliced drizzled with toffee and the chocolate dipped orange slices. We assure ourselves there's a bit of fruit in here at least. Other classic sweet treats include almond bread, spice-topped crispy pita chips, Florentines, jam drops, yoyos and savoury cheese biscuits. There are also Asian woven baskets in which to gather products in-store and make a personalised gift basket. Their decorated Christmas cakes are much sought after too.

HAWTHORN
271 Auburn Road
9813 3440
Mon–Fri 9am–5pm;
Sat 9.30am–5pm
Melway 45 F12
Map page 167

Knead

This delightful bakery has quickly settled into its local area with a great combination of interesting breads, breakfast and lunch choices, plus handmade sweets and cakes. The welcome here is always with a smile, but then why wouldn't you smile when you're surrounded by beautiful food? The shelves offer a range of different bread from baby baguettes to sprouted wheat, walnut, ciabatta, light rye and seeded rye. There's also a large selection of gluten-free breads (and other baked goods) for those with wheat intolerance. The array of other baked-on-site foods covers olive and anchovy foccacias, pies, quiches and pasties. The sweet selection is enticing too with hazelnut and lemon macaroons, meringues, marshmallows and brownies appearing regularly.

HAWTHORN
396 Burwood Road
9819 5883
Mon–Fri 7am–4pm;
Sat 7am–2pm;
Sun 8am–2pm
Melway 45 E10
Map page 167

Highlight
FESTIVE TREATS

Chocolate pistachio truffles, Phillippa's, page 21
For an Easter treat with a difference check out these delicious truffles. They are a stunning combination of Belgian couverture and Victorian cream rolled in vibrant green chopped pistachios.

Panforte, Fatto A Mano, page 12
Panforte is a wonderful Italian cake that is perfect for Christmas feasts. It's a firm, spicy-style nut cake that is thinly sliced and served with sweet wine. Buy this terrific treat by the wedge.

Sour cherry relish, Richmond Hill Café & Larder, page 57
This is a brilliant accompaniment made with sour cherries and muscat. It is delicious with roast duck, turkey or pork with crispy crackling.

Mini mince tarts, Replete Providore, page 122
Each December sees Replete's mini fruit mince tarts appear. They have a terrific crisp pastry base and a well-spiced nutty fruit filling with a star top.

La Tropezienne

La Tropezienne has settled nicely into its home in Glenferrie Road. There's always a warm welcome from the owners and the store has a laid back Provençal feel to it. Regulars have come to love their early morning visits for coffee with a little something to go – perhaps a raspberry croissant or almond brioche. As the morning unfolds other treats appear such as tomato tarts, quiche Lorraine and filled baguettes. Baguettes filled with camembert, chicken or ham and cheese are lunchtime favourites. Sweet treats are in abundance too with bags of mini Florentines and tiny meringues to take home. There's also beautifully prepared fruit friands, coffee éclairs, fruit tarts both small and large, plus lemon and olive oil cake. This is an authentic French treat.

HAWTHORN
780 Glenferrie Road
9818 1895
Daily 7am–6pm
Melway 45 D9
Map page 167

Laurent Boulangerie Patisserie

The name Laurent Boulangerie Patisserie has a certain stylish ring to it and this extends right through these stores and their products. Glamorous French-style cakes and pastries include fruit or chocolate éclairs, pecan, lemon, passionfruit or apple and almond tarts, plus the decadent Christine cake, Valrhona milk chocolate mousse and crème brûlée. Laurent's chocolate custard doughnuts are very hard to resist too. Savoury items are well covered, from filled baguettes, tarts and quiches at lunchtime to ham and cheese croissant, beef or chicken pies and of course quiche Lorraine. The French-inspired bread range is worth a good look too. There are almost a dozen stores around Melbourne. Call head office on 9543 2900 to find your closest store.

CITY
306 Little Collins Street
9654 1011
Mon–Sat 8am–6pm;
Sun 9am–5pm
Melway 1B L6
Map page 162

Cake decorating

There seems little doubt we're in the middle of a cake decorating boom. You only have to look at the amazing decorated muffins in food stores to see this in action. This is our pick of the places around Melbourne where you can source all the essential tools for this delicious hobby.

Cake Deco
This packed store just off Flinders Street is home to what has to be the biggest range of cake-decorating utensils in town. There are more cake tins, chocolate moulds, decorating utensils and specialist utensils than you can imagine. This is backed up by ready-to-use decorations and icing mixtures to create edible decorations at home.
Shop 7, Port Phillip Arcade, 232 Flinders Street, City; 9654 5335; www.cakedeco.com.au; Melway 1B M9; Map page 162

Greensborough Cake Decorating Centre
Anyone interested in cake decorating will find inspiration here. There's every decoration, tool, utensil and accessory imaginable. Cake tins and biscuit cutters come in every shape and size; icing, food colouring, chocolate buttons, cake mixes and choux pastry mixes are on hand too. Plus, you'll find all the candles, ribbons and ready-to-use cake decorations you could ever want.
Shop 2–5, 93 Grimshaw Street, Greensborough; 9435 0515; Melway 20 S2; Map page 171

Marg & Maree's
Lovers of cake decorating and bread baking will find much to enjoy here. There are all manner of flours from wholemeal and rye to organic white. There are also mixes to create choux pastry, muffins and shortbread. A large range of courses are held regularly, covering every aspect of bread and cake baking.
54 Bell Street, Heidelberg Heights; 9455 1611; Melway 31 H4; Map page 171

Merryday
If you're a cake-decorating devotee then Merryday is a place you should know about. There are displays of cake stands, cake tins, cake frills and ready-made decorations. Merryday also have ready-to-use cake mixes, icings and fondant available. Whatever you're interested in, you'll find all you need here.
Shop 3, 1291 Nepean Highway, Cheltenham; 9583 0022; Melway 86 J1; Map page 169

The Mixing Bowl
There's everything you'll ever need for creative baking here in downtown Burwood. Shelves are lined with cake tins in every shape and size imaginable, baking utensils, and bags of chocolate in dark, milk and white. Classes at night are offered to accelerate your skills and covers topics as wide as bread making, biscuits, cupcakes and decorating.
1387 Toorak Road, Burwood; 9809 4327; Melway 60 G6; Map page 167

Susie Q Cake Decorating Centre
Susie Q offers cake-tin hire, hand-moulded sugar flowers and everything in between for the cake lover. There's also a full selection of piping bags, icings and all the shiny decorations you'll ever need. If it all looks too difficult they also sell decorated cakes.
Shop 4, 372 Keilor Road, Nidree; 9379 2275; Melway 16 A11; Map page 163

Le Croissant

Stepping into Le Croissant in Burwood, one could be mistaken for thinking they had been transported to Paris. With the air of a French patisserie, and fantastic products to match, Le Croissant brings something special to the Melbourne bakery scene. The scene is set with an early morning visit where you may catch still-warm buttery or a chocolate-filled pain au chocolat. The sweet treats continue with sachertorte, opera gateau and chocolate-backed Florentine biscuits. Classic pastry includes platters of decorated choux pastry puffs and the awesome coffee or chocolate éclair fingers. Smaller sized treats include jam sandwich biscuits and prepacked selections of cats' tongues and crunchy macaroons that would be the perfect gift for the food lover in your life.

BURWOOD
1204 Toorak Road
9809 2263
Wed–Fri 7.30am–4.30pm;
Sat 7am–5pm;
Sun 7am–3pm
Melway 60 D5
Map page 167

Le Petit Gateau

Those looking for really exciting cakes with amazing flavour combinations and creative designs should look no further than Le Petit Gateau. It's headed up by Pierrick Boyer and you can even see the scores of pastry chefs hard at work through the viewing window. The cake displays showcase the products so well it makes it almost impossible to decide. Will it be the praline mud cake, the vanilla mille-feuille or the Manhattan? There's also a range of individual cakes such as Earl Grey mousse cake and the crisp lemon tarts; and don't forget the brownie and passionfruit chocolate gateau, which has to be tried to be believed. A select menu of hot chocolate and strawberries with chocolate fondue completes the package. This is one not to miss.

CITY
458 Little Collins Street
9944 8893
Mon–Fri 7.30am–5pm
Melway 1A G6
Map page 162

Let Them Eat Cake

If you ever wanted to see the true creativity of the pastry cooks art then look no further than Let Them Eat Cake in South Melbourne. Here unbridled creativity joins with pastry-cook skills and customers' ideas to create special-occasion cakes like no other. Pastry chef Chris Montobello always seems to have something new to show – perhaps a toy racing car, a giant wedge of cake, a globe of the world or a lady reclining in a martini glass – and, yes, they're all cakes. If you're after something smaller, then the display will certainly fill your needs. There is so much to chose from – giant lamingtons with cherry jam, individual bread and butter puddings, decorated gingerbreads and even cartoon character cupcakes. Don't miss a chance to visit Let Them Eat Cake!

SOUTH MELBOURNE
147–149 Cecil Street
9686 0077
Tues–Fri 7am–5.30pm;
Sat 7am–4pm
Melway 2K B2
Map page 168

Loafer Bread

Loafer is a tiny bakery just off the main shopping strip in Fitzroy North. The store doesn't have a huge display of bread and cakes, instead it takes a minimalist approach with simple bread racks and a glass-topped display of sweet things. The approach to bread at Loafer is organic, with natural ingredients and sourdough techniques. Their white unbleached, sprouted wheat, light rye and spelt loaves are particularly popular. If it's something sweet you're after then cast your eyes over the ever-changing daily display – glazed plum puff pastries, vanilla and chocolate swirl biscuits, gingerbread people and the much loved super seed slice. Sandwiches are prepared daily using their own breads and the coffee is Fairtrade, of course.

FITZROY NORTH
146 Scotchmer Street
9489 0766
Tues–Fri 8am–6pm;
Sat 8am–4pm;
Sun 9am–4pm
Melway 30 B12
Map page 164

Matisse Bread

Matti Malchi made his name baking bread in Adelaide – then decided it was time to head to Melbourne. He mostly services wholesale customers, so you'll find Matisse Bread at delis and food stores around town. His Moorabbin bakery has a large shop looking onto Chesterville Road, so the public also have direct access to his freshly baked sourdough. The daily selection includes the type of loaf you'd expect: sourdough baguettes, thick-crusted cobs and large white loaves – all terrific for sandwiches and rolls. Other standard loaves include wild rye, francese and a seeded loaf. More unusual breads include his potato herb loaf, kalamata olive sourdough, and walnut and poppy seed sour, which are all excellent with antipasto and dips.

MOORABBIN
1/161 Chesterville Road
9532 6182
Mon–Fri 8am–4pm;
Sat 8.30am–1pm
Melway 77 J8
Map page 169

Melissa Cake Shop

There a couple of reasons for visiting Smith Street Collingwood. One is to go shopping at Jonathan's butchers. The other is the opportunity to pick up a fantastic lunch or snack from Melissa Cake Shop. The favourite has to be the spanakopita – many people who know about Greek food agree it is one of this city's best. It's quite traditional with a stunning spinach and cheese filling wrapped inside layer upon layer of flaky golden filo pastry. If this isn't your thing there are other top choices here: tiropita (cheese), kreatopita (meat) and prasopita (leek) pastries. The sweet offerings are Greek delicacies such as baklava, crostoli, filo pastry filled with custard and rum babas. **Also at:** 661 High Street, Thornbury, 9484 4904.

COLLINGWOOD
118 Smith Street
9417 2643
Mon–Fri 7.30am–6pm;
Sat 8am–3pm
Melway 2C D10
Map page 164

Natural Tucker Bakery

Many food stores survive and thrive because of the huge range of foods they create in-store. Natural tucker proves you can create a smaller range and still be a long-running success. The bakery has been running for many years and attracts bread lovers from far and wide. The casalinga is the loaf many come for especially – and this is hardly surprising as it has a texture, flavour and taste you'll only find in a well-made sourdough loaf. There's also a sesame casalinga, 100 per cent rye, sourdough rolls and other daily specials. Healthy sweet treats include earthy apple scrolls, gluten-free Moroccan almond biscuits and date scones. Lunchtime also offers homemade soups and filled rolls. It's well worth a stop if you're heading along this section of Nicholson Street.

CARLTON NORTH
809 Nicholson Street
9380 4293
Mon–Fri 8am–6.30pm;
Sat 8am–3.30pm
Melway 30 A11
Map page 164

Noisette

Port Melbourne has been crying out for good food stores for some years now, and with the opening of places like Noisette, this is a process that is well underway. Using only the best organic flour, baker David Menard has created a selection of sourdough breads to suit every occasion. The sourdough cob is a great starting point with an excellent nutty flavour. Spelt bread has appeared on the menu too, alongside sunflower bread, baguettes, fruit bread and a wholemeal loaf. There's more besides bread with a large selection of patisserie to choose from in glamorous glass display cases. The chocolate and raspberry layered Matisse cake is a beauty and there's a selection of mini cakes. The buttery croissants are well worth a try here too.

PORT MELBOURNE
84 Bay Street
9646 9555;
Daily 6.30am–6pm;
Melway 2J D7
Map page 168

Highlight
AMAZING CAKES

Coffee éclair, Le Croissant, page 17
Le Croissant is tucked away in Burwood and presents stunning coffee éclairs. These light-as-a-feather choux pastry fingers are filled with coffee cream and glazed with coffee icing. They are an absolute taste sensation.

Jam doughnut, Baker D. Chirico, page 11
If you're partial to jam doughnuts, you need to pay a visit to Chirico in St Kilda. A mid-morning snack is rarely better than one of these jam-filled balls of sugary goodness.

Brownie and passionfruit chocolate gateau, Le Petit Gateau, page 17
Chocolate and passionfruit is not what many of us would call a classic flavour combination, but boy does it work. This amazing cake brings together a perfect balance of flavour and texture in every bite.

Fruit and nut muffins, Phillippa's, page 21
If you were going to create a stunning muffin you'd probably bring together a mix that includes fresh apple chunks, dried cranberries and crunch walnuts in a lightly spiced mix. That's exactly what's on offer here and they have a beautiful depth of flavour and texture.

Black forest roulade, Hausfrau, page 13
This is a light-as-a-feather chocolate sponge rolled with whipped cream and cherries. It is an absolute delight with a cup of their Genovese coffee.

Mini Paris Brest, Filou's, page 13
These mini choux pastry tartlets are a wonderful and tiny sweet indulgence. They offer crisp pastry filled with luscious praline-flavoured custard. Try stopping at just one.

Paterson's Cake Shop

This mini chain of family-run bakeries have a special place in the local food scene. From beginnings in Chapel Street, Windsor, there are stores in Bentleigh, Camberwell and South Melbourne. They aim to offer a blend of timeless products with a few contemporary items. This means apple charlotte and hazelnut gateau, fruit flans and coconut slice alongside chocolate yoyos and carrot cake. There are fruit cakes small, medium and large, and celebration cakes that can be decorated to suit any occasion. Watch out for those addictive cheese straws – once the packet is opened you can't stop until they're done. **Also at:** Shop 2, 332–338 Centre Road, Bentleigh, 9557 0943; 555 Riversdale Road, Camberwell, 9882 7190; 212 Clarendon Street, South Melbourne, 9682 1904.

WINDSOR
117 Chapel Street
9510 8541
Mon–Fri 9am–5.30pm;
Sat 9am–3pm
Melway 2P H1
Map page 166

Breakfast

There's more to a cooked breakfast than just eggs, bacon and sausages. Here are a few other interesting options from six breakfast hotspots around Melbourne. Enjoy!

The Botanical Hotel
Relax in the sunlit front section of the Botanical dining room and kick off with a revitalise juice – a terrific combo of melon, apple, grapefruit and mint. Then follow with their field mushrooms on toast, which will arrive at your table layered with roast tomatoes, avocado and iceberg lettuce. This is a real breakfast highlight with amazing textures and flavours.
169 Domain Road, South Yarra; 9820 7888; Melway 2L C2; Map page 168

Café Sweethearts
Classic breakfast dishes are the core business of this justly famous breakfast spot. Start with an OJ then move swiftly onto the eggs Romanoff, which appears as two soft poached eggs atop toasted muffins with sautéed spinach, a little hollandaise, basil and a simple tomato sauce on top. It's a terrific start to any day.
263 Coventry Street, South Melbourne; 9690 6752; Melway 2K C1; Map page 168

Gas Eatery & Supplies
Breakfast can be about much more than eggs and bacon. Take the baked beans with smoky ham at Gas for instance. Served with sourdough toast and a tall glass of blood orange, they make a heart-warming start to the day.
253 Coventry Street, South Melbourne; 9690 0217; Melway 2K C1; Map page 168

Las Chicas
This is one busy breakfast spot with hungry locals popping in before jumping on the tram and train and heading to work. There's plenty to choose from but an absolute favourite from the vegetarian menu is the toasted pide roll with mashed avocado and pan-fried mushrooms. With speedy, friendly service you'll soon be on your way.
203 Carlisle Street, Balaclava; 9531 3699; Melway 2P H9; Map page 170

Mr Tulk
Enjoy creamy cinnamon porridge with poached rhubarb at this inner-city hotspot. It's the perfect warming start to a day of study at the State Library. They make a seriously good coffee here too.
Ground Floor, State Library, 328 Swanston Street, City (enter via Latrobe Street); 8660 5700; Melway 1B P1; Map page 162

St Ali
The bircher muesli at St Ali is a beauty as it's studded with plump sultanas, has added coconut and wonderful zesty lemon yoghurt on top. Add a coffee of the day and you'll be set for the morning.
12–18 Yarra Place, South Melbourne, 9686 2990; Melway 2K D1, Map page 168

Phillippa's

The Phillippa's brand is synonymous with all that's good about the bread and baking scene in Melbourne. Having started as a single store in Armadale, their products are now available at farmers' markets and distributed to food stores around the state. Classic Phillippa's products include herbed spiced nuts, the earthy and beautifully textured pane francese rye, plus rosemary and vine fruit bread to serve with cheese. They also whip up outstanding muffins, friands, lemon tarts, brownies, shortbread, gingerbread and biscotti. The range goes into overdrive each Christmas and Easter with puddings, mince tarts, hot cross buns, white Christmas, stollen, panettone and much more besides. Not to be missed! **Also at:** 608 Hampton Street, Brighton, 9592 7340.

ARMADALE
1030 High Street
9576 2020
Mon–Fri 8am–6pm;
Sat 7.30am–5.30pm;
Sun 8am–5pm
Melway 59 A7
Map page 166

Pure Bread Bakery

Traditional sourdough breads states the sign on the front window and the store's appearance is in keeping with this promise. A huge mural of bread baking takes up one entire wall and sets the scene for the traditional display counter and wrought-iron display shelves. On offer is a good selection of classic sourdough, fruit breads and wholemeal loaves, among others. A selection of different bread rolls are offered too. The French sticks are popular and are a slightly lighter version of the white sourdough. A display of sweet treats takes pride of place here and includes a terrific walnut-studded carrot cake, which is spread with creamy icing and dotted with crunchy seeds. This popular local bakery is also home to lemon cakes, orange cakes and a much loved vanilla slice.

SURREY HILLS
114 Union Road
9836 3789
Mon–Fri 9am–5pm;
Sat 8am–2pm
Melway 46 H11
Map page 167

Silly Yaks Bakery Café

Silly Yaks Bakery Café – as the inventive name suggests – caters to sufferers of coeliac disease and other food intolerances. This store seems more café than bakery at times, but is still a good spot for those requiring gluten-free foods. As well as their staple breads, there are often fruit breads, scrolls, biscuits and sweets such as choc mud slice, gingerbreads, chocolate chip cookies, cheesecake slice and lamingtons on offer. Their cakes are also popular, ranging from baked cheesecakes to lemon meringue and fruit flans. Silly Yaks also offer a nice variety of ready-made coeliac-friendly meals such as sandwiches, soups, pastas and curries. There is even the Silly Yak's Beer, which is preservative, additive and gluten free.

NORTHCOTE
105 High Street
9482 3999
Tues–Fri 7.30am–4.30pm;
Sat–Sun 8am–5pm
Melway 30 E10
Map page 165

Sugardough Panificio and Patisserie

Sugardough is a top foodie location for Brunswick and the surrounding suburbs, drawing those who love freshly baked goods that are prepared by hand on-site. It also has a particularly Italian approach to baking, which really fits well with the area's culinary heritage. Hot-from-the-oven loaves include toscana, ciabatta, sourdough and wholegrain. There's vegetarian or meat pizza to go for those looking for a quick lunch or snack, or try a chicken makhani pie, beef roll, soup of the day or savoury tart. The cabinet is usually bursting with bomboloni (doughnuts) in an assortment of fillings, cherry friands and the beautifully textured tahini balls. The thick-as-syrup, on-tap hot chocolate is much loved too.

EAST BRUNSWICK
163 Lygon Street
9380 4060
Tues–Fri 7.30am–5pm;
Sat 7.30am–4pm;
Sun 8am–3pm
Melway 29 K9
Map page 164

Sunbeam Cakes

What a sweet little spot this traditional Aussie bakery is. Serving up classic cakes and sweet treats to bayside foodies young and old for over six decades, Sunbeam still has an old-fashioned friendly service about it that we love. Customers are well versed to take a number and know they'll be served in no time. This gives you a brief window of opportunity to browse the front window display and the array of sweet things inside. Will it be a traditional jelly slice or a mini Italian lemon meringue tart, or one of their apple- or custard-filled oblong doughnuts known as crusties? The selection also includes lamington fingers, jam tarts, vanilla slices, beestings and fruit cakes, plus decorated cupcakes and jam-filled monkey faces. Don't miss this Mentone institution!

MENTONE
129 Mentone Parade
9583 2091
Mon–Fri 7.30am–5.30pm;
Sat 7.30am–1.30pm
Melway 87 A6
Map page 169

Tanner's Swiss Patisserie

The outer Eastern suburbs are not exactly overflowing with top-quality bakeries, which is why we're always glad to have Tanner's Swiss Patisserie to visit in Syndal. It's beautifully decked out with wood panelled walls, dangling Swiss flags and original ornaments. As you might expect, the choices are along the central-European style. So, sacher torte, Black Forest gateau and vanilla slice are in abundance. They also whip up some excellent flaky croissants, fruit tarts, fruit Danishes and lemon tarts. If it's a real indulgent kick you're after then the double-decker vanilla slice was created with you in mind. Perfectly made buttery biscuits are available if you're after a treat to bring to afternoon tea, and the chocolate truffles are pretty popular too.

SYNDAL
232 Blackburn Road
9802 7265
Tues–Fri 8.30am–5.30pm;
Sat 8.30am–1.30pm;
Sun 9am–1.30pm
Melway 61 J12
Map page 171

Zimt Patisserie Bakery Café

Mont Albert residents love this Hamilton Street bakery, which is run by the talented Michael and Sue Leilder. The beautiful displays offer stunning cakes and pastries including strudel, berry tarts and biscuits. There is also a good range of savoury choices with gourmet pies, sausage rolls and various flavoured quiches. The opportunity to eat in-store is taken up with gusto by food-loving locals who eagerly vie for the tables. Whole decorated cakes are also a popular choice for celebrations, as are the colourful decorated cupcakes. Easter is celebrated here with gorgeous gingerbreads – ducks, rabbits, eggs and stars are all presented in beautiful colour. With a smart fitout, well-presented store staff and a production kitchen at the rear of the premises, this is a great spot for bakery lovers.

MONT ALBERT
38 Hamilton Street
9890 2382
Mon 7am–4pm;
Tues–Sat 7am–5pm
Melway 46 K10
Map page 167

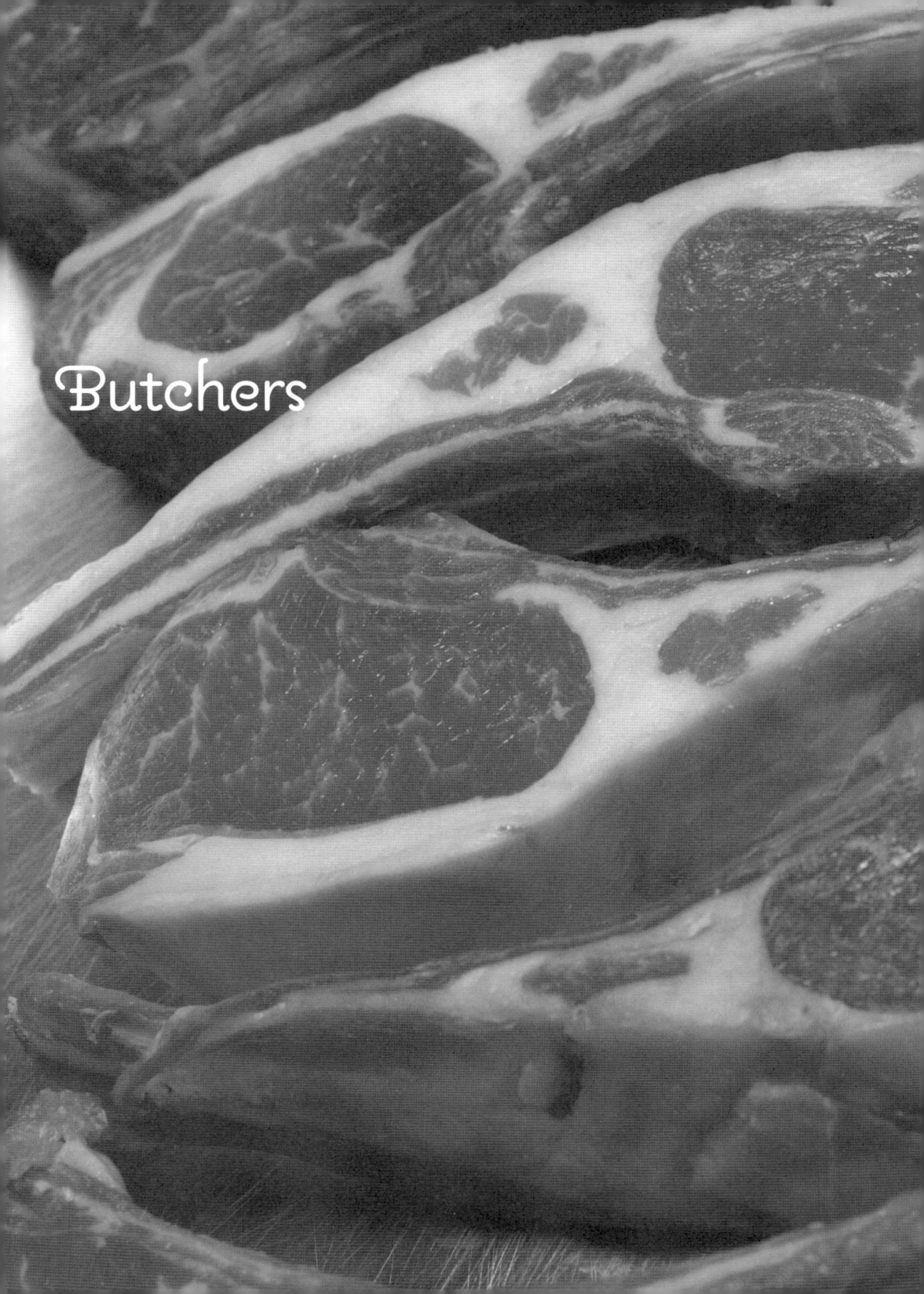

Butcher's shops, like most of our specialist food stores, are under increasing pressure from supermarkets. There's little doubt that for many people supermarkets offer a convenient way to shop. Luckily supermarkets can never compete on quality meats, smallgoods and real service and advice – aspects that good butchers have in spades. When visiting a topnotch butcher's shop, don't be afraid to ask for cuts that are not on display. A good butcher will often be able to prepare pork belly, bolar blade and thick-cut aged sirloin on request. Speaking of aged meat, we are noticing a lack of quality dry-aged meats around town. These meats have an amazing depth of flavour, tenderness and texture. So ask your butcher for dry-aged meats such as beef next time you're in-store. You never know what's out the back ageing to perfection!

Andrew's Choice

Andrew's Choice is a butcher with an influence way beyond its Yarraville location. For over a decade and a half this brand has been producing much-loved smallgoods to sell here and at delis and food stores across Melbourne. It's the cheese kranskys that are most well known and deservedly so. The on-site smallgoods production line also pumps out frankfurts, spicy debriciner, bacon, pastrami, ham and cold smoked pork loin. Fresh meats are in abundance here too: ready-to-cook kebabs and marinated lamb loins, burgers and sausages galore – it's hard to choose between the Italian salsiccia and New Zealand lamb, the South African boerewors and his hot Sicilian. Andrew's Choice is a star of the Melbourne food scene.

YARRAVILLE
24 Anderson Street
9687 2419
Mon–Fri 7am–6.30pm;
Sat 7am–2pm
Melway 42 A9
Map page 163

Belmore Biodynamic Meats

Belmore Biodynamic Meats started their business in Balwyn and are considered one of the leaders in the supply of biodynamic and organic meats. A recent move of location to Thornbury sees the business continue to offer great tasting, pesticide- and chemical-free meat and poultry. The products on offer contain no growth hormones, fertilisers or pesticides, and are grown on sustainable farms that adhere to strict guidelines. The move in suburb was to concentrate on wholesale but customers knocking on the door soon changed all that. A top selection here includes diced lamb or beef for curries and casseroles, legs of lamb, ready-for-the-oven rolled pork and organic poultry. Sausages are also offered including pure beef, chicken, Cornish, lamb and mint, and barbecue.

THORNBURY
137 Miller Street
9484 0469
Mon–Fri 7am–5pm;
Sat 7am–1pm
www.organicmeat
supply.com.au
Melway 30 C3
Map page 165

Bouchiers of Malvern Road

There's a particular sense of quality in the Bouchiers' stores that's apparent the moment you walk up to the counter. They have a knack of presenting meat in a manner that is so appealing. The friendly and informative service certainly helps. Choose from lamb loin stuffed with spinach and pine nuts, soy and pepper leg of lamb or veal cutlets coated with breadcrumbs, parmesan and parsley. The expertly aged porterhouse steak is awesome too. Smallgoods are covered by an array of sausages such as lamb and honey, beef, chipolatas and the new wagyu and mustard. **Also at:** Chadstone Shopping Centre, 1341 Dandenong Road, Chadstone, 8531 4387; David Jones Food Hall, Bourke Street Mall, City, 9643 2530.

HAWKSBURN
551 Malvern Road
9827 3629
Mon–Fri 6am–6pm;
Sat 6am–1pm
Melway 2M C10
Map page 166

Brenta Meats

For great tasting veal and pork, you can't go past Brenta Meats. This busy butcher's shop has been serving the Fairfield community for many years – and has built a reputation for offering quality meat along the way. Perennial favourites include the delicious osso buco, rolled pork and veal roasts. The range of sausages is extensive, and one of the most popular items on offer. Try the English pork (large or chipolata), pork and fennel or the bratwurst at your next barbecue. The huge Italian cotechino sausage is also available here. These need to be simmered and served as a hearty feast on cold winter's nights. Shelves in the retail area also offer a good selection of continental groceries.

FAIRFIELD
103 Station Street
9489 0820
Mon–Sat 7am–6pm
Melway 30 K10
Map page 165

The Chicken Pantry

For fantastic free-range birds you can't go past The Chicken Pantry. Located at the Queen Victoria Market, this store boasts every style and cut of chicken you could imagine. From chicken breasts to drumsticks, chicken wings to thighs, there is every possible option, and all of it is superb and hormone free. The whole chickens are a perennial favourite, while the free-range chicken, duck and quail eggs also make a mark. The Chicken Pantry also offers a nice range of quail, geese and duck products, along with fantastic chicken sausages. In the winter months, enjoy pheasant, hare and the peppered kangaroo fillets. There is excellent advice on hand from the friendly staff too. Join the queues on busy days and enjoy.

CITY
Stall 85–86, Dairy Produce Hall, Queen Victoria Market, cnr Elizabeth and Victoria Streets; 9329 6417
Tues 6am–2pm;
Thurs 6am–3pm;
Fri 6am–6pm; Sat 6am–3pm
Melway 2B C11
Map page 162

Continental Kosher Butchers

Continental Kosher Butchers started life in St Kilda and over time has grown to become one of the best-known kosher butchers in town. For years, the focus was on smallgoods, but as the business has grown, so too has the range of products on offer. Today, this store offers fine quality kosher meats such as beef, lamb and veal. There are ready-made products such as meatballs and sausages, along with barbeque chickens and a nice variety of offal. The ready-for-the-pan schnitzels are popular too. Brisket remains the top seller at Continental Kosher, but don't forget to look out for their traditional smallgoods such as salami and smoked chicken. This is truly a lovely and interesting place to shop.

MALVERN
155 Glenferrie Road
9509 9822
Mon–Thurs 8am–5pm;
Fri 8am–3pm
Melway 59 B9
Map page 167

Highlight
SNAGS

Chorizo sausage, Delicatess, page 53
Lovers of Spanish food and cooking should not miss these stunning sausages. They are beautifully made with a spicy coarse filling and an amazing flavour – available as mild or spicy varieties.

Chicken and parsley sausage, The Chicken Pantry, page 25
Chicken is often too lean to produce a beautiful sausage, but not here. The Chicken Pantry version is thin, packed with flavour and a real delight for a family dinner.

Rabbit and fresh thyme sausage, La Parisienne Pates, page 29
What a delicious treat these snags are. A fine rabbit filling that requires careful cooking so they are not dry. They are a real winner for autumn and winter cooking.

Wagyu and mustard, Bouchiers of Malvern Road, page 25
These sausages are a great way for first-timers to give wagyu a try. Serve with seeded horseradish mustard and mashed potato for a winning combination.

D. A. Di Censo & Sons

The Di Censo family are serious about their business, which is supplying the best quality meat and smallgoods they can. This makes for very happy customers indeed. Many come for the fresh meats on offer including things such as chemical-free chicken, good-quality steaks and excellent veal and lamb cuts. Others head straight for their favourite smallgoods – pancetta, salami, pastrami, strasbourg or bones for the winter soup pot. Then there are the famous sausages, all gluten and MSG free, including lamb and pesto, pork and basil, beef and chives, English-style pork and beef, plus specialty varieties such as the pork-and-veal combo Toulouse sausage. A small selection of groceries includes stock, mayonnaise, olive oil, capers and other pantry essentials.

DONCASTER EAST
Shop 24, Tunstall Square
9842 3078
Mon–Fri 6am–6pm;
Sat 6am–3pm
Melway 48 E2
Map page 171

Donati's Fine Meats

If you're looking for an example of Lygon Street's Italian food heritage then look no further than Donati's Fine Meats. Here in the white-tiled store, Italian-style meats are prepared and sold with great style – opera plays in the background, there's terrific art on the walls and customers can take the time to discuss a purchase to ensure it'll be just right. Veal is a strong feature with cuts such as scaloppini, shanks, osso buco and an excellent veal meat loaf with fresh herbs and garlic. Smallgoods too are incredibly popular with made-on-site ham, sausages and smoked chicken. Donati's is also one of the few remaining butchers where offal is featured. Heart, kidneys, tongue and liver are often available.

CARLTON
402 Lygon Street
9347 4948
Mon–Thurs 7am–6pm;
Fri 6am–6pm;
Sat 6am–1pm
Melway 2B G6
Map page 164

At La Bergerie, we offer you some of the finest foods to tempt your palate. Choose from our variety of fromage (cheese), charcuterie (small goods), epicerie fine (fine food) and French wines. Or ask us about cheese and gourmet platters; hampers; special events and tutored tastings.

Trading hours:
Tue to Friday 9am – 6pm
Sat 8am – 5pm   Sun 10am – 5pm
Closed on Monday

141 Maling Road Canterbury
Vic 3126 Australia
Tel +61 3 9830 7915
Fax +61 3 9830 7916
Email labergerie@aapt.net.au

Peter G Bouchier
Butchers of Distinction

Purveyor of fine quality meats and smallgoods. Located in Toorak and David Jones in Chadstone and the City.

We specialise in:
- Blackmores Wagyu beef
- Certified Angus
- Dry-aged beef
- A large range of game meat & poultry
- Award-winning gourmet sausages
- Local & imported delicatessen lines including foie gras & Spanish jamon

We also cater to the corporate & restaurant industry.

PETER G BOUCHIER
BUTCHERS
OF DISTINCTION

Peter G Bouchier

| 551 Malvern Road Toorak (03) 9827-3620 | David Jones Bourke St Melbourne (03) 9643-2530 | David Jones Chadstone Shopping Centre Chadstone (03) 8531-4387 |

Dunav Butcher

The window display here is not filled with pre-marinated chicken kebabs and ready-for-the-pan lamb fillets. Instead, it's a generous display of thick cut T-bone steak, whole blade steak and cuts for stews and casseroles. It's real meat-lover's territory with a strong Eastern European sense. Step inside and the aromas of on-site smoking and smallgoods will whisk you away. Beautiful hams, kranskys snags, kabana and salamis are all on display. A must-have are the cevapcici, a Balkan skinless sausage of minced pork and beef; cook slowly over charcoal for the best results. Shelves in the store are also packed with specialist foods – preserved cherries, preserved cabbage, horseradish, chocolate wafer biscuits and the much loved poppyseed cake.

SPRINGVALE
209 Springvale Road
9546 8582
Mon–Fri 7am–5.30pm;
Sat 7am–1pm
Melway 80 A8
Map page 169

Gruners

If you are looking for those hard-to-come-by smallgoods or sausages you can't go past Gruners in St Kilda. Peter Gruner has built a reputation of offering quality products, and his high standing is well deserved. The store was opened by Peter's father in 1958, and boasts a long tradition of providing tasty fare. Favourites include delicious smallgoods such as black pudding, bacon, cabanossi, hunter sausage and chorizo, sold hot or mild. The hams are legendary too. Customers can also pick up crispy roast pork and pastrami sliced to order. There is a great selection of fresh meats too, such as quality steaks and veal. This is an authentic taste of Eastern Europe in downtown St Kilda.

ST KILDA
227A Barkly Street
9534 2715
Mon–Fri 9am–5.45pm;
Sat 9am–2.45pm
Melway 2P C9
Map page 170

Hagen's Organic & Biodynamic Meats

For quality organic meats and poultry, you can't go past Hagen's fine selection. Two market shops are now operating at Prahran Market and the Queen Victoria Market, so there's double the chance of snaring some terrific products. Hagen's offers quality meats from some of the best organic providers in the country. The gluten-free sausages are incredibly good, as is the low-fat organic chicken mince. The porterhouse steaks are succulent and juicy, while the Moroccan lamb burgers have long been a favourite of ours. On the smallgoods side, checkout the sausages, thick-cut bacon and ham off the bone. The chicken schnitzels are pretty dammed fine too. **Also at:** Stall 16, Meat Hall, Queen Victoria Market, cnr Elizabeth and Victoria Streets, City, 9329 5534.

SOUTH YARRA
Shop 509, Prahran Market,
163–185 Commercial Road
9827 1899
Tues & Thurs 6am–5pm;
Fri 6am–6pm;
Sat 6am–5pm
Sun 10am–3pm
Melway 2L H9
Map page 166

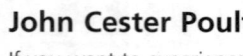

John Cester Poultry & Game

If you want to experience the best in poultry and game then this Prahran Market stall will fit the bill. The selection just gets better and better at John Cester. Recent trends have seen corn-fed chicken become available in all manner of cuts – the chicken drumettes and wings are particularly good. They are packed with flavour and terrific for junior dinners and making the best-quality stock. Quail, duck and kangaroo are also regularly available. Ready-to-cook foods include a great range of chicken sausages plus crumbed chicken schnitzels. The game selection increases over winter with wild boar, emu, wild hare and wild rabbit on hand. Chicken stock is here, too, as is chicken giblet gravy. And don't forget the turkey order for Christmas.

SOUTH YARRA
Shop 506, Prahran Market,
163–185 Commercial Road
9827 6111
Tues & Thurs 6am–5pm;
Fri 6am–6pm;
Sat 6am–5pm;
Sun 10am–3pm
Melway 2L H9
Map page 166

Jonathan's of Collingwood

Smith Street may not be one of this city's prime food-store locations but it's long been home to the wonderful Jonathan's of Collingwood butcher's shop. Fresh meats are stunning here, particularly the beautifully aged porterhouse steak. Lamb is another feature with trimmed tender cutlets a popular choice. Leg of lamb and marinated lamb rumps also feature strongly in the range. If it's smallgoods you're after then you're in the right place. The sausages are outstanding too: Italian pork and fennel, boudin blanc, merguez, chorizo and exceptional frankfurts. Christmas is huge here with customers clamouring for the famous Jonathan's ham and turkeys. If you're keen to add one to your table, make sure you get in early.

COLLINGWOOD
122 Smith Street
9419 4339
Mon–Fri 6am–6pm;
Sat 6am–2pm
Melway 2C D10
Map page 164

La Parisienne Pates

Lygon Street has long been the Italian heart of Melbourne – the place to buy Italian food and wine or enjoy an espresso. La Parisienne Pates shows the changing mood of this much loved inner suburb. The store is pure French style. In fact, you could well have stumbled upon it in a Paris laneway. There are terrines such as cracked pepper, duck and orange, rabbit and prune not to mention the fabulous textured pork rillettes. Toulouse, venison, rabbit and fresh thyme and boudin blanc sausages are also on hand. Classic French cheese, butter and jam are available too, along with a selection of sweet and savoury pastries. A stylish new café allows customers to enjoy café au lait, French tea and simple meals. You can even try out your French language skills. Bon appétit.

CARLTON
290 Lygon Street
9349 1852
Mon–Wed 9am–6pm;
Thurs–Fri 9am–6.30pm;
Sat 9am–6pm;
Sun 10am–6pm
Melway 2B G7
Map page 164

Lamont's Gourmet Meats

This bayside butcher has a quality approach to smallgoods and ready-to-cook meats. They're well known for terrific steaks – giant rump and rib eye in particular. They also do a serious trade in sausages with varieties such as fresh chorizo, pork and Viennese frankfurts. If you're after a taste test, come along to the regular Saturday barbecue. On the smallgoods side the kabana is eternally popular as is the Lamont's ham and smoked chicken. The bacon is hard to beat and ham hocks are usually available for soup. Christmas hams are big business here too in the lead up to the festive season. If you're after one you'll have to get your order in early.

HAMPTON
335 Hampton Street
9598 6269
Mon–Fri 8am–6pm;
Sat 7am–5pm
Melway 76 F6
Map page 169

Luv-a-Duck

Luv-a-Duck brings duck to the home kitchen with their variety of easy-to-prepare products. Staff are always on hand to offer advice on the wide variety of products that have been created by this innovative company. Peking duck remains the number one choice, and is available on its own or as part of a scrumptious dinner pack. The extensive product range includes duck breast and whole duck, Chinese-style duck half, marinated duck and shanks. The hands-on classes are a great opportunity to learn about the versatility of this fantastic dish. **Also at:** Spotlight Centre, Shop G22, 111 Cecil Street, South Melbourne, 9645 0122.

PORT MELBOURNE
228 Ingles Street
1300 649 000
Mon–Fri 9am–5.30pm;
Sat 9am–2pm
Melway 2B G7
Map page 168

Ormond Meat & Smallgoods

Ormond Meat and Smallgoods are specialists in continental meats. The selection here is always enticing and leaves customers with many dinner options. Naturally, pork is a firm favourite and ends up as delicious smoked hams, porchetta and an amazing array of sausages. The pistachio-stuffed pork has been a long-term favourite here too. Special Eastern European smallgoods extend to smoked tongue, spiced speck, kranskys, frankfurters and bratwurst sausages. The store also stocks a fine selection of fresh poultry along with European groceries. Cheeses are available too with classics such as gruyère, tilsit and edam. Bread includes hearty rye loaves, and the shelves are packed with mayonnaise, sauerkraut, relishes, mustard, spices, pickles, plus crackers, biscuits and chocolates.

ORMOND
634 North Road
9578 5049
Tues–Fri 8am–5.30pm;
Sat 7–11.30am
Melway 68 F9
Map 169

Paddy's Meats and Fine Wines

Irish butchers are few and far between around Melbourne, so thank goodness for Paddy's. The Irish selection ranges from the award-winning pork sausages (in various sizes) to bacon rashers, gammon (boiling bacon), Belfast burgers, corned beef and the classic black and white pudding. The rest of the selection covers the typical local butcher selection with porterhouse and T-bone steaks, roasting pork, lamb in all its cuts plus marinated legs of lamb. The selection is rounded out with smoked on-site cheese kransky and ham hocks, plus a huge array of sausages. Shoppers can even pick up a bottle of wine to go with their dinner. There's also a selection of imported groceries for those keen for a taste of home – Barry's tea, Tayto crisps, club orange bars and Bird's trifle mixes.

KEW
126 Cotham Road
9817 3859
Mon–Fri 7am–6pm;
Sat 7am–1pm
Melway 45 D6
Map page 165

Polkinghornes

Polkinghornes began with an approach to retailing that sees meats sourced from the farm going direct to the store. Beef is a huge seller here and Polkinghornes created their own cuts such as aga cubes for casseroling, shumi for Japanese-style dishes, plus ready-cut strips for stir-fries and minced beef. Prime porterhouse cuts are on hand for barbecuing, plus lamb cutlets and ready-made kebabs. The whole boned legs of lamb marinated in olive oil, lemon and herbs look excellent too. Sausages are on offer with flavours such as beef and ale. You'll also find poultry choices along with some ready-to-heat meals. Bags of freshly dug potatoes are also sourced on the farm and are delicious boiled and served with a little melted butter.

ALBERT PARK
125 Dundas Place
9690 4625
Mon–Fri 9am–7pm;
Sat 9am–5pm;
Sun 10am–5pm
Melway 2K A6
Map page 168

Prahran Continental Butcher

This has long been a favourite place to stock up on wonderful smallgoods and fresh meats in the continental style. They have beautiful choices for dinner such as bratwurst sausages, kranskys, veal weisswurst and thick or thin frankfurts. These are excellent with a side serve of sauerkraut and mild mustard. The liverwurst is a great treat. The hams, salami, meatloaves, pressed meats and white puddings are also popular choices. Bacon is on hand in lean or streaky style; the double-smoked streaky version is particularly good. Fresh meats, especially pork and beef, are a feature here too. A small selection of dill pickles, sauerkraut, horseradish and rye bread is usually on hand, along with continental cakes and biscuits.

PRAHRAN
170 Chapel Street
9510 2809
Mon midday–5pm;
Tues–Wed 8am–5pm;
Thurs 8am–6pm;
Fri 7.30am–6pm;
Sat 7am–2pm
Melway 2L H12
Map page 166

Rendina's Butchery

The opportunity to source organic and biodynamic meats is really growing around Melbourne. Firstly, there are more producers turning their conventional farms to this style of growing and, secondly, there's an increase in butchers specialising in these meats. Rendina's Butchery is one of the best in this field. They have an extensive range of beef, chicken, lamb and smallgoods to choose from – everything from dry-aged rump to lamb racks, chicken chops and topside roast. Smallgoods are also an essential part of their range with pancetta, salami, roast beef, kabana and strasbourg. The lean chicken sausage, flavoured with a hint of sea salt, pepper and white wine, is a beauty. If you can't get to Balwyn North, a selection of their smallgoods are sold through food stores across Melbourne.

BALWYN NORTH
253B Belmore Road
9857 6669
Mon–Fri 7am–6pm;
Sat 7am–1pm
Melway 46 E5
Map page 171

Rob's British Butchers

How lucky are we to have Rob Boyle in this food-obsessed city. After all, where else are you going to track down classic English smallgoods such as Cumberland sausages, pork pies and gammon ham? Or how about Cornish pasties, pork pies, steak and kidney puddings? Here at Rob's, of course. The display is beautifully arranged each day with all these plus his famous English pork sausages, short-back bacon and scotch eggs. Scots are well looked after here too, with haggis specially prepared for Burn's Night celebrations in January each year. Other products while not British in origin include sausages in flavours such as pork and sage, sweet chilli and plum, steak and onion, and boerewors sausages for expat South Africans.

DANDENONG
177 Lonsdale Street
9792 5188
Mon–Fri 8am–5pm;
Sat 8am–1pm
Melway 90 D8
Map page 171

Solomon Kosher Butcher

There's a terrific array of well-prepared meats and smallgoods on display here. First-time visitors should become familiar with the payment system. You choose your meats, and then pay at the cashier's window and your products will be in bags and ready to go. The substantial display offers rissoles and roasts, veal brisket and veal cutlets. Shoppers can also choose whole chickens, chicken in every imaginable cut and marinated chicken kebabs. Ready-crumbed chicken schnitzels, chicken nuggets and chicken Kiev are other popular choices judging by the way customers order them in large numbers. Smallgoods are stored in a separate refrigerated display, so things like frankfurts and cabanosi are offered alongside classic Jewish dips and salads.

ELSTERNWICK
140–144 Glen Eira Road
9532 8855
Mon–Thurs
7.30am–5.30pm;
Fri 7.30am–3pm
Melway 67 F1
Map page 170

Song Hiep

Song Hiep stands head and shoulders above the other butchers in this primarily Asian shopping area. For one thing they have an enormous range that covers both Asian and European cuts of meat. Add to this a massive selection at good prices and you have a terrific package. There are ducks, duck tongues and chicken in all its known cuts. Pork is particularly good here too, as you might expect, with pork shoulder, neck, belly and loin all featured. Western cuts include roasts, gravy beef, beef ribs and lamb chops, plus fresh sausages and kranskys. They've recently installed a flat screen TV and show clips on preparing the many cuts when you get home. With speedy service to boot, it really is a terrific local store.

SPRINGVALE
Shop G31, Springvale Shopping Centre,
46–58 Buckingham Avenue
9574 0833
Mon–Fri 8am–6pm;
Sat–Sun 8am–5pm
Melway 79 K10
Map page 169

Burgers

There are times when it's a burger and only a really good burger that will do the trick. The Melbourne burger scene has been undergoing considerable change with some chains being swallowed up by better run competitors. Here are a few current favourites.

Andrew's Hamburgers
This is a burger spot par excellence with over five decades in the trade. Join legions of fans for a perfect burger with the lot. The steak sandwiches are excellent too – accompanied by a brown paper bag of chips there's no better!
144 Bridport Street, Albert Park; 9690 2126; Melway 2K A6; Map page 168

Danny's Takeaway
Since the mid-1940s Danny's has been producing some of the best burgers in Melbourne. Try a burger with the lot for pure burger pleasure, with chips, of course!
360 St Georges Road, Fitzroy North; 9481 5847; Melway 30 C11; Map page 164

Grill'd
This is a fun, funky store with great grilled food to match. Check out the Mighty Melbourne or the always delicious crispy bacon and cheese option. There are terrific fries here too – not too thin, not too thick and salted to perfection. Store details at www.grilld.com.au.
754 Glenferrie Road, Hawthorn; 9819 0004; Melway 45 D9; Map page 167

Urban Burger
A terrific chain of burger bars with options covering beef, chicken and vegetarian. Love the Urban chick burger with salad and relish. Match with some UB thick-cut fries, aioli dipping sauce and you're set for a treat. See store details at www.urbanburger.com.au.
167 Bay Street, Port Melbourne, 9646 6030; Melway 57 C3; Map page 168

Trialto Meats

Trialto Meats is a store that always seems to be packed with customers, which is a problem all local butcher's shops would love to have. The appeal here is the huge array of top-quality meats combined with a friendly welcome and practical advice from the guys behind the counter. There's always some excellent veal on display with cutlets, brisket and spare ribs. Good choices also extend to marinated legs of lamb with Greek, Thai and Mongolian flavours available. Beef runs from ribs and roasts to rump and rissoles. The comprehensive range also includes Italian chipolatas, bratwurst, English pork and Chinese plum sausages. There are also dips, cheeses and Luv-a-Duck products to shop for. All in all it's quite a place.

ELSTERNWICK
397 Glen Huntly Road
9528 2612
Mon–Fri 7am–5.30pm;
Sat–Sun 7am–1.30pm
Melway 67 G3
Map page 170

Wangara Poultry & Game

The opportunity to access a range of meats usually only available to chefs is one not to be missed. That's exactly what's on offer at Wangara Poultry & Game, well-known wholesalers to Melbourne's restaurants. In the poultry area well-known local brands are a feature – with the wonderful Milawa and Hazeldene free-range chickens. There's also Glenloth corn-fed and Mickleham free-range duck. The list goes on with top-quality silkie chickens, pigeon and quail, pheasant, guinea fowl, duck and turkey. The game selection is equally extensive with emu and ostrich available in a variety of cuts, kangaroo and crocodile plus farmed and wild rabbits. Other well-known meat brands include Hopkins River beef, Blackmore Wagyu and Kurobuta pork.

KENSINGTON
Unit 1/321 Arden Street
9376 8188
Mon–Thurs 8am–4pm;
Fri 8am–3pm
Melway 2A B7
Map page 163

Wursthütte

This is a very popular spot for food-loving locals to stock up on top-quality meats and smallgoods. For almost two decades the team of dedicated butchers have been providing excellent products and service. Ready-to-cook lamb covers trimmed cutlets, lamb roast, loin and shanks for long, slow braises. Beef includes the classic cuts of sirloin, rump, T-bone and even ox tail in cooler months. Smallgoods are excellent here too with smoked chicken fillets, prosciutto, pastrami, corned beef and even smoked tongue. There are also bratwurst, knackwurst, cevapcici and Aussie barbecue sausages on offer. If you really want a meal in a hurry then check out the ready-meals range of sweet-and-sour pork, beef stroganoff, lamb curry and bolognaise sauce.

MALVERN
187 Glenferrie Road
9509 3359
Mon–Fri 8am–5.30pm;
Sat 8am–2pm
Melway 59 C8
Map page 167

The interest in top-quality chocolate continues unabated across Melbourne. Everyone seems keen to know about the latest chocolate shop to open or the latest chocolate truffle we've tracked down. Melbourne's chocolate lovers are aficionados who want their products handmade with great skill, freshly made before their very eyes and using only the very best couverture chocolate. You'll be pleased to know the quality and range of what's on offer is on the up and up. Well-known names like Koko Black, Max Brenner and Chocolateria San Churro continue to spread across the suburbs. We've also had the arrival of Ganache Chocolate in South Yarra to enjoy. So, get out there and explore – there's a world of chocolate waiting to be enjoyed right here in Melbourne.

Cacao Fine Chocolates

The name may be hard to pronounce, but the chocolates at Cacao are easy to enjoy! You'll love the amazing chocolate-coated jellies in flavours of lime, mango or raspberry. The wild passionfruit ganache chocolate is a beauty too, as is the honey bee, an addictive honey and milk chocolate praline in a milk chocolate shell. The Bastien mix of coconut and white chocolate is awesome; ditto the cocoa-rolled truffle noir. Cacao also offers chocolate Eiffel towers, nougat bars, tins of chocolate buttons and filled selection boxes. At Valentine's Day, Easter and Christmas there are beautiful creations such as marbled chocolate roosters, chickens and eggs. **Also at:** Shop 7/525 Little Collins Street, City, 9629 4955; Postal Hall, Melbourne GPO, 9662 4777

ST KILDA
52 Fitzroy Street
8598 9555
Daily 7am–7pm
Melway 2P A5
Map page 170

The Chocolate Lover

This chocolate-lovers stall is situated in the revamped concourse of the South Melbourne Market. Pierre-Olivier Stinzy has been creating beautiful chocolate products for some years now, so it's terrific to see him in a retail space. One display case is lined with decorated cakes in milk, dark and white chocolate. Another display is filled with outstanding handmade chocolate roses and designer chocolates: raspberry truffles, chocolate-coated ginger, double chocolate rocky road, giant chocolate truffles and many more. Gift boxes are filled and ready for the couverture lover in your life. Shoppers can also pick up the addictive chocolate mousse and get their hands on a cup of the thick-style Italian hot chocolate on tap. This is a terrific addition to this long-running foodie destination.

SOUTH MELBOURNE
Stall 34, South Melbourne Market, cnr Coventry and Cecil Streets
0411 474 493
Wed 8am–4pm;
Fri 8am–6pm;
Sat–Sun 8am–4pm
Melway 2K B1
Map page 168

MAGIC COOKING PRODUCTS

Cooking is no longer a chore with **Magic Cooking Products!**

MAGIC BBQ SHEET
Line your BBQ hot-plate with the BBQ sheet – even marinated food will not stick! No oil required even when cooking fish, eggs etc. After use just wash it clean and it's ready to use again. Re-use at least 1,000 times. Never scrub your BBQ hot-plate again. PRICE **$22.95**

MAGIC TOASTER BAGS
Make toasted sandwiches in your normal toaster – easy clean. Totally non-stick. Use hundreds of times – great hash browns, fish fingers etc. PRICE **$24.95**

LIMITED OFFER!

MAGIC OVEN LINER
Just place the oven liner on the bottom of your gas or electric oven. When spills occur, just wipe or wash it clean and replace in the oven. No more scrubbing or sprays to clean your oven. Will last for years. PRICE **$29.95**

Buy BBQ Sheet & Oven Liner
$49.95 (RRP $50.90) + $5 P&H
& receive a **FREE** set of **toaster bags**
valued at $24.95 **SAVE $27.90**

To order call **(02) 9144 4572**
or **www.magiccookingsheet.com.au** & mention this ad.

Chocolateria San Churro

When the first Chocolateria San Churro opened in Brunswick Street a few years back we predicated they would spread like wildfire. That's proven to be the case with stores now popping up across the suburbs. The appeal here is the Spanish tradition of creating long, thin doughnuts known as churros and serving them with warm chocolate dipping sauce (white, milk or dark). We're more partial to the dark dipping sauce than the others, but that's the beauty of the choices here. Besides the churros there are hot chocolates galore, ice-cream, chocolate shakes as well as a selection of chocolate truffles to enjoy. If you really can't decide between all the delicious treats then opt for a chocolate tapas plate. Visit www.sanchurro.com to find your nearest store.

FITZROY
277B Brunswick Street
9419 9936
Sun–Thurs 10am–11pm;
Fri & Sat 10am–midnight
Melway 2C B7
Map page 164

Chocolatier

You may not think of Ivanhoe as the chocolate hub of Melbourne but that's exactly where the well-known Chocolatier brand is based. They have a very cute shop on site, which is a wonderful showcase for the Chocolatier range. Shelves and cabinets display the products they have become famous for with pralines, truffles and filled chocolate gift boxes galore. Solid chocolate hearts come wrapped in foil for your favourite chocoholic; there are also scorched almonds and fruit jellies. Easter sees a huge array of good-quality chocolate eggs and novelties on display – everything from strawberries and cream eggs to praline or caramel-filled bunnies. There's even no sugar added milk and dark chocolate eggs. **Also at:** 444 Hampton Road, Hampton, 9598 1700.

IVANHOE
244 Waterdale Road
9499 7023
Mon–Thurs 9am–5.30pm;
Fri 9am–6pm;
Sat 9am–3pm
Melway 31 F5
Map page 171

Coco Loco

There aren't too many foodie highlights on High Street, Northcote, once you leave the Westgarth strip. That was until Coco Loco opened its doors. It's a beautifully designed space with a glam Middle Eastern feel from the glowing terracotta ceiling and the beautiful new timber display bar. The choices for chocolate lovers start with truffles flavoured with lemon myrtle, macadamia, pistachio and cardamom. The star of the show though has to be the hot chocolates. The difference is that they're made with cashew milk, which gives them lightness and texture you'll never get with regular milk. They're luscious and satisfying but not filling. The use of cashew milk also makes them suitable for vegans and coeliacs. Put this one on your must-visit list.

NORTHCOTE
219 High Street
9482 7033
Mon–Thurs 11am–3pm, 6pm–11pm;
Fri 11am–3pm, 6pm–1am;
Sat 11am–1am;
Sun 10am–11pm
Melway 30 F9
Map page 165

 Ganache Chocolate

This store has chocolatier Arno Backes at the helm, so you know it's going to be topnotch. Ganache is a chocolate store and café rolled into one delicious mouthful. The chocolates are made on-site so freshness is guaranteed. The display cabinets are packed with a showcase of sweet treats. Don't miss the Oriental spice chocolate or the mint leaf variety filled with peppermint fondant and ganache. There are also other stars such as the Mozart, Figaro, caramel dome and chocolate pyramids. The café area serves hot chocolates, beautiful patisserie and a selection of indulgent chocolate desserts. A terrific addition to the chocolate-lovers stores around Melbourne.

SOUTH YARRA
250 Toorak Road
9804 7485
Mon–Wed 8am–6pm;
Thurs 8am–8pm;
Fri 8am–10pm;
Sat 9am–10pm;
Sun 10am–8pm
Melway 2L J5
Map page 166

Haigh's Chocolates

There is something incredibly comforting about stepping into a Haigh's chocolate store: there's a sense of tradition, a range of chocolates we have come to know and love and always a warm welcome from the staff. Much loved favourites such as the giant peppermint frogs, gold foil–covered chocolate hearts, apricot delight, chocolate caramel fudge, scorched almonds, toffees and macadamia toffee brittle are classics, not forgetting after-dinner mints, peppermint crisp bars and coconut roughs. Haigh's signature selection boxes, which make terrific gifts, come in milk and dark chocolate. **Also at:** 26 Collins Street, City, 9650 2114; Shop 6, 191 Swanston Walk, City, 9662 2262; 715 Glenferrie Road, Hawthorn, 9819 5000; Shop 1, 501 Toorak Road, Toorak, 9827 8713.

CITY
Shop 7, Block Arcade,
282 Collins Street
9654 7673
Mon–Thurs 8.30am–6pm;
Fri 8.30am–7pm; Sat
9am–5pm; Sun 11am–5pm
Melway 1B L7
Map page 162

Koko Black

The team behind Koko Black has taken their brand to new heights with new retail spaces across Melbourne. The entire package is a beauty, from the jewellery-like cabinets through to stylish packaging. And the best chocolates? An almost impossible task, although a special mention has to go to the cinnamon milk chocolate ganache and the outstanding raspberry purée. The classic dark Belgian truffles are always a winner too. These are handmade, chocolate-dipped and rolled in cocoa over a three-day period. Their hot chocolate is perfect on a cold Melbourne day. **Also at:** 799 Burke Road, Camberwell, 9813 2111; Shop 4, Royal Arcade, City, 9639 8911; Shop B118, Chadstone Shopping Centre, 1341 Dandenong Road, Chadstone, 9530 9060; 52 Collins Street, City, 9663 5567.

CARLTON
167 Lygon Street
9349 2775
Mon–Thurs midday–11pm;
Fri midday–midnight;
Sat 11am–midnight;
Sun 11am–11pm
www.kokoblack.com
Melway 2B F8
Map page 164

Lizzy's Chocolate Creations

The display cabinet and shelves at Lizzy's are always filled with a terrific array of chocolate creations. The truffle selection offers flavours such as rum and raisin, Earl Grey, chilli, cherry and an excellent caramel style. Gift boxes in various sizes are filled with truffles if you don't want to choose. There are also sugar-coated fruit jellies to try and excellent rolled truffles. Easter sees a terrific selection of chocolate eggs and bunnies to give to the chocoholic in your life. Other specialty items include celebration cake plaques and chocolate numbers to decorate your next birthday cake. The Lizzy's hot chocolate is a treat too. Lizzy's offers great value for money and there's always a friendly welcome here.

CARNEGIE
172 Koornang Road
9568 0689
Mon–Thurs 9am–5.30pm;
Fri 9am–6pm;
Sat 9am–3.30pm
Melway 68 J5
Map page 167

Max Brenner

These stores have really put the fun into chocolate by creating a complete package of hot chocolates, iced-chocolate drinks, desserts and packaged chocolate treats to go. Wrap your hands around a warm mug of java dark orange chocolate on a cold winter's morning and you'll get the idea. Or cool down with an iced mocha frappe on a hot summer's day. You'll also find indulgent desserts and packaged chocolates – caramelised pecans, crispy waffles and chocolate thins are particular favourites. **Also at:** Shop GD 4 and 5, Little Menzies Lane, City, 9662 4442; Shop 2.208, Level 2, The Glen Shopping Centre, Springvale Road, Glen Waverley, 9803 5300; Shop 6302, Level 3, Highpoint Shopping Centre, Rosamond Grove, Maribyrnong, 9318 8388; 275 Clarendon Street, South Melbourne, 9696 0888.

CITY
25–27 QV Square, 210
Lonsdale Street; 9663 6000
Mon–Tues 8am–9pm;
Wed–Thurs 8am–10pm;
Fri 8am–11pm;
Sat 9am–11pm;
Sun 9am–9pm
www.maxbrenner.com
Melway 1B P2
Map page 162

Highlight
CHOCOLATE TREATS

Milk chocolate bar 49 per cent, Monsieur Truffe, page 39
This bar proves milk chocolate can be very good indeed. Enjoy the long flavours of berry and honey as each square melts in your mouth.

Crème brûlée, Xocolatl, page 39
This is a delicious dark chocolate heart filled with a luscious rich filling and dotted with a little silver foil on top.

Swiss truffles on a chocolate spoon, Ganache Chocolate, page 37
Imagine a Swiss truffle that is so carefully made it virtually explodes in your mouth. And to top it off it's served on an edible chocolate spoon.

Peppermint truffle bar, Haigh's Chocolates, page 38
Seriously good with just the right amount of peppermint to brighten the whole thing up.

Raspberry purée, Koko Black, page 38
This is an amazing chocolate-filled shell with a top layer of raspberry jelly and a lower blend of raspberry ganache. An absolute taste and texture sensation.

Menthe, Cacao, page 35
This imaginative combination of pecan marzipan and dark chocolate peppermint ganache is chocolate coated and topped with a vibrant green tile. You won't taste better.

Monsieur Truffe

What a talented fellow this Monsieur Truffe is. Not only has he grabbed the attention of Melbourne's chocolate fraternity with his truffles rolled in chopped roasted hazelnuts, now he's gone and produced a line of exquisite chocolate bars. The bars are couvertures sourced from specialist companies who create single estate and single variety products. The 68 per cent from Madagascar is a ripper while the 49 per cent milk chocolate from Venezuela will restore your faith in milk chocolate. The selection of truffles here is also exquisite and not at all sugary like many on the market. Flavours include pepper, lime, raspberry, orange, and an amazing sesame combo, which has to be tasted to be believed. This is a seriously good selection of chocolate from a seriously good chocolatier.

SOUTH YARRA
Stall 118B, Prahran Market,
163–185 Commercial Road
0417 917 576
Tues & Thurs–Fri 9am–5pm;
Sat 8.30am–5pm;
Sun 10am–3pm
Melway 2L H9
Map page 166

Xocolatl

Step into a Xocolatl store and you'll soon realise you are in a place where everyone is happy to come to work. But why wouldn't you when you meet chocolate lovers all day and tell them about the handmade creations on display. Staff are only too happy to run through the various chocolates beautifully displayed in glass-topped cabinets. Perhaps it'll be a small box today with a mix of dark, milk and white chocolate truffles? Or a selection of filled chocolates in flavours such as Baileys, summer fruit pudding or crème brûlée? Either way they're sure to please. Xocolatl has also built a name for itself as a top place for hot chocolates with added flavours of cinnamon and vanilla, chilli, orange or peppermint. **Also at:** 11 Strathalbyn Street, Kew East, 9857 0971; 115–121 Victoria Street, City.

CANTERBURY
123 Maling Road
9836 3100
Mon–Sat 9am–5pm;
Sun 10am–5pm
Melway 46 E11
Map page 167

Cooking classes

Whether you want to learn the basics or watch one of Melbourne's top chefs in action, there are cooking classes for all levels available. You can learn to cook everything from everyday Australian dinners, to Thai, Spanish, Italian and French food, as well as master bread making, cooking fish or decorating cakes. Not only that, all classes include tastings and you get to spend a couple of hours with like-minded people.

Bella Vedere
Headed up by talented chef Gary Cooper, this quaint cooking school is located above the wonderful Bella Vedere restaurant located at Badgers Brook Vineyard. The classes showcase Gary's philosophy on fresh and seasonal produce and highlights dishes taken from the restaurant menu.
Badgers Brook Vineyard, 874 Maroondah Highway, Coldstream; 5962 6161; Melway 277 B9

Beverley Sutherland Smith Cooking School
Beverley is one impressive lady. Not only has she published over twenty-seven books, and written numerous articles, her cooking school is one of the longest running in Australia with over twenty years under its belt. All classes take a seasonal approach to menus with delights such as soufflés, modern French menus, fabulous fish, chocolate desserts and dinner parties.
29 Regent Street, Mount Waverley; 9802 5544; www.beverleysutherlandsmith.com.au; Melway 70 G2; Map page 171

Elizabeth Chong
The Authentic Chinese Cooking course is never off the menu; the number of people who have come and mastered this skill and moved onto other classes such as Chinese Cooking for Desperate Housewives or Stir-fry Sensations is huge. Elizabeth is enthusiastic about all types of Asian cuisine, from Chinese and Thai to Vietnamese, and all are taught well.
Methodist Ladies College (MLC) Kew Campus, Barkers Road, Kew; 0419 889 570; Melway 45 E8; Map page 167

CAE Cooking School
The array of classes on offer covers every spectrum from Absolute Beginners, to Cup Cakes and seasonal suggestions such as Winter Desserts and Summer Seafood. Every type of cuisine is covered from Indian Vegetarian to Winter Greek Feasts and Thai Noodles. The classes are held in the Journal Canteen in Flinders Lane and hosted by various chefs, industry professionals and talented foodies.
253 Flinders Lane, City; 9652 0611; www.cae.edu.au; Melway 1B M9; Map page 162

Diana Marsland Cooking
Diana covers every type of class, from cooking fun for school children in the holidays through to hands-on pasta making, dinner-party skills and celebrity chefs showcasing their dishes. All classes take place in a warm and friendly atmosphere. Following each class, everyone sits down to eat and drink in the dining room. Classes are both hands-on and demonstration.
The Gables, 19 Brooke Street, Woodend; 5427 1155; www.dianamarslandcooking.com.au; Melway 609 G9

Essence Food Studio
Bark Beek offers a traditional kind of cooking class, and then he offers something quite different too. Many of the classes have a live music component and others are based around a performance. All focus on fine cuisine, demonstrated by Bark. Classes might include The Spice of Life, Mediterranean Magic or Northern Indian Feast.
7 Filippin Court, Werribee; 9742 3068; www.essencefoodstudio.com; Melway 206 A10

The Essential Ingredient Cooking School
The Essential Ingredient gang gathers together Australia's top chefs and puts them on display in this wonderful demonstration kitchen. Presenters including Teage Ezard, Greg Malouf, Guy Grossi and Stefano de Pieri appear regularly, as do visiting internationals. You can also learn other essential skills such as knife handling and there are hands-on classes such as pastry and sourdough bread making.
Prahran Market, Elizabeth Street, South Yarra; 9827 9047; Melway 2L H9; Map page 166

The French Kitchen
Di Holuigue celebrates forty years of teaching culinary excellence in 2009. During those years some 60,000 students have honed their skills on preparing excellent pastry, risotto, seafood and myriad other delights. All classes culminate in a feast of the dishes demonstrated, plus wine and plenty of discussion. Di also hosts annual food tours to Europe.
3 Avondale Road, Armadale; 9509 3638; Melway 58 J8; Map page 166

Gourmet Kids Cooking Workshops
Not only are these classes a lot of fun, with children getting to dress up with chefs hats and aprons, they are also educational. Classes are aimed at the two- to fifteen-year-old age group and there is a wide range of recipes to suit all levels, ages and skill. Most classes are hands-on and keep any child fully occupied.
1397 Malvern Road, Malvern; 9824 5979; www.gourmet-kids.com.au; Melway 59 E7; Map page 167

The Green Grocer Cooking School
Being one of the best organic greengrocers in town, the focus is on the seasonality of the produce and providing a link between the farm and table. Classes range from topics such as Vietnamese cooking to chocolate truffle making, cheese making and gluten-free cooking. A variety of presenters bring their expertise to the table, along with a glass of wine with which to enjoy the dishes created.
217 St Georges Road, Fitzroy North; 9489 1747; www.thegreengrocer.com.au; Melway 30 B12; Map page 164

Luscious Affairs
Melbourne caterer Liz Long heads up these interactive, lively classes at her Toorak kitchen. Classes run the whole gamut from cooking with kids, to a four-nighter of back to basics. You can also brush up your skills with duck four ways, dinner parties and sweet sensations.
Shop 9, Village Way Arcade, 501 Toorak Road, Toorak; 9827 7199; www.lusciousaffairs.com.au; Melway 2M E6; Map page 166

Meera Freeman Cooking Classes
Meera Freeman has been running cooking classes since 1990 and brings a wealth of knowledge to the table in her chosen fields of Italian, Thai, Vietnamese and North African cuisine. She personally hosts all the classes, which include a full dinner featuring the dishes taught and recipes. Classes run over a four-week period.
71 Barry Street, Carlton; 9348 2221; www.meerafreeman.com.au; Melway 2B C9; Map page 164

The Queen Victoria Market Cooking School
The classes here cover something for all tastes, from educational fun for kids in the school holidays to learning some secrets from Melbourne's top chefs, or showcasing the vibrant produce of the market. Expect classes such as Tasmanian salmon, Mother's Day brunch, Middle Eastern pantry basics or Spanish desserts.
69 Victoria Street, City; 9320 5822; www.qvm.com.au; Melway 2B C11; Map page 162

Savour Chocolate and Patisserie School
If chocolate is your passion and you want to learn how to make chocolate truffles, temper chocolate or create garnishes such as chocolate curls or fans, or even Easter eggs, book in here and roll up your sleeves. Get ready to bake, whisk, roll, knead and stir to create chocolate masterpieces you can then take home to enjoy.
126 Weston Street, Brunswick East; 9380 9777; www.savourschool.com.au; Melway 29 K10; Map page 164

Sunnybrae Cooking School
George Biron is back. After eight years, his hands-on classes return to the menu at his famous restaurant (now also open for Sunday lunches). It would be hard to meet someone more passionate than George and the range of classes varies from bread and pizza making, classic desserts and duck cooking to sausage making and offal Monday.
Sunnybrae, Birregurra; 5236 2276; www.sunnybraecookingschool.blogspot.com

Tony Tan Cooking Classes
Tony's new cooking school is as chic and classy as the man himself. Join him for one of his classes such as One Wok Wonders, Men@work, Thai Workshop or Tang Dynasty. Guest chefs from Melbourne and further afield join him, offering a diverse range of cooking styles and types. Tony also offers culinary tours to China during the year.
28A Lansell Road, Toorak; 9827 7347; www.tonytan.com.au; Melway 2M J4; Map page 166

William Angliss Institute of TAFE
Not only do the future generations of Melbourne's top chefs train here, but you can book in for one of their short courses. There's everything from sushi making, Asian noodles and pasta presca to classes for blokes, beginners and children. In addition, there is Shop & Cook, which is double the fun, covering cuisines such as Asian, Middle Eastern and African.
555 Latrobe Street, City; 9606 2111; www.angliss.vic.edu.au; Melway 1A C1; Map page 162

The local coffee scene is undergoing a revolution not seen since the post–Second World War influence of Italian migrants and coffee lovers. In recent years, much-loved local brands such as Genovese, Jasper, Quist's and Grinders Coffee House have been joined by a bevy of newcomers. South Melbourne's St Ali has been one of the leaders with a dedicated focus on single variety coffee. Also joining this movement has been the excellent Di Bella Coffee store in North Melbourne – again with roasting and café in one location. Tea also continues to be popular around Melbourne with fantastic products at places such as T2 and Oriental Tea House.

Beraldo Coffee

Whether you're looking for that perfect blend, a home plunger or your own espresso machine, Beraldo Coffee are on hand to provide expert advice. The coffee range at Beraldo is displayed in hessian-lined tubs and includes blends such as the Beraldo, Arabica and Makoroma options, as wall as beans from Costa Rica, Kenya, Indonesia and New Guinea. The popular choice remains the Beraldo Blend, a combination of seven different Arabica beans that they believe creates excellent quality espresso coffee. If it's coffee-making equipment you're after then Beraldo can help here too, from plungers and stove-top designs to automated machines for home use and grinders. You can even enjoy a coffee with a sweet snack while you're here.

NORTHCOTE
22 High Street
9482 2899
Mon–Fri 8am–5pm
Melway 30 E11
Map page 165

Cisco's World of Coffee

For over four decades Cisco's has been supplying Windsor residents with their regular caffeine fix. It was all pretty laid back for a while there until a recent influx of new restaurants, burger bars and fish and chip shops appeared on the scene. At least they'll have somewhere decent to source the best coffee beans. With so many years of experience and a huge selection of beans on display you can rest assured they'll be able to come up with a blend to suit every taste. Rich dark, smooth, fruit or mild, no matter your preference they'll be able to assist. Those looking for coffee-making equipment are well covered too with a large selection of brewers, plungers and even jugs for heating your milk. Tea is another feature, plus tea pots and all the accessories needed to make a perfect brew.

WINDSOR
106 Chapel Street
9510 7997
Mon–Fri 8.30am–5.45pm;
Sat 9am–5pm
Melway 2P H1
Map page 166

The Coffee Company

Step inside the door here and you'll know you're at a serious coffee retailer. Green (unroasted) coffee beans are stored in silver chutes while baskets of freshly roasted beans line the front of the store. The aromas will soon have you in caffeine heaven. There are a huge number of beans to choose from: African beans from Ethiopia, Kenya and Uganda; and Central and South American beans from Columbia, Costa Rica and Guatemala. There are also caffeine-free and certified organic options. Roasted nuts are huge here too with cashews, macadamias, peanuts, mixed nuts and many others on offer. Tea is well represented also with options covering black tea, green tea, herbal and fruit infusions. There's also a selection of coffee- and tea-making equipment available.

BALACLAVA
260 Carlisle Street
9534 6604
Mon–Fri 8.30am–6pm;
Sat 8.30am–5pm
Melway 2P H9
Map page 170

Coffee Mio

Coffee Mio is a large corner site on High Street dedicated to coffee beans and equipment for creating the perfect cafe latte. Large silver hoppers are filled with freshly roasted beans all ready to go. Varieties include Mio d'oro, espresso, moka extra, Colombian, plus organic and decaf options. A good selection of stove-top coffee machines are available on-site too covering all styles and budgets. If it's a machine for the home, office or café you're seeking, then checkout the room dedicated to such things. Large commercial machines from Gaggia include two, three and four group styles. Smaller options are also on offer. There are even cups and saucers if you want to have the very best of everything.

THORNBURY
807–811 High Street
9484 0776
Mon–Fri 8.30am–5pm;
Sat 8.30am–midday
Melway 30 F4
Map page 165

Cottle Coffee, Tea and Nuts

This tiny store, situated alongside the Cottle roasting area, is a real treat. Established in 1912, this store has a fantastic range of delicious coffee blends. Choose from the dozen or so freshly roasted coffee beans, or if you can't make up your mind opt for the store favourite Espresso Supreme. If you're not a coffee drinker then why not check out their delicious teas – try Cottle's own label of Irish breakfast tea or the soothing chamomile. There are snacks aplenty, such as chocolate-coated coffee beans, rice crackers and roasted nuts. There are also coffee pots, plungers and tea-brewing equipment to help you create the perfect drink at home. As South Melbourne heats up as a food-lovers destination remember Cottles were there before the rush.

SOUTH MELBOURNE
300 Coventry Street
9699 4121
Mon–Fri 9am–5pm;
Sat 9am–2pm
Melway 2K B2
Map page 168

Di Bella Coffee Roasting Warehouse

The Di Bella coffee business began in Brisbane and has now extended its reach to Melbourne with a terrific roasting warehouse and café in North Melbourne. The open plan of the store provides an excellent opportunity for coffee lovers to see the roasting process in action while their espresso is prepared. Coffee beans are sourced from estates around the world and roasted as required, so you are assured of freshness. Varieties range from Modena blend and certified organic to Fairtrade certified Rainforest Alliance. Education and training is another important aspect of Di Bella with customers invited to classes on using their equipment correctly to achieve the perfect coffee at home. With coffee equipment for sale and freshly roasted coffee beans ready to go, it's quite a place for coffee lovers.

NORTH MELBOURNE
19–21 Leveson Street
9329 2973
Mon–Fri 7am–5pm;
Sat–Sun 7.30am–4pm
Melway 2A J10
Map page 162

Highlight
CBD COFFEES

Brother Baba Budan
This tiny offshoot of St Ali in South Melbourne offers a great opportunity for city dwellers to enliven their day with a serious caffeine experience. You can go the traditional espresso machine product or try a brew coffee from the imported Clover machine.
359 Little Bourke Street, City; 9606 0449; Mon–Fri 7am–5pm, Sat 7.30am–5pm; Melway 1A K3; Map page 162

Federal Coffee Palace
This grand-sounding establishment is in fact an espresso machine tucked away behind the columns at the GPO. The excellent coffee it pumps out more than makes up for any lack of shop fitout. Order a strong long black and imagine you're in Rome.
GPO, cnr Elizabeth and Bourke Streets, City; 9662 2224; Mon–Sat 8am–6pm, Sun 8am–5pm; Melway 2F E3; Map page 162

Pellegrini's Espresso Bar
If it's a coffee experience you're after then look no further than Pellegrini's on Bourke Street. Pop up onto one of the red leather topped stools and enjoy a coffee that would compete with the best of them in Italy.
66 Bourke Street, City; 9662 1885; Daily 11am–11.30pm; Melway 1B T5; Map page 162

Quist's Coffee, page 48
Quist's may be tucked away on Little Collins Street but it's a great spot for CBD coffee lovers. Quist's have recently welcomed a limited edition, eagle-topped Victoria Arduino 'Venus Century' espresso machine into their store. Come and enjoy an espresso like no other in town.
166 Little Collins Street, City; 9650 1530; Mon–Fri 9am–5pm; Melway 1B Q6; Map page 162

Genovese Coffee

Coffee has become a seriously big business in Melbourne with new brands appearing each week, it seems. There's a lot to be said for knowing and trusting a long-running brand such as Genovese. Their signature red sign at cafés across town attests to their coffee being available in-store and is a drawcard for those who love their Super Brazil blend. Visit their headquarters in Coburg East and you'll get the opportunity to bag some freshly roasted beans, a new grinder or even an espresso machine. There are machines to suit home and commercial uses, machines for hot chocolate, branded cups and saucers, and even an on-site coffee school. Everything you could need in fact to get coffee perfection.

COBURG EAST
51 Moreland Road
9383 3300
Mon–Fri 9am–5pm;
Sat 9am–1pm
Melway 30 A3
Map page 165

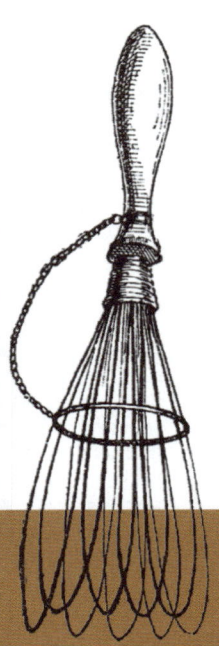

Books *for* Cooks

new & old books about wine, food & the culinary arts bought & sold

Australia's specialist independent cookery book store with over 20,000 new, out-of-print & antiquarian cookery & food & wine related books in stock

- right in the heart of Melbourne!

233-235 Gertrude St
Fitzroy Victoria 3065
Monday - Saturday 10-6
Sunday 11-5

Telephone: +613 8415 1415
Facsimile: +613 8415 1418
www.booksforcooks.com.au
shop@booksforcooks.com.au

FRESH CHEESE COMPANY
Mamma Lucia

bocconcini

mozzarella

mascarpone

parmesan

pecorino

ricotta

50 Weston Street,
Brunswick Vic 3056

Ph: 03 9381 2277

freshcheese.com.au

Grinders Coffee House

Many people take our coffee culture as an accepted part of the local food scene, but it hasn't always been that way. Some decades back Grinders Coffee House in Lygon Street was one of the few places to enjoy a great coffee and to buy beans to prepare coffee at home. The Grinders brand is now seen across the country, but the original store still offers a terrific coffee experience. On offer here are the classic Brazil Blend, Crema Caffe, House Blend, European Blend and Decafe plus the Giancarlo range, all prepacked and ready to go. There's a good selection of coffee beans ready to be ground to order too. Domestic coffee-making equipment is here and if you're in need of a Grinders latte then head to the Grinders Street Café next door.

CARLTON
277 Lygon Street
9347 7520
Mon–Fri 9am–5.45pm;
Sat 9am–5pm;
Sun 10am–4pm
Melway 2B G7
Map page 164

Jasper Coffee

Jasper is a brand that is much loved by coffee-loving Melburnians. You've only to see the swarms enjoying a latte at their Prahran Market Stall on a Saturday morning to see this in action. Jasper's original coffee blends are numbered one to ten and each has its own particular flavours and character. There's an organic blend and single-origin styles from Australia, Kenya, PNG and India all beautifully displayed in shiny silver buckets. Jasper is also passionate about Fairtrade coffee, which offers a better deal for those growing our coffee beans around the world. The Fitzroy store also stocks an extensive collection of local and imported chocolate. **Also at:** Stall 105, Prahran Market, 163–185 Commercial Road, South Yarra, 9827 8509.

FITZROY
267 Brunswick Street
9416 0921
Mon–Fri 10am–6pm;
Sat 9am–6pm;
Sun 10am–6pm
Melway 2C B7
Map page 164

Oriental Tea House

David Zhou has created a wonderful showcase for oriental-style teas within his yum cha restaurants. The fronts of the restaurants are dedicated to the teas with several on tasting daily. Many of them have particular attributes such as rose tea to assist blood circulation and lemongrass to improve digestion. There's also oolong tea (inner peace, harmony and digestion), white tea (high in antioxidants) and a selection of green teas. Fruit tea is also popular and ranges from blackcurrant and raspberry to vanilla and wild cherry. To complete your tea experience there is also a range of glass and earthenware tea pots in which to make your brew of choice, plus handmade cups and all the accessories you could wish for. **Also at:** 378 Little Collins Street, City, 9600 4230.

SOUTH YARRA
455 Chapel Street
9826 0168
Mon–Wed 10am–10pm;
Thurs 10am–11pm;
Fri–Sat 10am–11.30pm;
Sun 10am–10pm
Melway 2L J8
Map page 166

Quist's Coffee

More than seventy years in the one business is quite a feat and that's exactly what Quist's have achieved from early beginnings in Little Collins Street. They were the first coffee roasting business in the 1930s to hit Melbourne and proved a huge success. The coffee is now roasted on the city outskirts but the quality coffee remains. Drop by to source roasted coffee beans ground to your requirements – perhaps Brazil sachos, Kenya AA, Colombia or Costa Rica. There's also tea- and coffee-making equipment, plus cups and teapots to complete the job at home. Having a coffee made here has been taken up a notch with the arrival of a gleaming new Victoria Arduino 'Venus Century' espresso machine. It's one of only 100 in the world so order a latte and see this famous machine in action.

CITY
166 Little Collins Street
9650 1530
Mon–Fri 9am–5pm
Melway 1B Q6
Map page 162

St Ali

St Ali is a coffee roaster and coffee retailer dedicated to excellence. It's tucked away down a small laneway in South Melbourne, not that its location has stopped coffee lovers from tracking it down. Their green coffee beans are sourced from specialty growers far and wide – Brazil, India, Rwanda, Uganda, Mexico, Columbia and many more besides. The roasting is done in small batches, which allows the team to get the very best flavour from each variety. This means customers can choose from a variety of coffees that range from light and fruity to complex, deep and bittersweet. A great option at St Ali is their coffee of the day, as well as daily espresso blend, so there's a chance to try before you buy.

SOUTH MELBOURNE
12–18 Yarra Place
9686 2990
Mon–Sat 7am–5pm;
Sun 8am–4pm
Melway 2K D1
Map page 168

T2

If ever there was a store that would entice you to drink more tea, it would be T2. The range of tea is beautifully packaged and many are on tasting daily. There are classics such as China jasmine, Earl Grey, chamomile, peppermint, English breakfast and the lovely sencha tea, and innovative brews such as Turkish apple, botanica and magnolia garden. There are the world's most glamorous tea bags and even T2 biscuits to dunk! T2 also sell teapots and cups to match any of their specialty teas. **Also at:** Shop 140B, Chadstone Shopping Centre, 1341 Dandenong Road, Chadstone, 9530 4105; Galleria Shopping Centre, 385 Bourke Street, City, 1800 353 022; Shop GD 49, Level 2, Lonsdale Street Building, Melbourne Central, City, 1800 353 022.

FITZROY
340 Brunswick Street
9417 3722
Sat–Wed 9.30am–6pm;
Thurs–Fri 9.30am–8pm
Melway 2C B6
Map page 164

Toby's Estate Coffee and Fine Select Teas

Toby's Estate is well known to Sydney foodies as a brand dedicated to supplying the best speciality coffee and tea available. Well, Melburnians can now check out the entire range at their beautiful new retail store in Brunswick. Customers can watch beans roasting in front of their very eyes, choose from a selection of beans for home coffee making, see the huge range of teas and even enjoy a coffee in the spacious café area. The only difficulty is in choosing which coffee you'll take home. Will it be the Woolloomooloo Blend or the Sumatra Organic Fairtrade? Choosing tea is equally tricky with a massive range of green, black, herbal and semi-fermented teas available. There are also beautiful tea pots, home espresso machines and a mix of accessories to browse over. This is a great addition to the Brunswick food scene.

BRUNSWICK
29 Weston Street (enter from Charles Street)
9009 5462
Tues–Sun 7am–5pm
Melway 29 H9
Map page 164

Di Censo

Fine Quality Gourmet Foods

Di Censo's is a family-owned business that prides itself on its selected quality meats and excellent customer service.

From a family of eight generations of butchers, Di Censo's specialises in:

- Aged Meat • Award-Winning Sausages •
- Old-Style Small Goods •
- Pre-Prepared Meals • Cooking Advice •
- Christmas Hams - Honey - Natural Smoked - Baked •

ORDER AT alf@dicenso.com.au
Phone (03) 9842 3078 Fax (03) 9842 3182
Address 24 Tunstall Square Doncaster East VIC 3109

OPENING HOURS

Mon to Wed 7.00am - 6.00pm Thur to Fri 7.00am - 6.30pm
Saturday 7.00am - 3.00pm Sunday Closed

Crafting people
who create food you desire

Recipe for success

Combine a passion for food and fine wine, and add skills recognised around the world. Chefs, bakers, hotel managers, waiters and sommeliers are trained in first class facilities at Holmesglen's Centre for Hospitality, Cookery and Bakery.

Our diverse range of courses launch students towards a career in the dynamic food and hospitality industry. Apprenticeship, certificate, diploma and advanced diploma in:

- Bakery
- Cookery
- Food & Beverage
- Hospitality Management
- Patisserie

Call now
03 9564 6250 (Waverley)
03 9209 5938 (Moorabbin)

Victoria
The Place To Be

www.holmesglen.vic.edu.au

holmesglen

Delicatessens are essential local food emporiums offering a one-stop shop for all manner of foodie essentials. Traditionally this has been bacon, ham and salami, cheese, olives and tins of whole peeled tomatoes. The contemporary deli in Melbourne has evolved into something much grander and more exciting. The best delis now have an amazing array of products. They have become the place to source excellent sourdough bread, fresh pastas and pizza bases, antipasti, farmhouse cheeses, the freshest olive oils, great coffee, catering and ready-to-go meals. If you have such a store in your local shopping strip, keep up your patronage. It's a huge task to keep all of those food products at their best and the business rolling along. For it to thrive it needs you!

Albert Park Deli

This store is an essential part of the Dundas Place strip. It offers a terrific mix of deli and food store rolled into one, with a bustling café that spills out over the pavement outside. Shoppers can browse the selection of bread from Phillippa's, Irrewarra and other bakeries plus cheeses and other pantry essentials. The main thing customers do here is peruse the huge selection of take-home meals, such as beef lasagne, meatballs with tomato sauce and pasta, cannelloni, curries and casseroles. There's also pea and ham soup and an excellent egg and bacon slice. Sweet treats are also good here, particularly the jam doughnuts and the Lebanese spicy cake, which is packed with nuts, peel and semolina and flavoured with cumin and caraway.

ALBERT PARK
129 Dundas Place
9699 9594
Daily 6am–8pm
Melway 2K A6
Map page 168

Bill's Farm

The Queen Victoria Market has a huge range of delis to choose from – each one with their own terrific ingredients for keen cooks. Then there's Bill's Farm – standing head and shoulders above the rest. The difference with this deli is the incredible selection of products to choose from, combined with service from staff who really know their stuff. For starters cast your eyes over the selection of delicious cheeses, which includes local and European classics – buffalo mozzarella, parmigiano, British cheddar – and don't miss the barrel-ripened Greek feta. There's also Jane's sausages, smoked trout, dips and antipasti, plus local olive oil. The hit list continues with Persian fairy floss, butter, specialist preserves and the amazing imported Spanish jamon.

CITY
Stall 17–18, Dairy Produce Hall, Queen Victoria Market, cnr Elizabeth and Victoria Streets; 9328 2003
Tues & Thurs 6am–2pm;
Fri 6am–6pm;
Sat–Sun 6am–3pm;
Melway 2B C11;
Map page 162

Curds and Whey

In its early days Queen Victoria Market was awash with bulk cheese and butter stalls. Now in the twenty-first century this is the one remaining example of this style of retailing. Curds and Whey, expertly guided by owner Anna Burley, is a popular corner site with one side dedicated to bulk cheeses and the other to more specialist cheeses and foodie products. The bulk cheese counter is particularly busy with products mostly from around Victoria – the Drouin tasty is a favourite. Bulk butter is another drawcard: salted butter for spreading on toast, and unsalted for cooking and baking. The smaller counter has a great selection of farmhouse cheeses, plus terrific pâtés and terrines. Don't miss the excellent honey on tap too.

CITY
Stall 12–13, Dairy Produce Hall, Queen Victoria Market, cnr Elizabeth and Victoria Streets
9326 9009
Tues & Thurs 6am–2pm;
Fri 6am–6pm; Sat 6am–3pm
Melway 2B C12
Map page 162

Delicatess

Delicatess ticks all the boxes when it comes to creating a great modern deli. The selection in the chilled cabinet is well chosen with all manner of olives, grilled and marinated vegetables, and the best smoked salmon from Tom Cooper. This sits alongside an extensive cheese selection with the wonderful La Luna cheese, imported European classics and many local favourites. All the accompaniments for your cheese platter are on hand too from quince paste and dried muscatels to excellent breads from Phillippa's and Irrewarra. Smallgoods are exceptional here with the best three-year cured Spanish jamon, plus chorizo sausage, Italian prosciutto, smoked chicken fillets and leg ham on offer. There are just so many good things here – don't miss it.

SOUTH YARRA
Stall 706, Prahran Market, 163–185 Commercial Road
9824 1752
Tues 6am–5pm;
Thurs–Fri 6am–6pm;
Sat 6am–5pm
Melway 2L H9
Map page 166

Eurodore

Port Melbourne has finally received a terrific all-in-one delicatessen and food store. And locals are loving the opportunity to pick up terrific ingredients close to home. The place is beautifully decked out and has an almost French style about it. The staff know their products too, which is an important part of any stores success. The long refrigerated counter contains terrific hams, bacon and smallgoods, plus a great selection of local and European cheeses. Local foodie brands also feature on the shelves. There's also excellent olive oil, fresh breads, pasta and foodie gifts. You can even slip into the café for a refreshing glass of wine after all that shopping. Customer events are also hosted here with visiting winemakers, cheese lovers and food producers.

PORT MELBOURNE
271 Bay Street
9646 3499
Sun–Thurs 8am–6pm;
Fri–Sat 8am–10pm
Melway 2J F4
Map page 168

The French Shop

The dedication to retailing great cheese and dairy foods is apparent with just one glance at the French Shop. Yes, French cheese is a real focus here with classics such as brie, camembert, Roquefort and washed-rind styles, as well as a number of goat cheeses. Cheese changes from day to day so take the time to ensure you're getting your chosen wedge just how you like it. Alongside these are other European classics including luscious taleggio and soft blue gorgonzola from Italy, plus English cheddar and gorgeous butters. The French Shop is also renowned as a place to source beautiful terrines, pâté and rillettes and a select range of antipasto ingredients. Imported and local jams, marmalades, Maldon sea salt, Italian pastas and French mustard also feature here.

CITY
Stall 1–2, Dairy Produce Hall, Queen Victoria Market, cnr Elizabeth and Victoria Streets; 0419 347 631
Tues & Thurs 6am–2pm;
Fri 6am–6pm;
Sat 6am–2pm
Melway 2B C11
Map page 162

Kazachor

Visiting Kazachor is a little like stepping back in time to when Eastern European delis were prolific and multilingual ladies looked after everyone with great efficiency. Today at Kazachor that's still how it's done. Everyone takes a number and waits for one of the deli ladies to call you up. The Bentleigh locals certainly know the system and it goes off without a hitch. The stunning display of smallgoods is the reason most people shop here. It's a tempting display of smoked chicken fillets, awesome Polish and German sausages, chicken kabana, delicious smoked hams, liverwurst and so much more that pulls the crowds. The selection also covers marinated herrings and smoked salmon. Shelves here are filled with imported instant packet soup mixes, biscuits and imported jams.

BENTLEIGH
480 Centre Road
9557 4028
Mon–Fri 9am–6pm;
Sat 9am–5pm;
Sun 9am–3pm
Melway 77 E1
Map page 169

La Bergerie

Melbourne is a city where you'd think there would be great cheese shops on every shopping strip. Well, in reality they are few and far between. So, think how lucky Canterbury residents are with La Bergerie on their doorstep in Maling Road. Here the lure of aged cheddar, ripe brie and perfectly matured blue cheese becomes a reality. As with all good cheese shops there is an opportunity to taste before you buy and the over the counter advice is excellent. They are strong on European classics here with aged comte, gruyère and the award-winning Cashel blue from Ireland. Besides cheese there's a top selection of beautiful terrines, special pastas, sweet treats and olive oil. The excellent Gundowing ice-cream from north-east Victoria is also available.

CANTERBURY
141 Maling Road
9830 7915
Mon–Fri 10am–6pm;
Sat 8.30am–6pm;
Sun 10am–5pm
Melway 46 D11
Map page 167

Laikon Deli

There are times as a food lover when you want a classic Greek delicatessen. Well, Laikon Deli is a terrific example of just that and it's been servicing the needs of Bridge Road locals for many years now. You know it's good from the window display of dangling prosciutto, salami and pancetta, plus the extensive selection of beautifully displayed dried fruits and nuts – apricots, dates, figs, sultanas and currants alongside almonds, pistachios, walnuts and pine nuts. The selection of dried legumes is excellent with everything from chickpeas and borlotti beans to lentils and lima beans. There's also good-quality hams and bacon, plus cheeses galore, olive oil, pasta and pasta sauces. If you're in need of a sweet treat then don't miss the dried figs stuffed with walnuts.

RICHMOND
324 Bridge Road
9428 8495
Mon–Fri 7.30am–6pm;
Sat 6.30am–5.30pm
Melway 2H B6
Map page 166

Ludo The Good Food Store

Ludo is a store we're very familiar with, mostly because we assisted owners John and Rose Hudson to get the place up and running. It's proven to be a much loved foodie hangout in the bayside area. Early morning it's the place for coffee to go and breakfast. From midday it's a favoured lunch spot with a delicious array of fresh salads, pies, tarts and sandwiches on offer. Then there's the produce side of the business with a select range of olives and antipasti, smoked salmon, farmhouse cheese, rare roast beef, hams, salami, jamon and prosciutto from top-quality producers. There's sourdough bread fresh daily and beautiful sweet treats to enjoy. The shelves are filled with the best confectionary, olive oil, Asian and Middle Eastern ingredients and spices for the home cook.

SANDRINGHAM
5 Waltham Street
9598 5488
Mon–Fri 8.30am–5pm;
Sat–Sun 9am–5pm
Melway 76 G9
Map page 169

Le Croissant

Est'd 1969, Le Croissant is one of Melbourne's oldest French Patisseries.

Tradition and experience are the most important ingredients in producing our authentic hand made pastries. Using all natural ingredients, we offer a selection of freshly baked pastries including hand made croissants, biscuits, tarts and cakes.

1204 Toorak Rd Camberwell ~ Ph: (03) 9809 2263 ~ Open Wednesday thru til Sunday (Closed Mon & Tues)

Highlight
DELI FOODS

Barrel-ripened feta cheese, Bill's Farm, page 52
The Greek-made barrel-ripened feta has to be tasted to be believed. A cracking combo of sheep and goat milk is combined, and then ripened in timber barrels until it's fresh and zesty. It's a million miles removed from commercially made salty feta.

Barossa smoked chicken, Delicatess, page 53
These beautifully made fillets are juicy and carefully smoked to perfection. Try one sliced and tossed through hot penne with tender green peas, parmigiano and chopped fresh mint for a sensational dinner in a hurry.

Freshly made ricotta, Mamma Lucia
A direct-to-the-public cheese factory where cheese fans go to on Saturday mornings to pick up tubs of freshly-made, still-warm ricotta. It's a real treat.
50 Weston Street, Brunswick; 9381 2277; Mon–Fri 8.30am–4.30pm; Sat 8.30am–1.30pm; Melway 29 H9; Map page 164

La Luna goat's cheese, Richmond Hill Cafe & Larder, page 57
Year in and year out we recommend cheeses from Holy Goat. One taste of their beautifully balanced, full-flavoured La Luna cheese will make you a fan for life too.

Milawa Cheese Shop

David and Anne Brown are pioneers of the local farmhouse cheese-making industry. They established Milawa Cheese Company in 1988 in north-east Victoria and haven't looked back since. They also run this cheese shop in Carlton North to showcase their range to cheese-loving Melburnians. Many of their early cheeses are now considered classics – King River gold, for example, with its pungent gutsy aroma and flavour. The aged Milawa Blue is another popular cheese. Other farmhouse producers are represented here too with dairy products from Tarago, Timboon, Meredith and Woodside, and Hunter Valley Cheese also gets a look in. The shop plays host to other top foodie products from the Milawa region, including Milawa mustards, honey and quince paste.

CARLTON NORTH
665 Nicholson Street
9381 1777
Mon–Fri 10am–6pm;
Sat 9am–2pm
Melway 30 A12
Map page 164

Nick and Sue's Gourmet Deli

Camberwell Fresh Food Market has been home to Nick and Sue's Gourmet Deli for over two decades now – and what a range they've created. Many of the foods are prepared on-site, which is definitely one of the keys to their success. Check out the grilled kalamata olives, baked ricotta, grilled eggplant and Spanish sardines to taste the difference for yourself. No wonder they have so many loyal customers. The deli is a terrific spot to pick up a loaf of Phillippa's bread to accompany your antipasto. Aviv bagels are on hand and are perfectly filled with a spread of horseradish and the in-house smoked salmon. There's also salads, soups, pasta and sauces and cheeses to choose from, plus almond bread, panforte and coffee. All in all it's an excellent place to shop.

CAMBERWELL
Shop 17–19,
Camberwell Market,
519 Riversdale Road
9882 8795
Tues, Thurs & Fri 7am–6pm;
Sat 7am–4pm
Melway 59 J1
Map page 167

Pete 'n' Rosies

Pete 'n' Rosies is a stalwart of the Prahran Market scene and one of the delis that led the way into serious cheese retailing in the 1990s. Today the cheese selection still includes all the big names – King Island for brie and aged cheddar (the black wax is particularly good), Tarago River's gorgonzola-inspired blue cheese, plus buttery brie from Jindi. The deli is also home to big name products from people such as Charmaine Solomon (curry pastes), Maggie Beer (quince paste and verjuice), Phillippa's (spiced nuts and brownies) and Jonathan's (hams and sausages). Add to this a well-stocked bread area, olive oil, spices, condiments and antipasti, and you have a complete package.

SOUTH YARRA
Shop 713, Prahran Market,
163–185 Commercial Road
9826 1260
Tues 6am–5pm;
Thurs–Fri 6am–6pm;
Sat 6am–5pm
Melway 2L H9
Map page 166

Pickadeli

South Melbourne Market has undergone a transformation in recent times. The main shopping aisle has been renovated and upgraded with beautiful-looking stores at which to browse and shop. The appeal of Pickadeli is both its size and its products and service. Rather than just a counter, customers can step inside and browse the extensive selection. The enormous chilled display cabinet is home to fresh ravioli from producers like Alligator, and excellent meats including ham, prosciutto and roast beef. The cheese counter is always worth a look too, with a good selection of locally made and imported cheeses to choose from. The grocery selection includes products such as biscuits, olive oil, arborio rice and dried pasta.

SOUTH MELBOURNE
Shop 4–5, Food Court,
South Melbourne Market,
cnr Coventry and Cecil Sts
9696 3160
Wed 7.30am–4pm;
Fri 7.30am–6pm;
Sat–Sun 8am–4pm
Melway 2K B1
Map page 168

Polish Deli

Just looking at the delicious choices on offer at the Polish Deli would make any shopper salivate with hunger! With salami hanging overhead and a display cabinet lined with enticing smallgoods, there is a plethora of choices on offer. Specialty Polish and German smallgoods and foodies products are the main focus. Spicy chilli kabana, double-smoked cabanosi, lean roast pork, black pudding, pork crackling – the selection seems endless. Other popular food with the crowds who congregate here on Saturday mornings includes short back bacon, smoked eels and rye loaves. There are mayonnaises and pickles, sauces from continental Europe and black puddings aplenty. With hundreds of meats and only so much time, you'll never run out of things to try.

CITY
Stall 5–6, Dairy Produce
Hall, Queen Victoria Market,
cnr Elizabeth and Victoria Sts
9348 9211
Tues & Thurs 6am–2pm;
Fri 6am–6pm; Sat 6am–3pm;
Sun 9am–4pm
Melway 2B C11
Map page 162

Richmond Hill Cafe & Larder

RHC&L continues to offer a cheese shopping experience like no other in this town. It is an extraordinary feat when you consider the business has been operating for over a decade and none of the original partners are now involved. Cheese retailing takes incredible skills if you're to do it right. This means maturing the cheese in an environment that is totally controlled in terms of temperature and humidity, then bringing the mature cheese to the retail cheese room at just the right time for cheese lovers to enjoy. The larder also offers goodies to accompany your cheese including sourdough bread, British cucumber pickle and caramelised fig and quince preserve. The house-label jams and marmalades, relishes, chutneys and mustards are also worth a good look.

RICHMOND
48–50 Bridge Road
9421 2808
Sun–Thurs 8.30am–5pm;
Fri–Sat 8.30am–6pm
Melway 2G G5
Map page 166

The farmers' market principle is simple: all stallholders must produce their own goods. The farmers' aim is to use minimal or no chemicals in production and can only claim organic and biodynamic growing by certification. These farmers bring their produce, often picked or dug up in the twelve hours before the market, into the city for us all to enjoy. Some only travel a small distance, others come from further afield. Following the principle of reducing food miles, it has to be Victorian produce, with most coming from a radius of 200 km. Exceptions are made for the amazing citrus fruit from the north-west. You can chat to growers about the produce, pick up cooking tips, hang out, meet long-lost friends and stock up for the week. BYO own bags as all markets have a strong sense of preserving our environment. For further information on new farmers' markets visit www.farmersmarkets.org.au.

Boroondara Farmers' Market

This bustling farmers' market has seventy stalls on a regular basis and focuses on primary produce. You can just about source your whole week's shopping here from Little Creek Cattle Farm beef, Alloway Buffalo, Garfield fish farm and Kartanji Park lamb. Add breads from Phillippa's, organic loaves from Hope Farm and gluten-free savouries from an Affair to Remember. The Smokehouse provides smoked trout, salmon and chicken, green eggs for free-range googies and Alpine Olive Oil. There are also trestle loads of seasonal fruit and vegetables, including organics from the likes of Fernleigh Farm. The barbecue gets fired up early for bacon and egg rolls and the queue for the coffee machine is popular.

HAWTHORN EAST
Patterson Reserve, Auburn Road
9278 4444
Third Sat of each month
8am–1pm
Melway 59 E3
Map page 167

Cardinia Ranges Farmers' Market

Borderline as a regional farmers' market, this bustling market draws on the true spirit of farmers' markets to pull in all local farmers and breeders in the Cardinia Ranges area. The pork and lamb comes from heritage breeds, more celebrated for their flavour, a local beef producer has just joined the gang, and farmed barramundi completes the protein side. Organic vegetables abound. These vary depending on the season, but you might see pumpkins, tomatoes, potatoes and carrots on offer. Spring heralds the arrival of asparagus from nearby Kooweerup. Autumn sees chestnuts, hazelnuts, walnuts and quinces to tempt us. Every three months they celebrate the best of the season with a festival: apple and chestnut, Beasty (the animals of Cardinia) and asparagus to name a few.

PAKENHAM
Pakenham Racecourse, Racecourse Road
5945 0403
Second Sat of each month
8am–midday
Melway 317 F8

Highlight
MARKET TREATS

Di's rhubarb – Collingwood, Gasworks, Slow Food and Veg Out
You will find Di come rain or shine selling her unique, and self-developed, rhubarb. Cooking instructions come free, and there's her fabulous jam, chutney or rhubarb tarts for a small price.

Glenora Heritage
What you find at the Glenora Heritage stall largely depends on the season, but there's always lettuce, radishes and rocket. Summer sees heirloom tomatoes and baby carrots. Depending on the season they may go foraging for wild mushrooms in autumn and nettles, but other than that it's all grown on their property just outside Kyneton.

Gypsy Pig – Gasworks and Slow Food
Gypsy Pig is so named because one of the bloodlines they have saved is called Gypsy. This free-range pork is bred in West Gippsland, the old breeds represent a wonderful old-fashioned flavour and are a taste sensation. You can buy just about every cut, plus bacon, sausages and even bones for your dog.

Moondarra blueberries – all markets except Cardinia
These wonderful organic blueberries are probably the best blueberries in the world. Grown in Gippsland, fresh fruit is available January to April, with frozen fruit and trees available the rest of the year.

Collingwood Children's Farm Farmers' Market

This market was the first inner-city market back in 2002. It is probably the most beautiful farmers' market with its backdrop of gum trees and the Yarra Valley, and the best of urban and rural producers showcase their wares. Approximately one-third are original stallholders, such as Mt Zero and Di's rhubarb. Depending on the season, expect to find sixty to seventy farmers. There is cheese from Holy Goat, Maffra cheese and Red Hill cheese; organic milk and butter from Gippsland; and bread from Hope Farm and St Andrew's bakeries, as well as Turkish bread. Seventy-five per cent of stalls are vegetables, with a large proportion of those being organic and an increasing number of bio-dynamic growers. Add in coffee and a big breaky and it's a perfect way to spend a Saturday morning.

ABBOTSFORD
St Heliers Street
9417 5806
Second Sat of each month
8am–1pm
Melway 2D C9
Map page 165

Gasworks Farmers' Market

This market has a lovely, quite different, setting among the artists studios set within the remaining walls of the South Melbourne gas plant. Fruit and vegetables dominate: breads come from nearby Il Fornaio, Greg Brown and Knead in Hawthorn. The Mt Bellview Welsh Black beef from north-east Victoria is extraordinary, as is the Gypsy Pig from Gippsland. Newcomer to the regional cheese-making scene is Blue Bay from Mornington. Check out their European range including kefir, fresh curds, mozzarella and crumbly hard cheeses. Stalwarts such as Mt Zero display their wares: olives, olive oil, tapenades, lentils and beetroot relish. Glenora Heritage has the best range of salad leaves, baby carrots and turnips, plus heritage tomatoes and field mushrooms.

ALBERT PARK
Gasworks Arts Park,
21 Graham Street
8606 4200
Third Sat of each month
8.30am–1pm
Melway 2J H7
Map page 168

Kingston Farmers' Market

Run by the local council in conjunction with the Rotary Club and community groups, this market's operation means you'll be parked and shopping before you can say 'hug a tree'. Organiser Vicky Davidson tells us that it's relatively small with fifty to sixty stalls, depending on the season. There is venison, lamb, beef, barramundi, free-range chicken and buffalo, plus two cheese stalls, Red Hill and Blue Bay, and bread from Hope Farm, Phillippa's and Greg Brown. You will find fruit and vegetables of every persuasion, along with free-range eggs, cakes, puddings, olive oils and Sri Lankan pastes. A local makes fruit sorbets in summer; you can also find vegetable and herb seedlings, hydroponic tomatoes, mushrooms, nuts in autumn and stone fruit in summer.

HIGHETT
Sir William Fry Reserve,
cnr Nepean Highway and
Bay Road
9581 4735
First Sat of each month
8am–12.30pm
Melway 77 G11
Map page 169

Slow Food Melbourne Farmers' Market

A welcome addition to the farmers' market scene, Slow Food brings its philosophy to an everyday level. Their main criteria are to support local produce, reduce food miles, and maintain traditional cooking and growing methods. In line with this, you will find no hydroponics at this market and like other farmers' markets it's plastic bag free, so BYO recycled bags. Surrounded by the buildings of the convent, you have to look well into all nooks and crannies to find every stallholder. Vegetables are a huge drawcard with them coming from nearby areas such as Werribee, Cranbourne, Wandin and Keilor. Look out for all our favourites: Petty's Orchard with their heritage apples, Mt Zero, Di's rhubarb and Gypsy Pig.

ABBOTSFORD
St Heliers Street
9416 2099
Fourth Sat of each month
8am–1pm
Melway 2D C9
Map page 165

Veg Out St Kilda Farmers' Market

Veg Out has its particular St Kilda feel, with an amazing local vibe. Community groups feature here, such as a local school selling cakes or an environmentally aware group. There are loads of organic vegetables, including garlic, fresh greens, root vegetables and salad vegetables. Look out for the amazing pistachios in autumn, real stone fruit in summer and citrus fruits in winter. The Moondarra blueberries are the best in the world, completely organic and sure to sell out early. Make a beeline for the Glenora Heritage Produce, Andrew Woods eclectic vegetables, Petty's Orchard and Mt Zero to round out your shopping experience. Like all farmers' markets it's plastic bag free, so BYO recycling bag, a healthy appetite and the anticipation of fresh vegetables picked the day before from the farm.

ST KILDA
Peanut Farm Oval, between
Chaucer and Spenser
Streets
0407 411 198
First Sat of each month
8.30am–1pm
Melway 2P B10
Map page 170

Fine food stores

Where would we be without these fine food stores? Innovators such as John Portelli, Syd Weddel and Simon Johnson bring us quality products from all four corners of the globe. They introduce us to new flavours, which over the course of a couple years become staples in our pantries (just think about the 1990s hero – sun-dried tomatoes). We can visit them direct to see the range of what has grabbed their eyes on buying trips to Europe; no doubt, much of this range will end up in a food store close to you. Not quite in the same league, but still offering us the best of all the local and imported products, is Leo's and David Jones. Their dedication to bringing us the best products under one roof, with quality service, is amazing. They are in a class of their own.

David Jones Food Hall

The David Jones food halls gather together in one place all the top brands from across Australia and the world. There are shelves and shelves of olive oils, jams, relishes, curry pastes, biscuits and chocolates. Each food hall has a Peter Bouchier butcher's shop (see page 25), fresh fish, fruit and vegetables, and bread from Phillippa's. The cheese counters are amazing, with the best of local and imported farmhouse cheeses, and there is a tempting cake section where you can pre-order celebration cakes. It's also a great place to grab a quick bite to eat – the sushi and oyster bars are particularly good. **Also at:** Lower Level, Chadstone Shopping Centre, 1341 Dandenong Road, Chadstone, 8531 4444.

CITY
Bourke Street Mall
9643 2222
Mon–Wed 9.30am–6pm;
Thurs 9.30am–7pm;
Fri 9.30am–9pm;
Sat 9am–7pm;
Sun 10am–6pm
Melway 1B M5
Map page 162

Enoteca Sileno

Since 1953, Enoteca has brought us quality Italian ingredients such as parmigiano reggiano, olive oil, vincotta, balsamic vinegar and pasta to our tables. The original store was upgraded and moved to this superb new location, which also houses the Vino Bar and Restaurant and function centre, home to their cooking classes and wine-appreciation classes. The care and attention to detail that John Portelli and his team take to choose the best ingredients and then describe them is second to none, contributing greatly to their success. The shelves are stocked with pasta of all shapes and sizes and price brackets, as well as the Ferron arborio rice. The range of extra virgin olive oils and aged balsamics is amazing. The cheese room is home to the hunks of reggiano and legs of air-dried prosciutto.

CARLTON NORTH
920 Lygon Street
9389 7000
Mon–Wed 9am–6pm;
Thurs–Sat 9am–9pm;
Sun 10am–4pm
Melway 29 K12
Map page 164

> ## Highlight
> ### BEST PRODUCTS
>
> **Parmigiano reggiano, Enoteca Sileno, page 63**
> The Extra Testa Parmigiano Reggiano DOP, is a classic Italian ingredient that has found its way into discerning Melburnian kitchens. It is cured with love and Caroli extra virgin olive oil for at least three years, which gives it a delicious flavour and gorgeous rich nuttiness.
>
> **Saffron, The Essential Ingredient, page 64**
> Saffron, cultivated from the stamens of the *crocus sativus*, is an essential ingredient in traditional Mediterranean dishes such as paella and bouillabaisse. The saffron comes from Spain and before use it is imperative to soak the threads in warm water.
>
> **Sapori Sienna Cake, Mediterranean Wholesalers, page 65**
> This is a traditional Italian sweetmeat made from candied fruits, spices and almonds. This round cake is customarily served at Christmas time, but is a firm favourite with all Italian families.
>
> **SJ Pasta Sauces, Simon Johnson, page 65**
> SJ Pasta Sauces are a pantry staple and come in five different styles – rocket, chilli, basil, cherry tomato and puttanesca. They have a minimum of 83 per cent sweet ripe San Marzano tomatoes from Southern Italy and are made during the summer months when the tomatoes and basil are in season. They are chunky, sweet and free of additives and preservatives.

The Essential Ingredient

Located right in the heart of Prahran Market, this store sells a wide variety of ingredients to Melbourne's top chefs, home cooks and passionate foodies. There are many different aspects to this retailer: cooking classes (see page 41); homewares, books and kitchen equipment (see page 98). All sourced with care to bring you the best product at the best price. Their own label covers everything from vinegars, olive oils, capers and salt, and they also stock the best from other local and imported producers. They represent Peter Watson, Greg Malouf and Kennedy & Wilson. Every kitchen gadget, peculiar and not so peculiar ingredient, pot, bottle opener, toothpick, serviette, apron or food item you require can be found here.

SOUTH YARRA
Elizabeth Street
9827 9047
Mon–Thurs 9am–5pm;
Fri 9am–5.30pm;
Sat 8am–5pm;
Sun 10am–4pm
Melway 2L H9
Map page 166

Leo's Fine Food & Wine

Leo's are wonderful supermarkets for one-stop quality shopping and great convenience. Leo's offer household products at great prices, but their range of quality and gourmet products, still at good prices, sets them apart. The meat section is enough to turn any vegetarian: rolled-lamb roasts, juicy steaks, tender chicken kebabs and flavour-packed sausages. The deli section is impressive with local and imported cheeses, in all price brackets, plus take-home meals and antipasto ingredients. Breads come from Phillippa's, Irrewarra, La Madre and Dench. Products from Simon Johnson, Christine Manfield, Maggie Beer and regional producers such as Cunliffe and Waters fill the shelves. December sees the Christmas shop open upstairs, full of edible presents. **Also at:** 133 Burgundy Street, Heidelberg, 9458 4866.

KEW
26 Princess Street
9853 8314
Daily 7am–10pm
Melway 45 C6
Map page 165

Mediterranean Wholesalers

One of the biggest independent food shops in town, people come from all across Melbourne to stock up on the bargain prices of the Italian goods here. The deals are so good that everyone ends up spending more than anticipated. You may come for one can of tomatoes, and end up with a slab. The shop is split into different sections. There are dry goods (including pasta and arborio rice), tinned tomatoes, tomato sugo, tinned beans and jars of sun-dried tomatoes, artichokes and olives. The deli section at the back is home to all the great Italian cheeses, salami, pork and fennel sausages, salt cod and antipasto items. You can also find cookware, wine and spirits (including limoncello), a bakery and a coffee spot (enjoy in-house or take home).

BRUNSWICK
482 Sydney Road
9380 4777
Mon–Thurs 9am–5.30pm;
Fri 9am–7pm; Sat
8.30am–2pm
Melway 29 H7
Map page 164

Peter Watson

Peter's smart black packaging can be found in all good food stores across Victoria. He is most famous for his spices, which are all small-batch produced to ensure freshness. The range also includes dressings, marinades, mueslis, jams, chutneys, sweet sauces and mustards. Attention to detail ensures that the quality is always the highest and new products are added constantly. The wholesale side of the business sends out products to all kinds of food stores, while the two small shops allow Peter a creative outlet for small batches of seasonal products. Herbs and spices cover everything from allspice to thyme, including blends such as kashmiri masala, ras el hanout and zaatar. **Also at:** 113 St David Street, Fitzroy, 9417 0209.

SOUTH MELBOURNE
6 Union Street
9699 2566
Summer:
Wed–Sun 10am–4pm;
Winter:
Wed–Sat 10am–4pm
Melway 2K C2
Map page 168

Simon Johnson, Purveyor of Quality Foods

The name 'Simon Johnson' is synonymous with quality. His dedication sees him purchasing products from over eighty different producers around the world, such as Duchy Originals, Valrhona and Ortiz. With seven stores across Australia, plus a huge wholesaling business, you can pop into one of his three Melbourne stores to buy the ingredients that the top chefs use and produce for him. Big names include Jamie Oliver, Christine Manfield, Mariage Frères tea, Joseph olive oil and Ferran Adria. His own brand represents great value and covers all bases: pasta, sauces, olive oil, sweet treats, pastry shells, mayonnaise, salt and curry pastes to name a few. Special mentions must go to the cheese room and the range of chocolate; both are outstanding. **Also at:** 12–14 St David Street, Fitzroy, 9486 9456; Shop FO27, 1341 Dandenong Road, Chadstone.

TOORAK
471 Toorak Road
9826 2588
Mon–Fri 10am–6.30pm;
Sat 9am–5pm;
Sun 10am–4pm
Melway 2M F6
Map page 166

Fish and seafood

We're all advised to eat more fish and seafood as a part of our diet – but in order to cook the best fish we need dedicated fishmongers in our local high street. Also, we all want a place where we can be guaranteed that the seafood on display is really fresh. A good fishmonger can assist with all of this. Start going there regularly and they'll offer advice on what to buy based on previous purchases. Fishmongers are usually pretty keen cooks too and full of good advice on what to do with your chosen item in the kitchen. Some fishmongers are also starting to do part of the cook's job too with prepared seafood patties; marinated whole and filleted fish; and kebabs ready for the grill. Cooking a healthy and delicious fish dinner has suddenly become a whole lot easier.

Aquanas Seafood

This is a newcomer on the seafood retailing scene although the family behind the venture has been in the seafood wholesaling scene for many years. The place certainly looks swish with a large counter containing all manner of good things from the sea. The aim here is to make cooking seafood as easy as possible for the home cook. This sees seafood soups such as crab bisque and clam chowder available to take home and heat. There are also sweet chilli fish cakes, seafood lasagne and smoked trout cannelloni in an ever-changing menu. This is set alongside a selection of top-quality, ready-for-the-pan seafood. All the favourites are available from salmon, flathead and rockling, to more speciality items such as sardine fillets and vongole.

HAWTHORN
734 Glenferrie Road
9815 1028
Mon–Fri 10am–6.30pm;
Sat 9am–3.30pm
Melway 45 D9
Map page 167

Canals, The Seafood Appreciation Centre

The silver Canal's sign has been welcoming seafood lovers for about ninety years, and what a job they do. Shopping at Canals is just like it should be – you have a chat with the person behind the counter, discuss what's good on the day and what you feel like cooking; then there's a sale and you trot off home with something delicious. There's a daily selection of fresh fish on ice here – it could be snapper, salmon, whiting or flathead depending on the season. Shellfish can also feature blue swimmer crabs, scampi, mussels and freshly opened oysters, which are especially good when the juices are retained in the oyster. Other good things on offer include smoked salmon, smoked ocean trout, and gravlax by the slice.

CARLTON NORTH
703 Nicholson Street
9380 4537
Tues–Thurs 9am–5.30pm;
Fri 8am–6pm;
Sat 8am–midday
Melway 30 A11
Map page 164

Clamms Fast Fish

Two main options loom at Clamms Fast Fish – to purchase delicious seafood and cook at home, or enjoy a few things from the takeaway fish and chips menu. Those going down the home-cooking line can choose from the freshest seafood prepared and ready to go. Marinated whole snapper can be cooked on the barbecue hotplate or baked to perfection, and prawn kebabs and salmon kebabs are all perfectly sized for the frypan. The selection runs across a daily catch that can include tuna steaks, calamari, marlin, rockling, blue grenadier, salmon, scallops and so much more. There's also ready-to-eat sushi, sushi platters, cooked prawns and crays in season. When it comes to fresh seafood Clamms are hard to beat!
Also at: 93 Dundas Place, Albert Park, 9690 8969.

ST KILDA
141 Acland Street
9534 1917
Daily 9am–9pm
Melway 2P B9
Map page 170

Claringbold's Seafoods

Even if you're not thinking of buying seafood the awesome display at Claringbold's always seems to draw us over for a quick look. This 'quick look' usually results in a change to the dinner menu to incorporate some amazing-looking fish or shellfish we just have to try. Fresh fish runs from well-known varieties such as Atlantic salmon, snapper, flathead and whiting to more exotic options including coral trout, wild barramundi, swordfish and the best yellow fin tuna. Crays, crabs, scallops, oysters and mussels also feature. Claringbold's is also renowned for their sushi display, which is all made on-site daily with the pick of the day's catch. Other specialist foods to look out for include the cooked king crab legs from Alaska, which are really outstanding.

SOUTH YARRA
Shop 510, Prahran Market,
163–185 Commercial Road
9826 8381
Tues & Sat 6am–5pm;
Thurs–Fri 6am–6pm;
Melway 2L H9
Map page 166

Conway

For just on three decades Conway has been supplying the public with a top array of fresh and frozen seafood. All through the day steady streams of fish lovers come to browse and buy from the display. The fresh range depends on the catch of the day – so can range from salmon, trevally, skate, flake and blue eye – both as whole fish or filleted. Live crays are available to pick from a tank if you want to be assured of freshness. Other seafood essentials include smoked salmon, marinated mussels and smoked trout. Frozen supplies include soft-shell crabs, prawns, scallops, calamari and much more besides. With a new building underway on the corner of Wingfield Street the shopping here is going to become even better than before.

FOOTSCRAY
11–17 Wingfield Street
9689 3400
Mon–Fri 7.30am–5.30pm;
Sat 7.30am–2pm
Melway 2S H8
Map page 163

Dandenong Arcade Fish Supply

The Dandenong Arcade is not the most glamorous shopping site we've come across, but nestled alongside the local cafés and coffee shops is a really terrific array of fresh fish. Weekends are pretty packed here as shoppers vie for the fresh seafood at the Dandenong Arcade Fish Supply. Prices are very affordable, which no doubt adds to its attraction. Not only that, the fish look great too. A typical choice of whole fish can include trout, leather jacket, whiting, mullet golden bream and tiny sardines. A small selection of shellfish covers prawns and mussels primarily. Just pick your fish, weigh and pay, then have it prepared to your liking. The efficient fishmongers will soon have you on your way home with the makings of a terrific meal.

DANDENONG
Shop 6, 236 Lonsdale Street
9792 9267
Mon–Thurs 8am–5pm;
Fri 8am–6pm;
Sat 8am–5pm
Melway 91 E6
Map page 171

Ducgo Live Seafood

There aren't too many places to buy live seafood around Melbourne, but this well-known Box Hill fishmongers is one outlet. Ducgo has a long row of bubbling tanks filled with many different varieties of fish and shellfish. There's live parrot fish, silvery coated barramundi, Murray cod and even a tank filled with masses of slippery eels. Also on offer most weeks are tiny prawns whizzing around in their own tank, plus menacing-looking mud crabs, lively crayfish and farmed abalone. All the shopper has to do is choose a likely looking specimen from the tanks and the staff will catch and dispatch it for you. A small selection of fresh filleted fish and frozen fish is also available.

BOX HILL
4–6 Cambridge Street
9899 9668
Mon–Fri 9.30am–6.30pm;
Sat 9am–6pm;
Sun 10am–4pm
Melway 47 D10
Map page 171

Fegari Seafood

Fegari Seafood has established itself as a one of this city's best outlet for fresh seafood. Take a few steps inside the door and you'll soon understand why. A massive ice-filled counter holds the day's catch, there's soothing music playing, easy on the eye lighting and a warm welcome. Customers can see Ari working away on fish large and small all through the day, so they are in no doubt this is a super-fresh product. Daily picks might be flathead fillets, marlin or tuna, rockling, hapouka or even their quite delicious fish patties packed with spinach and fresh herbs. The whole smoked trout are excellent too. If you ever needed an excuse to start eating fresh seafood again, it's here at Fegari Seafood.

HAMPTON
425 Hampton Street
9533 4411
Tues–Fri 8.30am–6pm;
Sat 8.30am–4pm
Melway 76 G5
Map page 169

Ferg's Fish

Fish lovers who live in the bayside area of Melbourne are well served with top seafood retail outlets such as the two Ferg's Fish stores. At both Hampton and Beaumaris shoppers have access to a large range of ready-to-cook seafood dishes. Perhaps it'll be the marinated salmon with lemon, Spanish onion and dill, or the prawns with chilli and ginger. Choices also run to ready-to-cook mussels, seafood kebabs, calamari, cooked crayfish and even smoked salmon. Ready-to-heat noodles and pasta are available and would be perfect to toss through the marinara mix. Excellent advice is given to assist with cooking when you get home. There are also platters of seafood available for parties and celebrations. **Also at:** 327 Hampton Street, Hampton, 9598 7426.

BEAUMARIS
Shop 18, South Concourse
9589 0699
Mon–Fri 9am–6pm;
Sat 8am–4pm
Melway 86 D7
Map page 169

Kingfisher Seafoods

Kingfisher Seafoods is tucked away in the corner of Camberwell Market. From this small stall comes some of the freshest and best-quality seafood in this part of Melbourne. The display of whole fish is always outstanding, with garfish, snapper, bream, flathead, whiting and salmon featured. Alongside this are cooked crays, smoked trout, green prawns, calamari and oysters. Staff are always happy to chat about the best way to cook the different seafood on offer and to prepare it ready for you. You may want to bake snapper fillets, pan-fry whiting, whip up a Thai prawn curry or barbecue salmon fillets. No matter the dish it'll be cleaned, filleted, de-boned and ready to prepare the moment you get home.

CAMBERWELL
Shop 11, Camberwell Market, 521 Riversdale Road
9882 4467
Tues & Thurs–Fri 7am–7pm;
Sat 7am–5pm
Melway 59 J1
Map page 167

Fish and chips

There's no doubting Melburnians' love of fish and chips. It's one of the most popular family takeaway meals going. Here we've selected the places that stand head and shoulders above the local fish and chip shop – places where they care about the oil they use and the freshness of the seafood in the cabinets. They're also places where the owners move beyond the basics to offer interesting new tastes, such as Greek fish soup, tempura battered flake and fish burgers.

Blufish
Blufish is just the spot for beautifully battered sea bass and a serve of crispy chips. Other options include calamari salad, seafood skewers and the heart-warming Greek fish soup.
16 Centre Place, City; 9663 0738; Melway 1B M8; Map page 162

Cerberus Kiosk
Cerberus Kiosk is a top spot to enjoy fish and chips and views across the bay to the CBD. Don't miss the tender battered calamari rings and excellent battered scallops. Grab a serve of chips or indulge in one of the many seafood packs on offer.
Boathouse 212, Half Moon Bay, Black Rock; 9533 4028; Melway 85 H2; Map page 169

Clamms Fast Fish
Fresh and fast could be used to sum up the Clamms experience. Terrific packs offer a mix of good things – fish bites, calamari rings, potato cakes, king prawns, chips and battered scallops. As unlikely as it sounds they're coated in a soft batter and still juicy inside.
141 Acland Street, St Kilda; 9534 1917; Melway 2P B9; Map page 170

D'lish Fish
Being situated on the end of Station Pier means this can be one busy spot, but they do get the simple things just right – beautifully battered flake, good-quality chips and crumbed calamari rings.
3/105 Beach Street, Beacon Cove, Port Melbourne; 9646 0660; Melway 2J A6; Map page 168

Fish Bar
If you're a fan of crispy-coated calamari rings, are looking for gutsy-flavoured fish bites and a serve of excellent chips, then Fish Bar is a must. You can relax and enjoy the views over Docklands.
25 New Quay Promenade, Docklands; 9670 5410; Melway 2E E4, Map page 163

Fish Tank
With a great-looking display and speedy service, Fish Tank is Brighton's favourite. Classics of crumbed calamari, mini battered flake fillets and crunchy chips are on hand alongside Thai salmon patties, chilli prawn skewers and baked fish.
20 Church Street, Brighton; 9592 0697; Melway 67 D11; Map page 170

Hooked
Pile into Hooked for hand-cut chippies, battered scallops and tempura battered flathead. Don't miss the battered king prawns too, they are fantastic. A fish burger is also available for those who like their dinner between bun halves.
172 Chapel Street, Windsor; 9529 1075; Melway 2L H12; Map page 166

Red Mullet
This is Glenferrie Road's fish and chip hot spot. Eat in or out from a menu of grilled, baked or fried fish, salt and pepper squid, Thai fish and veggie burgers. There are lots of set-price packs too.
210 Glenferrie Road, Malvern; 9500 9338; Melway 59 C8; Map page 167

M & C Seafoods

M & C Seafoods is a wholesale store that welcomes retail customers too. Choose from the self-serve chilled cabinets brimming with fresh varieties of fish such as tuna, snapper and flathead, salmon, whiting and red mullet. Calamari, crabs and scallops also make an appearance, as do oysters. The display usually contains prawns both cooked and raw. Green raw prawns are perfect for making skewers for the barbecue. M & C Seafoods also label all of their seafood as either local or imported, so you always know what you are buying. Many shoppers like the self-serve aspect of M & C and the value for money they provide.

PRESTON
3 Reserve Street
9416 9311
Wed–Fri 7am–5pm;
Sat 7am–3pm
Melway 31 B4
Map page 165

O'psaras on Portman

This shopping strip's reputation as a Greek food hub is growing by the year, so it's no surprise to find an excellent seafood store in Portman Street. The display here is always enticing with an ever-changing array of whole fish and pan-ready choices. The display always looks incredibly fresh with whole snapper, whiting, sardines and tuna alongside more unusual varieties such as pike, gurnard, bay salmon and leatherjackets. As you would expect in an area known for its Greek cooking, there's calamari and cuttlefish aplenty, plus oysters, scallops and mussels to whisk home for dinner. Service is always spot on too, so make O'psaras a regular stop between leaving work and arriving home to cook dinner.

OAKLEIGH
32 Portman Street
9569 7946
Tues 7am–5.30pm;
Wed–Fri 7am–6pm;
Sat 7am–12.30pm
Melway 69 F7
Map page 169

Prosser's

Prosser's has been in the business for almost eight decades, and is still an incredibly popular Queen Victoria Market fresh seafood stall. It's one of the first stalls most people see at the market and it has a top selection of whole and filleted fish along the expansive counter. All tastes and budgets are covered by barramundi, kingfish, snapper, tailor and morwong. The list goes on with popular picks such as salmon, trevally, mussels and flathead. Prawns are big here too, with something for every dish and any budget. Service is always on the ball with lots of people behind the counter ready to look after your every need. Prosser's is a big drawcard at Christmas and Easter with queues out the door onto Elizabeth Street – yes, it's that popular!

CITY
Stall 30, Queen Victoria Market, cnr Elizabeth and Victoria Streets
9329 0992
Tues & Thurs 6am–2pm;
Fri 6am–6pm;
Sat 6am–3pm
Melway 2B C11
Map page 162

Theo's & Sons Fresh Seafood

Every now and then a store opens that sets the bar for others to follow – well this is one of them. Not only do Theo's have a dedicated team of shuckers opening oysters as needed through the day, they'll also serve them up with their juices still intact in the shell if you prefer. The provenance of each variety is provided too, so you know exactly what you're getting and where it's from. Theo's are very fussy about the fish they provide to customers. The range will only include the best of the day's catch. They also supply freshly cooked to order lobsters, so let them know an hour ahead and it'll be ready and waiting to go. Their next step in customer service is prawns cooked to order. Now if that isn't service, we don't know what is.

SOUTH YARRA
Shop 502, Prahran Market, 163–185 Commercial Road
9826 4288
Tues & Sat 7am–5pm;
Thurs–Fri 7am–6pm;
Sun 10am–3pm
Melway 2L H9
Map page 166

Vasiliki Fresh Crayfish Supply

Melburnians have a love affair with cooked crayfish. They're there when we gather for family celebrations, hot summer days, Christmas lunch and when we just feel like being indulgent. Vasiliki specialises in these very sea creatures from around the islands of Bass Strait. All you need do is pick up the phone, call in your order and it'll be cooked and waiting to pick up in no time. You have to wonder why anyone would bother with a precooked cray from a fishmonger with this type of service available. Shoppers can also get their hands on freshly opened oysters from along the east coast and Tasmania, King Island crabs, crayfish tails (if you're not up for the whole cray), Tasmanian scallops and even smoked salmon. It's quite a place for lovers of the best and freshest cooked seafood.

ST KILDA
173B Barkly Street
9534 2106
Mon–Thurs 8am–1pm;
Fri 8am–2pm;
Sat 8am–midday
Melway 2P C9
Map page 170

Win Sam Seafood and Butcher

Glen Waverley gained a top seafood place when Win Sam opened a few years back. The range here is so varied it's hard to know where to start really. From ready-to-cook salmon cutlets and fillets to the huge selection of prawns, the cabinet is full of good things. If it's whole fish you're after that's here too, and friendly staff can have it cleaned and prepared for you in no time. There are also fish balls and pre-prepared seafood products for including in Asian soups and stir-fries. Oysters, scallops, calamari and mussels also appear here. An array of fish tanks keep live seafood on hand if you want it super fresh.

GLEN WAVERLEY
99 Kingsway
9574 8888
Daily 9am–6pm
(not public holidays)
Melway 71 C2
Map page 171

Yumi's Kosher Seafoods

Yumi's Kosher Seafoods may look like a simple seafood outlet, but it's so much more that that. The Yumi brand extends beyond the seafood on offer to a range of top-quality dips sold at supermarkets and food stores across Victoria and NSW. A couple of outstanding flavours include the sweet potato and cashew dip, as well as the delicious egg salad. The Yumi's mayonnaise is a beauty too. As the sign in the window states, the fish here is 100 per cent kosher and 100 per cent fresh. Salmon features extensively as a fresh fish as well as chunks of hot smoked salmon. Thin-sliced cold smoked salmon is also on hand. The fresh selection is offered whole or filleted and regularly features salmon, tuna, trout and other kosher friendly varieties.

RIPPONLEA
29 Glen Eira Road
9523 6444
Tues 7am–4.30pm;
Wed 7am–5pm;
Thurs 7am–5.30pm;
Fri 7am–3pm
Melway 67 E1
Map page 170

Greengrocers

The local greengrocer is an essential service in every local shopping hub. It's a place where you can gather the latest seasonal ingredients, meet like-minded foodies, have a chat about what you're cooking and go home inspired and stocked up for days of great cooking. It could be chestnuts, grapes and figs in autumn, wonderful salad ingredients and berries over summer, asparagus, basil and mangoes each spring or potatoes, parsnips, swedes and turnips for winter cooking. There's also the opportunity to go to the source of your ingredients. Fresh produce is in abundance at our many markets with specialist stallholders such as Michael Mow and Damien Pike at Prahran Market. There are farm-gate sales around regional Victoria and the the wonderful Aumann Family Orchard on a hillside near Warrandyte. Now that's fresh!

Albert Park Fruit Palace

This long-running 'fruit palace' offers local residents a good array of in-season fruit and vegetables, with plenty more besides. There's always a good selection of potatoes, tomatoes, fresh greens, apples, pears and citrus on hand. The time of year will dictate which varieties are at their best but they provide all the essentials needed for everyday meals. Specialist ingredients appear from time to time too, including some excellent mushrooms in late autumn. Mangoes and stone fruit always feature predominately when available. The array of fresh-cut flowers at the front of the store is always enticing, and will enliven the kitchen perfectly. If you enjoy a one-stop shop, then have a good browse along the selection of dried fruit, nuts, dairy, juices and groceries at the rear of the space.

ALBERT PARK
91 Dundas Place
9690 4383
Mon–Fri 7am–8.30pm;
Sat–Sun 24 hours
Melway 2K A6
Map page 168

Aumann Family Orchard

The Aumann Family Orchard is nestled on a hillside near the town of Warrandyte. It's a rural setting and really fits in well with the grown-on-farm approach the shop promotes. Stepping in here is like walking into a pretty nice packing shed. There are large wooden tubs filled with all sorts of farm-grown fruit. The great thing here is they pick fruit when it ripe, so it's full of flavour and read to enjoy. Over summer this tends towards stone fruit such as peaches plus white and yellow nectarines, including the Zee Sweet variety that can be enjoyed slightly crisp. The range also extends to cherries, apricots and nashi. As the weather cools into autumn and winter, plums, pears and apples appear in store. There are ready-to-eat varieties such as Fuji, red delicious, pink lady and Priscilla.

WARRANDYTE
150 Harris Gully Road
9844 3464
Summer: daily 8am–6pm;
Winter:
daily 8.30am–5.30pm
Melway 35 A6
Map page 171

Biviano & Sons

This is a greengrocer who can offer a lot more than fresh fruit and vegetables. It's more a mini food store really with a terrific array of fresh produce surrounded by kitchen essentials. A recent addition to the store is a towering flower stand in the middle of the retail space. The fresh produce always looks terrific and loyal locals love the extensive range of potatoes, apples, pears, bananas, lettuces and melons that always feature. Salad ingredients and fresh herbs are also excellent here. Chilled cabinets offer dips, yoghurt topped with fruit purée and farmhouse cheeses. There are also organic fruit juices, pastas, olive oil and much more besides. There's always so much to choose from here and good value to boot.

FAIRFIELD
98–100 Station Street
9489 0087
Mon–Thurs 6am–7pm;
Fri 6am–8pm;
Sat 6am–5pm;
Sun 7am–5pm
Melway 30 K10
Map page 165

Damian Pike, Wild Mushroom Specialist

There are plenty of options when shopping for fresh produce at the Prahran Market, but there's only one Damien Pike. For over two decades he's been standing head and shoulders above his competitors as 'the' place for specialist ingredients. Mushrooms are what he is particularly well known for and his selection of cultivated and wild mushrooms (in season) is outstanding. This includes Swiss brown, button, shiitake, enoki and oyster mushrooms most of the year, plus wild orange pine and slippery jack mushrooms in autumn. Imported truffles usually appear around September and October. Besides fungi, Damien has the very best plums, lettuces, zucchini flowers, oranges and blood oranges, Roma tomatoes, baby carrots, cabbages and so much more.

SOUTH YARRA
Stall 116, Prahran Market,
163–185 Commercial Road
9824 0805
Tues & Sat dawn–5pm;
Thurs–Fri dawn–6pm;
Sun 10am–3pm
Melway 2L H9
Map page 166

Devola's

From the fresh flowers displayed outside to the cool produce-filled interior this store is a boon for locals. There's always a good selection of everyday produce needs as well as specialist seasonal ingredients. Good fresh fruit extends from the standards of apples, pears, oranges, stone fruit and bananas to interesting options such as pomegranates and beautiful berries. On the vegetable side there's typically a great selection of potato varieties for different uses, plus capsicums, zucchini, eggplants, carrots and even podded peas for those without the time to pod them. There are also fresh chillies, garlic, greens, ginger and bean sprouts – in fact, everything you need for Asian cooking. Other goodies here include dried fruit, nuts and the excellent Summer Snow fruit juice.

BRIGHTON
616 Hampton Street
9592 5635
Mon–Fri 6.30am–7pm;
Sat 7am–5pm;
Sun 7.30am–4pm
Melway 76 G3
Map page 169

Fresh Generation

Fresh Generation has a prime location in I Shed at the Queen Victoria Market. It's set at the end of the organics aisle and is a popular stop for shoppers who really care about what they buy and cook. The stall seems to shout out seasonality and presents the very best produce growers have to offer. In the cooler months it could be Red Otway potatoes, beautiful rhubarb and freshly picked wild mushrooms such as orange pines and slippery jacks. The warmer months bring amazing chillies, Mr Tran's tomatoes and heirloom tomato varieties such as green zebras and black Russians. Blood oranges, baby green beans, pineapples, sweet navel oranges and pink grapefruit also feature. Special ingredients are always offered for tasting, so you know exactly what to expect when you get your ingredients home.

CITY
I Shed, Queen Victoria
Market, cnr Elizabeth and
Victoria Streets
9329 3909
Tues & Thurs 6am–2pm;
Fri 6am–6pm; Sat 6am–
3pm; Sun 9am–4pm
Melway 2B C11
Map page 162

Napoli Quality Fruit Market

Napoli Quality Fruit Market is a fresh fruit and vegetable store in laid-back Williamstown. Aside from quality fresh produce, there are plenty of essential daily ingredients on offer too. This selection is varied and covers Irrewarra bread, pesto, hummus and lots of other dips and antipasti. Customers can stock up on muesli, preserves, jams and even pickled onions. Smoked salmon is also on hand along with cheeses, smallgoods, antipasti, juices and yoghurts. The main game here is fresh produce, so beautiful lettuces, herbs, apples, citrus fruits and pears are available as well as berries, bananas, pumpkins, potatoes and parsnips. There's always a warm welcome and good advice too. You'd be more than happy if this was in your local shopping strip.

WILLIAMSTOWN
68 Ferguson Street
9397 6164
Daily 6am–7pm
Melway 56 C8
Map page 163

Scicluna's

Scicluna's offers terrific value-for-money fresh ingredients and a whole lot more. This spacious store has a certain beach theme about it with thatched roofs over the fresh produce. It certainly makes for relaxing shopping. The seasons are always apparent in the array of fresh ingredients. Autumn, for instance, sees a great array of apples, pears and citrus backed up by chestnuts, almonds and walnuts. Similarly, summer is the time for wonderful stone fruit (apricots, peaches and nectarines), as well as melons and fresh strawberries, raspberries and blueberries. You can select from good-quality smallgoods, many pre-sliced and ready to eat, plus good-quality cheeses, yoghurts, fresh meat, snack foods and dried fruit. **Also at:** Shop 152, Bayside North Shopping Centre, Beach Street, Frankston, 9781 2777.

MENTONE
2–4 Como Parade
9585 5586
Daily 7am–7pm
Melway 86 K6
Map page 169

Top Shelf Fruits

There's not a lot of space to spare at this terrific Beaumaris greengrocer, but no one seems to mind as the selection on offer is just so good. All the basics are well covered with potatoes, carrots, fresh greens, carrots and tomatoes in abundance. On the fruit side there are masses of apple varieties, plus pears, oranges, grapes, melons and pineapples. Exotics are also covered including a mix of mushroom varieties during the autumn season. The rear of the store is like a mini delicatessen with shelves and refrigerated cabinets jam-packed with olive oil, pizza bases and antipasto such as roasted capsicum, marinated eggplant and olives. There are also staples such as Murray River salt, cheeses, yoghurt and a good selection of biscuits. It's always a busy spot but the queues seem to clear quite quickly.

BEAUMARIS
Shop 1, South Concourse
9589 2170
Daily 6am–6pm
Melway 86 D7
Map page 169

Toscano's of Kew

Toscano's is a family-run greengrocer par excellence. Their loyal customers wouldn't dream of going anywhere else to pick up their everyday seasonal and specialist produce. This comes down to careful choices at the wholesale market, wonderful fresh looking displays and excellent service – all of which is rarely achieved by food retailers. They have all of this here in spades and it's apparent from first glance. There are colourful fresh displays of apples, pears, oranges and lemons, fragrant fresh herbs, stunning stone fruit each summer, full-flavoured tomato varieties, earthy potatoes and so much more. Autumn sees olives, walnuts, almonds and wild mushrooms on hand. Add in friendly service and great cooking advice and you have a terrific offer. **Also at:** Shop FF3, Victoria Gardens, Victoria Street, Richmond, 9429 6064.

KEW
217 High Street
9853 7762
Mon–Thurs 8am–6pm;
Fri 8am–7pm;
Sat 7.30am–1pm
Melway 45 C6
Map page 165

Tunstall Fresh

Tunstall Fresh is so busy they've had to move premises recently, but Doncaster East customers can rest easy as they're still in the same shopping strip. The attraction is the excellent array of fresh produce that always takes a seasonal approach, peppered with good specialty ingredients. So, in autumn for instance they will stock plenty of apples, pears, grapes and rhubarb, as well as fresh chestnuts and quinces. On the vegetable side at this time of year they are big on potatoes, pumpkin, mushrooms and onions, and interesting ingredients such as olives, endive and fennel to back this up. Because the store is so busy you know the turnover is excellent, so nothing hangs around for too long. The friendly, speedy service on the checkouts completes the picture beautifully here.

DONCASTER EAST
11–12 Tunstall Square
9842 1820
Mon–Wed 7am–7pm;
Thurs–Fri 7am–7.30pm;
Sat 7am–2pm
Melway 48 E2
Map page 171

Vegetable Connection

There are a number of terrific food stores dotted around Melbourne that bring an organic approach to food retailing that encompasses fresh produce alongside grocery and pantry goods. Vegetable Connection in Fitzroy is one such place. Step inside the doors here and you can't help but be inspired to cook. There's always cane baskets filled with the freshest ingredients, a seasonal supply of heirloom tomatoes, figs, pears, mandarins and walnuts in autumn for instance. Much of what's here is organic and clearly labelled. The rest of the store is stocked with good-quality groceries. Customers can stock up on muesli mixes, legumes, preserved lemons, cordials, chocolate, yoghurt and dried fruits. A good selection of cheeses from local dairies is also offered.

FITZROY
255 Brunswick Street
9417 2788
Mon–Sat 9am–7pm;
Sun 9.30am–6pm
Melway 2C B8
Map page 164

Ice-cream and gelato

The history of this city's ice-cream and gelato scene has a particularly Italian leaning. Stores set up decades ago around Carlton led the way and for many people it was their first taste of top-quality gelato. A lot of these shops are still serving frozen treats to a loving public and in recent years they have been joined by a new generation of stores, which have also found an adoring clientele. The groovy-looking Trampoline, for example, with their fun product names and welcoming stores, and Fritz Gelato with its delicious combo of gelato and freshly cooked doughnuts have become favourites. We're also long-standing fans of the creative frozen treats at 7 Apples Gelato in St Kilda, Il Dolce Freddo in Lygon Street and the much-loved Jocks in Albert Park. All are perfect places for a cooling cone on a hot summer's day.

Casa del Gelato

There's almost three decades of gelati-making experience at Casa del Gelato, so you know you're in good hands when you step up to the counter at this Lygon Street hot spot. If it's a hot summer's night, getting to the counter may take a while, but it'll be worth the wait. The award-winning passionfruit and mango gelati are definitely worth a try here, if you can ignore the rich, creamy chocolate gelato that is. Other terrific options include lemon, coconut, boysenberry, nougat and caramel. Those who usually have to overlook gelati because they are lactose intolerant are in the right place. If you really can't choose then order a little of a few different flavours and enjoy them in a cup or cone as you wander along Lygon Street.

CARLTON
165 Lygon Street
9347 0220
Summer: daily midday–midnight;
Winter: Tues–Sun midday–late
Melway 2B F9
Map page 164

Fritz Gelato

Fritz Gelato continue to provide excellent frozen treats. Organic ingredients are used where available so you know you're getting a really special product. The range includes gelati, sorbet, frozen yoghurt and low GI options. Favourite flavours include butterscotch, cool mint and honeycomb crunch, bounty, nectarine and peach. Flavours of the month also appear including Anzac biscuit in April, plum sorbet for December and hot cross bun in March. The organic cinnamon and sugar-rolled doughnuts are excellent here too. **Also at:** 334 Bridge Road, Richmond, 9427 9898; Shop 2, South Melbourne Market, cnr Cecil and Coventry Streets, South Melbourne, 9681 3109; Stall 120, Prahran Market, 163–185 Commercial Road, South Yarra, 9826 6114.

ST KILDA
11A Fitzroy Street
8598 9090
Daily midday–midnight (later on hot summer nights)
Melway 2N J6
Map page 170

Il Dolce Freddo

The gelati here is the real McCoy with fresh seasonal fruit churned with great skill into two dozen or so daily flavours. There's always a warm welcome too as Donna and her team greet hundreds of gelati lovers until late into the night. Wonderful richer styles include the every popular rocher, chocolate and Snickers, which is made with hazelnuts instead of peanuts. Lighter fruit styles include the luscious yoghurt-based fruity de bosco, as well as mango, passionfruit, coconut and coconut with pandan. If you prefer nutty flavours then you won't want to miss the macadamia flavour, it's particularly good with a mini scoop of coffee gelati on top. If you're really up for a challenge then the pungent durian gelati should be on top of your list.

CARLTON
116 Lygon Street
9639 3344
Daily 12.30pm–late;
closed Mondays in winter
Melway 2B F10
Map page 164

Jock's Ice Cream & Sorbets

You have to love a store where they really worship the product they sell – which in the case of Jock's is handcrafted gelati and sorbets. There's a palpable sense of fun and pleasure here with an ever-changing seasonal selection and staff who are only too happy to offer tastings. Flavours in the ice-cream range vary from classic vanilla, chocolate, berry or passionfruit, and hazelnut to the exotic – look out for gingerbread, honey pokey, Turkish delight, pistachio, black rice pudding and the caramel-like fig ripple. Try a tasting or two, and then choose a flavour or three in a cup or cone. There are also freshly made biscuits for dipping and enjoying with your chosen cone including chocolate and pistachio, hazelnut and orange, and baby cones for junior gelati lovers.

ALBERT PARK
83 Victoria Avenue
9686 3838; Summer:
Mon–Thurs midday–9pm;
Fri–Sat midday–11pm;
Sun midday–10pm; Winter:
Sun–Thurs midday–8pm;
Fri–Sat midday–9pm
Melway 2J J8
Map page 168

Limonetto

We're big fans of Limonetto for a number of reasons. First up it's the actual building itself, which is shaped like a giant waffle cone and decorated with groovy fluro lights in the ceiling. It also seems completely natural to be enjoying gelati when near the water, in this case on the edge of the rapidly expanding Docklands. And of course there's the gelati itself, which always looks so very appealing and never veers into that too sweet stage. Try the dark, brooding almost savoury chocolate flavour to see this in action. It's a ripper. The marzipan-flavoured pistachio is also a winner, as is the creamy caramel dotted with chunks of honeycomb. Last, but certainly not least, there's the Limonetto flavour, which is zesty, mouth puckering and everything a proper lemon gelati should be.

DOCKLANDS
New Quay Promenade
9642 5001
Summer: Mon–Fri 11am–
10pm; Sat–Sun 11am–late;
Winter: Mon–Fri
11am–7.30pm;
Sat–Sun 11am–late
Melway 2E E4
Map page 163

7 Apples Gelato

What a hot spot Acland Street has turned into, from the original cake shops, which always attract a crowd, to the onslaught of cafés in recent years. The other attraction here is the wonderful 7 Apples Gelato. There are often queues until late into the night, but the wait is well worth it. A long-running favourite of ours here is the yoghurt gelato, a refreshingly light option for hot summer days. Other zesty styles include raspberry, blood orange, passionfruit and an excellent green apple variety. If it's a richer experience you're looking for then check out the peanut butter, tiramisu, crème caramel, honeycomb and croccantino. The rum and raisin is an absolute beauty. There are classics on offer too such as chocolate, vanilla and white chocolate, plus sorbets, smoothies and juices to choose from.

ST KILDA
75 Acland Street
9537 3633
Summer: daily
10.30am–late;
Winter: daily
10.30am–10.30pm
Melway 2P B9
Map page 170

Highlight
FABULOUS FLAVOURS

Lickerish, Trampoline, page 81
This not too sweet, wonderfully textured gelati is an adult's delight. It's chock full of aniseedy flavours and excellent textures.

Rum and raisin, 7 Apples Gelato, page 80
Imagine the creamiest, smoothest gelato topped with sticky syrup and plump raisins. As good as it sounds, it tastes even better!

Macadamia, Il Dolce Freddo, page 80
It's extremely difficult to pick just one flavour from the range at Il Dolce Freddo. A recent favourite was the macadamia, which has a wonderful coarse nutty texture – perfect with a mini scoop of coffee gelati on top.

Panettone, Tutto Bene, page 82
This awesome gelati is packed with flavours of toasty panettone, such as candied fruit, spice, raisins and yeasty sweet bread. It's like an Italian Christmas in every mouthful.

Fig ripple, Jock's Ice Cream & Sorbets, page 80
A standout autumnal ice-cream that is made with poached fresh figs. It crackles with tiny fig seeds and a beautiful caramel/butterscotch background flavour. A real beauty.

Hot cross bun, Fritz Gelato, page 79
This delicious combination of spices and fruit really hits the spot. It's like a creamy hot cross bun in a tub – perfect for Melbourne's Easter weather!

Trampoline

Trampoline has made a big impression since appearing on the local gelati scene a couple of years back. Their colourful store fitouts and fun approach to service have made them a firm favourite with young gelati lovers in particular. Not that the products are in any way altered for kids' tastes. No, these are big bold flavours that really make an impression. The zesty, tongue-tingling passionfruit for instance is a beauty; it's loved by young and old alike. Ditto the wild berry, coffee crunch, deep mint and lemon sorbet. Trampoline also offer their own version of a choc dipped gelati cone known as a mushroom, plus handmade cakes for all occasions and Christmas ice-cream puddings. **Also at:** Chadstone Shopping Centre; Swanston Street, City; Doncaster and Malvern; Acland Street, St Kilda; Southbank. Call head office for store details: 8416 0315.

FITZROY
381 Brunswick Street
9415 8689
Daily midday–late
Melway 2C B6
Map page 164

Tutto Bene

There's something particularly adult about the gelati on display at Tutto Bene in Southgate. They all seem to have been made with the minimum of sweetness, and in doing so retain the real flavours that went into them. Perhaps it's the Italian approach to making gelati, or simply Simon Humble's personal style. Either way it really works. The display can include mango, limoncello, lime, Baileys or cherry almond. There's also a light-as-a-feather zesty mandarin option, a delicious torrone flavour with hints of almondy nougat and an awesome panettone gelati. It's not just Melburnians who have fallen for these gelati, Simon Humble's chocolate, strawberry, hazelnut, vanilla and Ferrero Roche flavours recently took out a swag of medals at the Royal Sydney Show. It's a top spot to pick up a gelato and enjoy a wander along the Southbank promenade.

SOUTHBANK
Mid level Southgate
9696 3334
Daily midday–late
Melway 2F F7
Map page 168

Indian and Sri Lankan food

The stores that supply Melburnians with the ingredients and foods for Indian cooking are spread far and wide. There's Bangla Sweets & Curry Café in Fitzroy, where shoppers can get their hands on excellent traditional sweets plus a selection of tasty snacks and nibbles to keep hunger pangs at bay. Curry Creations at Prahran Market is another Indian hot spot. Here chef-quality curry pastes and simmer sauces will make whipping up your Indian feast a breeze. If you really want to explore and browse through different stores then the shopping area centred on Foster Street, Dandenong, is what you need. Now known as Little India it offers food stores that sell curries, Bollywood movies, sweets and even traditional clothing if required. Hindustan Imports just outside Dandenong is also worth a visit for amazing spices, dried fruits and nuts.

Bangla Sweets & Curry Café

Bangla is mostly known as an informal Brunswick Street café. But the attraction for food lovers is the opportunity to get their hands on some excellent Indian sweets without having to travel to food stores in Dandenong. Besides the location, what's also appealing here is the sweets are very well displayed. Each one is labelled and there is helpful advice is on hand. The orange halwa puddings are popular, so too the pretzel-shaped, gold-flecked jalebi. Burfi, an Indian sweet made from condensed milk and sugar, comes in almond, vanilla and cashew flavours. Savoury snacks are available here too with bags of roasted nuts, Bombay mix, namak para (cumin and caraway spiced fried pastry strips) and many more besides – perfect snacks to accompany a Bollywood movie night.

FITZROY
199 Brunswick Street
9417 1877
Daily 11.30am–10.30pm
Melway 2C A9
Map page 164

Calcutta Sweets

Indian sweets are incredible treats that come in myriad flavours, shapes and styles. Dandenong offers a number of stores that specialise in these foods, mostly clustered in and around Foster Street, a shopping strip recently titled Little India. Calcutta Sweets is one of the best of these stores. Service can be a bit hit or miss as staff don't always engage with customers, but just keep asking questions and choosing from the display. The rasmalai made from paneer and nuts is worthy of a sample, as is gulab jamun, a condensed milk dough cooked in sugar syrup with cardamom and rosewater. Burfi comes in besan (chickpea), almond, cashew, coconut, chocolate and gaajar (carrot) flavours. Many come with a sprinkle of gold or silver leaf, signifying wealth. This is a top spot to grab a delicious curry and naan bread lunch too.

DANDENONG
52E Foster Street
9793 8101
Mon 10.30am–7pm;
Tues–Sun 10.30am–9pm
Melway 91A D8
Map page 171

Curry Creations

For authentic Indian curry without the hassle, head to Curry Creations at Prahran Market. Their cute corner stall is a popular stop for food lovers doing the rounds of the market. What they're looking for are the restaurant-quality simmer sauces to create dishes such as hot vindaloo, chicken korma, rogan josh and butter chicken. All you need do is pick up the remaining ingredients from the other market traders and you're on the way to a quick and delicious meal. Thai green, Thai red, rendang and tandoori pastes are also on hand here. There's also a selection of beautiful chutneys to add interest to everyday meals, along with essentials such as rice, pappadums and spices. For an authentic taste of India you can't go past Curry Creations.

SOUTH YARRA
Shop 712, Prahran Market,
163–185 Commercial Road
9827 1344
Tues, Thurs, Fri & Sat
8am–5pm
Melway 2L H9
Map page 166

Hindustan Imports

What a wonderful temple to Indian cuisine. This delightful store, perched on the front of a massive warehouse full of Indian food, offers excellent products at amazingly good prices. Whole aisles are dedicated to certain foods. The dried fruit and nuts aisle offers Iranian green sultanas, smoked almonds, cashews, pepitas, dried apples, dates and many more besides. The spice aisle is the same with everything from saffron to vibrant green cardamom pods. Shoppers can also get their hands on stone mortar and pestles, grinding stones, Indian cooking pots and a massive selection of snack foods. As Hindustan are wholesalers, their products are available in commercial quantities if needed. So if you want a 10 kg bag of Sri Lankan red rice, no problem. Smaller qualities are available.

DANDENONG
50 Greens Road
9794 6640
Mon–Sat 8.30am–5.30pm;
Melway 95 F3
Map page 171

India Bazaar International

Foster Street is one of the main shopping strips in this part of town and this store offers a good range of Indian, Pakistani, Fijian and Sri Lankan ingredients. These are displayed over a fairly large area and include many different varieties and brands of rice: jasmin, basmati and many more besides. Other essential ingredients include cooking oils and tins of ghee, ready-to-use curry pastes and a gamut of spices to make your own pastes at home. Wander the aisles and you'll come across dried fruits and nuts, chickpeas, lentils, spicy sauces, interesting dessert mixes and many other exotic products. The fridges play host to cheeses, yoghurts and other dairy foods. The entire upper section of the store is dedicated to Bollywood DVDs and CDs.

DANDENONG
77 Foster Street
9794 7010
Daily 10.30am–7.30pm
Melway 91A D8
Map page 171

Indian Impex

This corner store is an excellent place to get your first taste of shopping for Indian ingredients. It's always well stocked and is as clean as a whistle. Advice is happily provided, so don't hesitate to ask about the many ingredients in-store. Browse the well-displayed aisles for excellent spices and spice blends, rice, lentils, chickpeas and other staples of Indian cooking. Also on offer is flour made from chickpeas, red and green lentils, packets of pappadums and tins of ghee. Packet mixes are popular too, and not a bad way for the time poor to whip up Indian breads and desserts. All manner of curries come pre-prepared if you want to give them a try.

DANDENONG
187–189 Thomas Street
9708 5518
Daily 9am–9pm
Melway 91A E7
Map page 171

Highlight
SPICES

Cardamom
Cardamom is best purchased as vibrant green pods. Inside are the aromatic seeds that provide the mild yet distinctive cardamom flavour. An essential component of many curries and poaching liquids, it is also useful as a breath freshener after a spicy meal.

Kaffir lime leaves
These leaves are used whole in broths for flavour, or finely shredded for salads and marinades. Each leaf has two oval sections and a pungent citrus flavour. They are available fresh, frozen and dried.

Saffron
Saffron is one of the world's most expensive spices, with each thread coming from the centre of the crocus flower. Luckily, only a few threads are needed to enjoy saffron's aroma and flavour.

Sichuan pepper
The small red berries aren't actually a member of the pepper family, but they have a peppery taste. It is best toasted before use in classic dishes such as salt and pepper calamari. Also known as Szechwan pepper.

Sumac
These red berries are usually available crushed and ready for use. Sumac has a sweet yet lemony tang to it which is excellent sprinkled over food from the barbecue and warm salads.

Vanilla
This is becoming an increasingly expensive spice to use in the home kitchen. Ensure you are getting the very best quality with plump, soft vanilla pods. Use in sugar syrups, poached fruit, custard and panacotta mixtures.

MKS Enterprises

MKS Enterprises offers so much for those who really love Indian and Sri Lankan food and cooking. If you love to whip up curries and other specialities, MKS is just for you. There are hard-to-get frozen vegetables such as baby okra and fenugreek, plus a good selection of coconut cream and coconut milk, sesame seeds and flour for making chapati and naan breads. Rice is available in 1 kg, 2 kg, and even 25 kg bags in specialist varieties such as red, basmati, patna and sona masur, a variety used to make biryani. There's a selection of imported instant cake and snack mixes and the quality of spices is impressive. The other great attraction here is the café, which is housed alongside the rows and rows of Bollywood videos and DVDs. Great-tasting curries, rice dishes and samosa are always on offer.

DANDENONG
23 Pultney Street
9701 3165
Sun–Thurs 9am–8pm;
Fri–Sat 9am–9pm
Melway 91A E8
Map page 171

Punjab Sweet & Indian Takeaway

Punjab Sweet & Indian Takeaway is set just off the main Little India strip of Foster Street, but that doesn't stop it being a popular spot for locals. As with many of these stores its part sweet store and part café. There are myriad curries, samosa, pakora, naan breads and pappadums to enjoy daily. For us, however, it's the sweets treats that are the standouts here. Rich in sugar, they are a deeply significant part of Indian culture, being enjoyed after a meal or at special festivals and events. The most prevalent varieties such as burfi, jalebi and gulab jamun are all here. The burfi is particularly good, in flavours such as coconut, pistachio and mango. Some are even topped with gold leaf.

DANDENONG
2B Mason Street
9792 1694
Mon 10am–8pm;
Tues–Fri 10am–9pm;
Sat–Sun 11am–9pm
Melway 90 D7
Map page 171

Italian food

Italian food and cooking is a hugely important part of the local food scene. Over the years, Italians have brought us cafés and coffee businesses, butcher's shops, pasta places, delicatessens and much more – and always with great style, too. That tradition continues today with top food stores such as King & Godfree and Lygon Food Store in the heart of Italian Carlton. There's also the amazing Enoteca Sileno further up Lygon Street with its combination of stunning aged cheeses, imported olive oil, balsamic vinegar and vast selection of wine. In fact, Italian food is so entrenched it's hard to imagine cooking without parmigiano, extra virgin olive oil, prosciutto, salami, pasta and tomato sugo. It's not just hard, it's almost impossible. Long live our love affair with all things Italian!

Alligator Brand

Since the mid-1990s Alligator has been supplying quality pastas that rival the best in town. Their freshly made products are quickly whisked out to food stores, delis and restaurants around town. They are also available direct from their Yarraville production kitchen. Large commercial packs are on hand as are smaller retail packets, so choose one to suit the need. Beautifully filled ravioli in flavours of roasted pumpkin and parmesan, mushroom and garlic, and smoked salmon and dill are perennial favourites. Other specialties include spinach and ricotta cannelloni, delicious sweet potato gnocchi and flavoured pastas such as squid ink linguine. Selected frozen bulk packs of ravioli and cannelloni are also available, along with ready-to-heat pasta sauces.

YARRAVILLE
1–3 Taylor Street
9687 0870
Mon–Fri 7am–3.30pm
Melway 42 C10
Map page 163

Cardamone

There's something about the way Italians run supermarkets that is so incredibly appealing. Yes, there are aisles lined with all the household essentials, but the food on offer has a 'real' feel to it. Head to the grocery area to stock up on all the Italian basics such as sugo sauces, olive oils, balsamic and peeled tomatoes. Lovers of fresh bread will find crusty pasta dura and loaves of ciabatta here too. The delicatessen section is also a firm favourite, with its selection of salami, prosciutto, hams and other good things. There's also antipasti, marinated olives and delicious cheeses – classics such as ricotta, provolone, parmigiano and remano. The excellent range continues with tinned tuna, homemade soups, pasta sauces and fresh pasta.

FAIRFIELD
143 Station Street
9481 0586
Mon–Thurs 8.30am–7pm;
Fri 8.30am–8pm;
Sat 8am–5pm;
Sun 10am–3pm
Melway 30 K10
Map page 165

Donnini's Pasta

Since the early 1980s the Omizzolo family have been creating terrific fresh pasta for food-loving Melburnians. The selection is always colourful and enticing with gnocchi, filled tortellini and ravioli alongside short and straight pastas such as spaghetti, linguini, shells and rigatoni to name just a few. The range of flavours is enticing including a very special saffron and pepper pappardelle, which is perfect served with a tomato and olive sauce. The roasted artichoke, pine nut and ricotta agnolotti is a beauty too. If you really want the meal ready for you there's a selection of pasta sauces, basil pesto, grated parmigiano and lasagne. **Also at:** 74 Maling Road, Canterbury, 9888 5722; 525 Malvern Road, Hawksburn, 9826 9199; 140A Upper Heidelberg Road, Ivanhoe, 9499 5150.

CARLTON
398 Lygon Street
9347 1655
Mon–Fri 9.30am–5.30pm;
Sat 9.30am–5pm
Melway 2B G6
Map page 164

Farinacci's Fresh Pasta

There's a certain feeling of quality that comes from seeing food prepared before your eyes. Farinacci's offers just that experience as they create fresh pasta in their Caulfield kitchen/store. Customers can see the pasta machines and preparation kitchen just behind the display counter. Pasta choices vary on a daily basis but they often range from specialty styles such as duck or chicken and leek ravioli, to potato gnocchi and filled cannelloni tubes. Simpler options include ribbons of tagliatelle and fettuccini and lasagne sheets. Sauces with cream-based and tomato-based varieties are available. Pasta cooking instructions and times are available if you want to ensure dinner will be just right. Customers can complete the Italian feast by picking up a tub of their tiramisu.

CAULFIELD
662 Glen Huntly Road
9528 6076
Mon–Fri 7am–5pm;
Sat 9am–midday
Melway 67 K4
Map page 170

Gervasi Foodworks

Those looking for an intimate, Italian-oriented shopping experience around Brunswick should look no further than Gervasi Foodworks. This Italian *supermercato* offers a full range of local and imported goods, from pasta and polenta to anchovies and olive oil. Shoppers shouldn't bypass the astonishing array of smallgoods and antipasti available at the deli. Grab a number and browse the selection of olives, artichokes, eggplant and sun-dried tomatoes while you wait your turn. There's also sliced-to-order prosciutto and salami on offer. An extensive cheese selection offers pre-packed ricotta, provolone, mozzarella, grana and parmigiano. Gervasi also boasts its own butcher's department, offering freshly made Italian pork sausages that are not to be missed.

BRUNSWICK
870 Sydney Road
9386 0170
Mon–Wed 8.30am–6pm;
Thurs 8.30am–7pm;
Fri 8.30am–8pm;
Sat 8am–4pm;
Sun 9.30am–4pm
Melway 29 H4
Map page 165

Italian Gourmet Deli

Every cook needs access to good Italian ingredients and this store in downtown Dandenong does exactly that for local foodies. It's a classic-looking store with a great feeling of tradition. There are long shelves filled with essentials such as whole peeled tomatoes, diced tomatoes and bottles of tomato sugo. You'll also find jars of pesto, marinated olives, tuna, sardines and legumes galore, as well as lentils, chickpeas, borlotti beans and all the dried ingredients for hearty soups. Naturally, pasta is here too in its many guises from penne and rigatoni to gnocchi, vermicelli and lasagne sheets. Smallgoods are either pre-sliced, pre-packed and ready to go or sliced to your preference. Parmigiano, antipasti, prosciutto, salami and fresh sausages are also here.

DANDENONG
Shop 1,
11 Langhorne Street
9792 5121
Mon–Sat 9am–5pm
Melway 91A E7
Map page 171

Highlight
ITALIAN FOOD

Arborio rice
This is a short-grain rice traditionally used in northern Italy to make risotto. These short fat grains soak up liquid during the cooking process and become plump and full of flavour. The rice should be stirred well during cooking and finished with parmigiano reggiano.

Balsamic vinegar
Real balsamic is made using the solero method. This takes many years and intensely concentrates the flavour of the vinegar. The time taken in production makes it quite expensive, but only a few drops are needed to enjoy its amazing sweet/sour flavour.

Olive oil
There is little doubt that extra virgin olive oil is the best for our health and our cooking. When buying olive oil look for one that has been made recently (within the past twelve months is best). The oil should have a balance of fruitiness, bitterness and pungency.

Parmigiano reggiano
Considered one of the kings of cheeses, it's hard to imagine cooking without it. The best parmigiano is bought in a chunk and grated or shaved as needed. Add it to risotto, omelettes, soups and salads.

Polenta
This is a ground cornmeal used in Italy to produce a soft mixture to accompany stews such as osso buco. It can also be set into a firm block before cutting into wedges. These can then be grilled or pan-fried until golden brown.

Prosciutto
Prosciutto is a salted air-dried ham made from a leg of pork. The best prosciutto is aged for more than twelve months and should be sliced quite thinly. It can be served as part of an antipasto, put onto a cooked pizza or wrapped around figs, warm chestnuts or melon slices.

King & Godfree

If there were awards for longevity in the food retail sector, King & Godfree would surely have a tonne of them. Kicking off over 120 years ago, they've seen amazing changes to the Lygon shopping precinct. With many of the original food stores becoming cafés and restaurants it's great to see K&G still doing well. There's a fantastic assortment of Italian foods and alcohol on offer here. Wine, beer and spirits take up the majority of floor space, and there is fine array of deli items on offer – favourites include the grilled capsicum, sun-dried tomatoes, salami and artichokes. The store also stocks a wide assortment of local and imported items such as pasta and ready-made sauces, delicious cheeses, rice and olive oil. And to top it all off, a great selection of imported chocolates.

CARLTON
293–297 Lygon Street
9347 1619
Mon–Sat 9am–9pm;
Sun 11am–7pm
Melway 2B G7
Map page 164

Lygon Food Store

Lygon Food Store is an integral part of the Carlton food scene. For years it was one of the few places to source excellent parmigiano reggiano, provolone, taleggio and other classic Italian-style cheeses. Today Lygon Food Store continues in its tradition of providing quality produce. It has expanded to include a buzzing café area, including simple fare such as panini brimming with quality ingredients. The deli today largely specialises in Italian and local cheeses plus antipasti. There is also a fine selection of smallgoods including porchetta, prosciutto and salami. The shelves hold a wide selection of olive oil, vinegar and dried pasta. The coffee is pretty good too and there's plenty of chocolate, nougat and other Italian treats to go with it.

CARLTON
263 Lygon Street
9347 6279
Mon–Sat 7am–5.30pm;
Sun 8am–5pm
Melway 2B G7
Map page 164

Monaco's Continental Delicatessen & Foodstore

Most food stores succeed because they choose a location that has other like-minded retailers nearby. Monaco's proves you can be out on your own and still thrive. The store has recently doubled in size and this has allowed for the range to grow substantially. Now there are fresh ingredients and lots of supermarket basics alongside its more traditional continental choices. A chiller cabinet includes all manner of salad ingredients and everyday cooking basics. This ranges from balsamic vinegars and olive oil on the shelves to the deli selection of marinated olives, chunks of parmigiano, salami, prosciutto and sausages. Continental cakes and biscuits feature here too. Specialist food brands are also available from Maggie Beer, Phillippa's and Peter Watson.

CAMBERWELL
523–525 Camberwell Road
9889 7198
Mon–Fri 8am–8pm;
Sat 8am–7.30pm;
Sun 8am–7pm
Melway 60 B4
Map page 167

O'Heas Bakery & Deli

O'Heas doesn't need other shops nearby to attract a crowd – it stands alone and has a loyal band of followers. Get in early for delicious still-warm loaves and rolls from the wood-fired ovens. The ovens churn out an amazing array of breads and sweets, including baguettes, rolls, pizza bases, crusty scone bread and treccia (twisted) loaf. Also worth checking out are the jam and chocolate sandwich biscuits, and almond and hazelnut macaroons. The cake selection includes cannoli – vanilla, chocolate and ricotta with chocolate shavings. There's also everything you need to put together an Italian feast: olives, grilled eggplant, roast eggplant, artichokes, Italian-style sausages, cheeses, salami, ham and prosciutto sliced to order.

COBURG
203–205 O'Hea Street
9354 8070
Mon–Fri 6.30am–7pm;
Sat–Sun 7am–3pm
Melway 17 E11
Map page 165

Oliv

Melbourne has very few stores dedicated to olive oil, and Oliv in Hawthorn is one of those. They are a specialist in their field, and look after the needs of food lovers in Hawthorn and surrounding suburbs. There are always oils on tasting, so customers get to try before they buy. Oils here are sourced from Australian producers such as Red Rock, Mount Zero and Kyneton as well as many Italian brands. Oliv offers a wide variety of marinated olives and olive pastes, at-home marinating kits and olive-oil products such as soaps and body balms. There's also a good selection of olive books, kitchen utensils and stainless-steel olive pourers. Best of all, there is always someone on hand to help you in selecting the best olive oil for your needs, whether it is a fruity or spicy blend.

HAWTHORN
328 Auburn Road
9818 2375
Mon–Fri 8.30am–5.30pm
Sat 9am–3pm
Melway 59 F1
Map page 167

Oliveria

If you're looking to source the very best olive oil then make a beeline for Oliveria in Prahran. They gather only extra virgin olive oil from specialist producers around Australia, New Zealand, Spain and Italy. What's also terrific here is the opportunity to try the olive oil before you buy. This means customers are guaranteed to purchase oil that suits their taste (oil with their preferred balance of fruitiness, bitterness and pepper) and what they want to use it for at home. There's a lot more than just olive oil here too, with exclusive marinated olive brands, polenta, arborio rice, crisp breads and even chocolate-coated almonds that look like green olives. Oliveria also have stunning ceramic oil decanters, beautiful platters and olive-wood bowls, olive-based cosmetics and even an olive-leaf tea.

PRAHRAN
Prahran Central Shopping Centre, cnr Commercial Road and Cato Street
9510 0690
Mon–Fri 9am–5.30pm;
Sat 9am–5pm
Melway 2L H9
Map page 166

The Pasta Eater

There's something so very enticing about the aromas of simmering pasta sauces wafting from the kitchen. It's exactly the thing you want to happen as it proves beyond a doubt that beautiful things are being prepared fresh for you to enjoy. The welcome here is always warm and the display enticing. Perhaps it'll be the cannelloni today ready to be baked with a simple tomato sauce, or a meat lasagne or even a vegetarian version layered with ricotta, spinach and a tomato and basil sauce. All are fresh and ready to pop into the oven at home. There's also spaghetti, fettuccini and tagliatelle plus sauces and grated parmigiano to go. Sweet treats to complete the meal include nougat and panforte. Pasta cooking pots, olive oil and vinegars are also on hand if you need to re-equip the home kitchen.

BLACK ROCK
17 Bluff Road
9589 6676
Mon–Fri 10am–6pm;
Sat 9am–1pm
Melway 85 K4
Map page 169

Traditional Pasta Shop

This is one popular stall at the Queen Victoria Market if the crowds on a Saturday morning are anything to go by. It's hardly surprising really as pasta can be a very economical and nutritious way to feed a family. The Traditional Pasta Shop's display is packed with tagliatelle, gnocchi, ravioli and many other pasta shapes and styles. And all of it is freshly made too. The popular standards run along the lines of spaghetti, fettuccine and tagliatelle. There's also a customer demand for gnocchi and ravioli. There are all the other ingredients here for a pasta meal including tomato, bolognese, creamy mushroom, basil and pine nut, and carbonara. Packets of grated parmigiano are on hand too and ready to go.

CITY
Shop 3–4, Dairy Produce Hall, Queen Victoria Market, cnr Elizabeth and Victoria Sts
0424 868 459
Tues & Thurs 6am–2pm;
Fri 6am–6pm; Sat 6am–3pm; Sun 8am–4pm
Melway 2B C11
Map page 162

Yarra Valley Pasta

Since its inception more than ten years ago, Yarra Valley Pasta has grown to become an indispensable supplier of quality pasta and sauces. The company prides itself on using quality products such as free-range eggs and GM-free flour, and many of the recipes have been handed down from generation to generation. Yarra Valley Pasta offer both snap-frozen and fresh pasta and sauces. Snap-frozen dishes include ravioli filled with chicken and veal, trout and goat's cheese, and roasted fennel, mascarpone and walnut, while their fresh pastas include cracked black pepper fettuccine, lemon and parsley linguine, and beef lasagne. At Prahran Market they also showcase other quality foods from the Yarra Valley. Not to be missed!

SOUTH YARRA
Stall 118A, Prahran Market, 163–185 Commercial Road
9824 1887
Tues, Thurs & Sat 6am–5pm;
Fri 6am–6pm;
Melway 2L H9
Map page 166

Kitchen equipment

There comes a time when you realise that your kitchen needs a bit of a spruce up. Not so much your stove and bench tops, but more so your everyday equipment and accessories. Perhaps it is time to get rid of the saucepan with the dodgy handle, the slightly chipped platters and the wobbly chopping board. Well, rest assured, Melbourne is well served with specialist kitchenware stores that can assist with this task. Commercial-quality equipment is available at London & American Supply Stores, which sells everything from chef's uniforms to chopping boards and knives. Chef's Hat in South Melbourne offers a massive selection of great kitchen products, as does The Essential Ingredient. The home cook also needs new inspiration and ideas from time to time, too. And there's no better way to replenish the cookbook shelf than with a visit to the unbeatable Books for Cooks.

Books for Cooks

Recipe books are the lifeblood of each and every cook. It's through them that ideas are passed between people who will probably never meet. They can be packed with the latest cooking ideas, have detailed instructions on making pizza in a wood-fired oven, making salami at home, or even present recipes last cooked hundreds of years ago. Books for Cooks is a repository of all these and so much more. As Melbourne's only specialist food and wine store it's a magnet for people from far and wide. Alongside the cookbooks (which cover virtually every cuisine) there are books on food history, sociology and a terrific selection of facsimile editions, periodicals and food magazines. It's a wonderful place to browse for new kitchen treasures.

FITZROY
233–235 Gertrude Street
8415 1415
Mon–Sat 10am–6pm;
Sun 11am–5pm
Melway 2C C11
Map page 164

Chef's Hat

Do you want to shop where the chefs shop? Then Chef's Hat is just for you. Located opposite the South Melbourne Market it offers a range of products for home and commercial kitchens that is second to none. The store is set up like a supermarket – getting lost in the maze of cups, saucers, pots and pans is half the fun. Wander the aisles here and you'll be presented with every shape and size of plate, bowl, cup, saucer, glass, platter, knife, fork and spoon you could conceive of. There are cooks' knives for domestic and commercial uses by all the leading brands, and chopping boards in timber and synthetic materials. There are also coffee pots in varying styles, as well as gadgets galore – graters, choppers, peelers and tools you didn't even know you needed. The value for money is second to none.

SOUTH MELBOURNE
131 Cecil Street
9682 1441
Mon–Fri 9am–5.30pm;
Sat 10am–4pm;
Sun 11am–4pm
Melway 2K B1
Map page 168

Highlight
ESSENTIAL KITCHEN EQUIPMENT

Kitchen timer
To keep your cooking up to the minute and ensure kitchen perfection, invest in a kitchen timer.

Microplane grater
This handy piece of equipment is terrific for grating anything: parmesan, ginger, citrus, zest, palm sugar – and it does the job in half the time of a traditional grater.

Muffin papers
Flash new printed styles in gold, silver and white are especially good for creating celebration muffin cakes.

Silicone pastry brush
If you haven't experienced the joys of using a silicone pastry brush, now's the time. It provides better coverage, is heat resistant and doesn't lose its bristles like most traditional brushes.

Spatulas
Rubber moulded spatulas are flexible and designed to get all the mixture from bowls and ensure cakes are perfectly mixed.

Salad spinner
An absolute essential for summer salads – leaves must be dry so that they can be coated properly in dressing.

The Essential Ingredient

Every food lover's needs can be found under the one roof of this spectacular emporium from the upstairs cooking school to the fabulous foods on offer. The kitchenware side of the business brings together products designed for the home cook as well as the professional kitchen. There's a huge selection of cutlery, plates, bowls and other tableware. Shelves are lined with all sorts of bakeware: cake tins, baking mats, spatulas, rolling pins, baking beans, muffin tins and almost everything else you could ever wish for. The latest and greatest cookbooks are also on display. There are also knives, terracotta baking dishes, barware, coffee equipment and so much more. The extensive range is backed up by knowledgeable staff who are as keen about cooking as their customers.

SOUTH YARRA
Prahran Market,
Elizabeth Street
9827 9047
Mon–Thurs 9am–5pm;
Fri 9am–5.30pm;
Sat 8am–5pm;
Sun 10am–4pm
Melway 2L H9
Map page 166

Kuche

There are kitchenware stores in virtually every shopping centre and local retail strip in Melbourne. But few of them are as well presented as Kuche in Beaumaris. The store is always decked out in beautiful things, you can see them appearing in your kitchen and on your dining table in a flash. Smart bakeware, cake tins and muffin pans, plus all the wooden spoons, utensils, oven mitts, tea towels and aprons you will ever need. There's also weighing scales, chopping boards, stainless-steel colanders and cooks knives. If you're looking to inspire kitchen skills into a tiny tot, check out the range of specially designed baking and cooking kits. With saucepans and fry pans, platters and bowls, even specialist food products, you're sure to find a new must-have product.

BEAUMARIS
26 South Concourse
9589 7188
Mon–Fri 9.30am–5.30pm;
Sat 9am–4pm;
Melway 86 D7
Map page 169

London & American Supply Stores

This store's city location makes it a prime spot for chefs and apprentice chefs to get kitted out with all the gear they need. There's a corner dedicated to chef's uniforms stocking everything from hats to boots, plus a counter dedicated to knives of all shapes and sizes. Prominent knife brands such as Global, Mundial, Victorinox and F. Dick Knives are all on offer. The remainder of the store is given over to excellent home kitchen equipment and utensils. Chopping boards, kettles, coffee plungers, salad spinners and cake tins of every shape and size are available. Knife sharpening is available every Friday for those not skilled at using a sharpening stone. There is also a nice supply of culinary books on offer.

CITY
483–485 Elizabeth Street
9329 7181
Mon–Fri 9am–5pm;
Sat 9am–3pm;
Sun 10am–3pm
Melway 2B C12
Map page 162

Minimax

There's a certain feeling of pleasure that comes with walking through a Minimax store. Browsing through the displays you just know you're in kitchen heaven. There are oven mitts with matching aprons, juicers, Minimax food processors and Kitchen Aid mixers, plus toasters, colourful kettles, beautiful teapots and weighing scales. Contemporary kitchen gadgets range from parmesan shavers and egg timers to groovy vegetable peelers. The latest release cookbooks are on hand if you need inspiration for dinner, plus saucepans, measuring jugs, whisks, spoons and cooks' knives. A huge range of tableware is also available from plates and cutlery to cocktail shakers, glassware, placemats and napkins. **Also at:** 10 Church Street, Brighton, 9592 4533; 582 Burke Road, Camberwell, 9813 0888.

HAWKSBURN
585 Malvern Road
9826 0022
Mon–Thurs 9am–5.30pm;
Fri 9am–7pm;
Sat 9am–5.30pm;
Sun 10am–5pm
www.minimax.com.au
Melway 2M D10
Map page 166

Roost

There are some excellent places to shop for good quality kitchenware around Melbourne but there's only one Roost. The sheer size of the place is the first thing you notice with a huge ground floor and open mezzanine level. What's also apparent here is the enormous range and how beautifully it's all displayed. There's everything you'll need to set a beautiful table for that upcoming dinner party: glassware, plates, cutlery and platters in the latest designs and colours. Your kitchen can also be stocked with the latest platters, tea towels, casseroles and serving utensils. A selection of essential kitchen utensils and gadgets are also on hand and are perfect as gifts for foodie friends. If the shopping gets too much, relax for a coffee at the in-store café.

MALVERN
256 Glenferrie Road
9509 7166
Mon–Fri 9.30am–6pm;
Sat 9.30am–5.30pm;
Sun 10am–5pm
Melway 59 C8
Map page 167

Scullerymade

The quality of the products here never veers off track – it's always the best of the best. This means it'll last the distance in your kitchen. The excellent range is backed up with excellent service and advice to help with choosing the perfect pan to prepare paella, the right whisk for whipping fluffy omelettes and the perfect piping bag for your chosen decorating task. The product range also extends to pasta making and cutting equipment, cake tins and baking utensils of all sizes, a terrific selection of knives and more wooden spoons than you thought possible. Crockery and table utensils are also covered here as are bowls for cooking the Christmas pudding, plus useful kitchen gadgets such as egg timers and rolling pins. Long may it stay just so.

MALVERN
1400 High Street
9509 4003
Mon–Fri 9am–5pm;
Sat 9am–1pm
Melway 59 E8
Map page 167

Markets

There is no doubt that all of Melbourne's fresh-produce markets are on the up and up. Patronage is certainly on the rise – you've only to try to get a car-parking space to see that in action. Shoppers, it seems, are looking for value for money and a better quality shopping experience than the local supermarket. Our markets offer this in spades. All of our markets have been going through serious refurbishment, too. South Melbourne Market's main food aisle is like a swish city food hall, with the added bonus of food-loving people behind the counters. Ditto for Queen Victoria Market and its newly completed fish and meat hall. Footscray Market is looking more orderly all the time and Preston continues to draw huge crowds of hungry foodies. It all bodes well for the future of food shopping.

Camberwell Fresh Food Market

Camberwell Market continues to offer local shoppers an intimate market experience with around two dozen stalls all under the one roof. There's a great mix of delis, butchers, fishmongers, cafés and florists here, so the full weekly shop can be done in the one place. The main central area is home to Camberwell Market Fruit & Veg (Shop 12), which offers a terrific range of everyday and specialist ingredients. Alongside this is Prospect Wines (Shop 12A), which always seem to have a couple of special wines on tasting – perfect if you're looking to pick up a bottle or two to go with dinner. Looking onto this space are stands such as Kingfisher Seafoods (Shop 11) and its array of terrific-looking fish and shellfish. Deli shoppers are well served here too with the much-loved Nick and Sue's (Shop 17–19) as well as Peter's Continental Deli & Nuts (Shop 22 and 24) and Camberwell Market Deli (Shop 6). Helena's Cakes (Shop 21) offer a good selection of cakes, biscuits and slices, including a gluten-free range. Other specialist stores include The Provado Food Store (Shop 25) if you're in need of a coffee to keep you fuelled up for the shopping trip. Sweeties (Shop 11A) can provide all the sweet treats, dried fruits, nuts and pulses you'll ever need. And don't forget to pick up a bunch of fresh blooms from Al's Flower EFX (Shop 14) to brighten up the dining table.

CAMBERWELL
521 Riversdale Road
9539 1361
Tues & Thurs–Fri 7am–7pm;
Sat 7am–5pm
Melway 59 J1
Map page 167

Highlight
MARKET TREATS

The Borek Shop, Stall 95–96, Queen Victoria Market
For the most amazing spicy lamb and vegetable or spinach and cheese borek (Turkish pizzas) check out The Borek Shop in the Deli Hall.

Coffea Café, 519–521 Elizabeth Street, City
Coffea is the place at the Queen Victoria Market for a top coffee and a wedge of their excellent castagnaccio slice, which is made with chestnut flour, rosemary and pine nuts.

Aptus Seafoods, Stall 25, South Melbourne Market
To fortify yourself during a busy shopping expedition slide on up to the oyster bar at Aptus for a few freshly opened oyster shots. They are the perfect market treat.

Yoyo Sushi, Camberwell Market, Shop 11B
Sushi is one of the most popular snacks on the go and Yoyo Sushi is the perfect place to pick up a hand roll or two at Camberwell Market.

Footscray Market

Footscray Market continues to be known for its vast array of Asian meats, poultry and seafood stalls. John and Kevin's Fresh Fish (Stall 119) remains a winner with its enticing selection of flounder, prawns, squid and blue grenadier. Best Kay Seafood (Stall 117) is the spot to pick up great-looking coral trout and red snapper, while YK Fresh Fish (Stall 128) has a good selection too including blue swimmer crabs. T. H. Butcher (Stall 130) has a terrific range of Asian and European cuts such as pork ribs and belly alongside steak and sausages. Quality Poultry Supplies (Stall 107–116) is worth a look for eggs, duck, quail, turkey wings and every cut of chicken ever invented. Head to Pelekan Deli (Stall 97) for all your deli needs, including bacon, salami, olives and imported Bulgarian feta. Rina's Coffee (Stall 110) is also worth a look when stocking up on nuts, dried fruit and snack foods. Coffee and coffee equipment are here too. Cedar Fruit Supply (Stall 204) stocks excellent ingredients including very good Asian greens and herbs such as Vietnamese mint, curry leaf, Thai basil and saw-leaf coriander. If you're after a savoury snack to enjoy on the way home, then check out the Turkish pizzas and pies at Nada's Takeaway (Stall 250).

FOOTSCRAY
cnr Hopkins and Leeds Streets
9687 1205
Tues–Wed 7am–4pm;
Thurs 7am–6pm;
Fri 7am–8pm;
Sat 7am–4pm
Melway 42 D4
Map page 163

Food tours

This book is a good guide for you to discover more about the food secrets of Melbourne, but nothing beats being taken around by a professional. Each tour is bound to teach you something you didn't know before and there are always plenty of tastings to keep you happy.

Chocoholic Tours
Since 1995, Suzie Wharton has led groups through the streets of Melbourne searching out the best chocolate treats. Today, her range of tours always covers chocolate, but also includes historical, brunch, treats and sweet temptations. All tours are walking and last approximately 1½ hours.
9686 4655 or 0412 158 017;
www.chocoholictours.com.au

Foodies' Tours of Melbourne
Hosted by co-author Allan Campion, you have the choice of numerous tours. The city walking tour takes food lovers through the hidden arcades and alleys discovering the best chocolate, coffee, egg tarts and dumplings. Bus tours go further afield and explore South Melbourne and the Prahran Market with gelati, chocolate, olive oil, coffee and other European foodie tastings along the way.
0408 555 679; www.melbournefoodtours.com

Melbourne's Chinatown with Elizabeth Chong
Who better to show us the highlights of Chinatown than the Empress of all things Chinese? Elizabeth Chong's knowledge of and passion for Chinese food comes through on these tours, and who else can take you behind the scenes, one of the kitchens to see the chefs in action?
0419 889 570

Mushroom hunts in May
Cameron Russell leads these foraging tours through Main Ridge looking for slippery jacks and pine mushrooms – and being very careful to avoid the poisonous variety. Once you have worked up an appetite, it's back to T'Gallant for a taste of these wonderful mushrooms, beautifully complemented by pinot noir.
T'Gallant Winery, 1385 Mornington–Flinders Road, Main Ridge; 5989 6565

Queen Victoria Market Foodies' Tour
Some people come here every week to shop and others are bewildered by the hustle and bustle of Melbourne's biggest market. The tour not only gives a background into the market's history and why it's so important to Melburnians, but also takes you through all the halls, introducing you to remarkable stallholders and a taste of their wares.
Queen Victoria Market, cnr Elizabeth and Victoria Streets, City; 9320 5835; Melway 2B C11; Map page 162

Secrets of Sydney Road
Hosted by Gamil Abou-Lehaf, these cultural and cuisine tours of Sydney Road are a wonderful insight into fascinating Middle Eastern cuisine. Highlights include visits to bakeries, butchers and grocery stores, and lunch with Gamil, who explains the culture of the dishes.
9652 0611; www.cae.edu.au

Prahran Market

Prahran Market plays host to a delicious array of top Melbourne delis, butchers, fishmongers and fruiterers, so many that shoppers are totally spoilt for choice. Fish lovers can head to Claringbold's (Stall 510) for the most beautiful seafood display in the market, while Theo's (Stall 502) is the place for oysters, crayfish, prawns and pan-ready fish. Meat lovers can go organic at Hagen's (Stall 509) or check out the awesome range at John Cester Poultry and Game (Stall 506). For the best in fresh produce visit Damian Pike (Stall 116) who is a specialist in seasonal ingredients and mushrooms. Don't miss his neighbour M. J. Mow (Stall 108) for the best in freshly dug potatoes, plus horseradish, garlic, onions, swedes and parsnips. The selection of fresh produce at Ripe Organic Grocer (Stall 7–8) is always inviting too. Our favourite deli is Delicatess (Stall 706) for great cheese, antipasto, jamon and prosciutto. Yarra Valley Pasta Shop (Stall 118A) is choc-a-block with beautiful pastas, sauces and good things from producers in the Yarra Valley. Then stock up on the very best chocolate truffles by visiting Monsieur Truffe (Stall 118).

SOUTH YARRA
163–185 Commercial Road
8290 8220
Tues & Thurs dawn–5pm;
Fri dawn–6pm;
Sat dawn–5pm;
Sun 10am–3pm
Melway 2L H9
Map page 166

Preston Market

Parking is tight around Preston Market, but that shows just how popular this produce market is with local food lovers. It's an incredible multicultural mix here with shoppers and stallholders of many nationalities rubbing shoulders. Not a lot changes here in terms of the stalls. We still like Preston Hai Xuong Daily Fresh Fish (Stall W195) for a top selection of fresh seafood, while Nick's Proud Chicks (Stall W184) is our pick for duck, rabbit, turkey, quail and chickens. In the deli section check out Vita's Deli & Fresh Pasta (Stall C223) where customers can see their homemade ravioli, gnocchi and agnolotti prepared on-site. Farinacci Deli (Stall C239–240) is excellent for antipasto, while Ivan and Maria Slavonija's Deli (Stall C234) offers an outstanding display of continental smallgoods that includes dozens of salami, bacon, sausages and smoked pork. Rhubarb Rhubarb Organics (Stall 137–138) has the best range of fresh organic produce, plus groceries, bottled milk and sourdough bread. For a perk up before you tackle the car park again, grab a coffee and a chocolate macaroon from Preston Coffee Centre (Stall C215). If you need to stock up on a few bottles of red for the weekend then check out ReWines, which offer wine direct from the barrel.

PRESTON
2/30A The Centreway
9478 3130
Wed & Sat 8am–3pm;
Thurs 8am–6pm;
Fri 8am–8pm;
Melway 18 F11
Map page 165

Queen Victoria Market

What's not to like about a CBD produce market that has been serving the community for more than 125 years? At the Peel Street end (Shed B), don't miss G & C Fresh Produce (Stall 61–63). In I shed check out The Fresh Connection (Stall 83) for potatoes, fungi and other good things. In the Deli Hall take a look at the Polish Deli (Stall 5–6) for smallgoods galore, Bill's Farm (Stall 17–18) for the latest foodie treats, Curds & Whey (Stall 12–13) for butter and cheddar, plus M & G Aaiafa (Shop 66–70) for sourdough breads. The Chicken Pantry (Stall 85–86) is a must-visit stall for free-range chicken. Check out Happy Tuna (Stall 27) for the freshest yellow fin tuna and marinara mix and the Seafood and Oyster Spot (Stall 28) for freshly shucked oysters. Meat lovers can try Jenkins (Stall 12) for female pork and bolar blade, then Jago's (Stall 19) for osso buco and rack of lamb. McIver's Coffee & Tea (Stall 101–102) is the place for teapots and knitted cosies. If hunger pains kick in then a spinach and cheese borek from The Borek Shop (Stall 95–96) should do the trick.

CITY
cnr Elizabeth and Victoria Streets
9320 5822
Tues & Thurs 6am–2pm;
Fri 6am–6pm;
Sat 6am–3pm;
Sun 9am–4pm
(limited stalls open)
Melway 2B B11
Map page 162

South Melbourne Market

South Melbourne Market has just been through a period of refurbishment and improvement that has led to a wonderful new central aisle lined with delis, fishmongers, butchers and food stores. These delicious-looking stores have added a new lease of life to existing retailers and attracted a couple of newcomers along the way. Rita's Nuts and Coffee (Stall 18–19) has long been a favourite for mostly Australian-produced dried fruit, nuts and legumes. Aptus Seafood (Stall 25) is looking terrific too and offers the sea's bounty, great service and oysters opened to order. Tom's Organic Meats (Stall 30) offer an enticing selection of well-bred lamb shanks, legs of lamb, pork and beef. Cheese lovers are spoilt for choice with Emerald Deli (Stall 23–24), and their walk-in cheese room is packed with creamy triple creams, washed rinds and cheddars. Theo's Deli (Stall 16–17) is the place in the market for sliced meats with an excellent array of antipasti, dips and other foodies' essentials. W.B. Smith (Stall 114–116) sells every kitchen utensil and products you'll ever need. Fritz Gelato (Stall 2) is the perfect spot for organic cinnamon doughnuts or a cooling gelati. For fresh ingredients don't miss The Potato Man (Stall 50) for a terrific selection. There is also Fruits on Coventry (Stall 46–48) for wonderful seasonal produce and service.

SOUTH MELBOURNE
cnr Coventry and Cecil Streets
9209 6295
Wed 8am–4pm;
Thurs 8am–4pm (Cecil Street food area only)
Fri 8am–6pm;
Sat–Sun 8am–4pm
Melway 2K B1–2
Map page 168

middle eastern food

There's a growing interest in the use of Middle Eastern ingredients in the home kitchen. This has been spurred on by Greg Malouf's wonderful cookbooks and the growth of restaurants specialising in this style of cooking. Gathering the ingredients means making a trip to a specialist retailer such as those in this chapter. They spread from Dandenong and Murrumbeena to Preston and Brunswick, so most of Melbourne is well covered. The terrific thing about these stores is they tend to be one-stop shops. Shelves are lined with top-quality dried fruits and nuts, aromatic spice blends, pistachio-topped halva, sweet and sour pomegranate syrup, beautiful feta, yoghurt, pastry and so much more – a food-filled Aladdin's Cave of exotic ingredients.

Al-Alamy International Coffee & Nuts

This well laid out Middle Eastern food store, tucked away just behind Sydney Road, is arguably the best Middle Eastern food store in the area. As is the norm for these outlets, it combines bakery, café and retail space into one. The bakery corner pumps out haloumi pastries, feta and spinach pies and pizzas by the oven load. The centre of the store features a couple of rows of glass-topped boxes, each filled with a different product. Customers can self-serve dried dates, cranberries, figs, crispy fruit chips, zaatar, burgul, cracked wheat, chickpeas, almonds and pine nuts – all manner of good things really. There are lots of other essentials here too, including halva, tahini, pomegranate juice and a selection of baklava and sweet treats.

COBURG
Shop 4–6, 51 Waterfield Street
9355 8866
Mon–Sat 7am–9pm;
Sun 7am–7pm
Melway 29 H1
Map page 165

A1 Bakery

The buzz around A1 Bakery has been unchanged since they opened their doors – it's a buzz that says if you want an authentic Australian–Lebanese food experience you'll find it here. It's 'the' place to visit on a Saturday morning to browse for specialist ingredients and leave hours later having had lunch, sweet treats, coffee and with amazing products to try at home. The shelves are home to giant couscous, rose water, orange-blossom water, pomegranate molasses, sheep's milk feta, pistachio halva, fairy floss and much more besides. The rear bakery section pumps out zaatar-topped pizzas, lamb pizzas, plus melt-in-the-mouth cheese and spinach pastries through the day. **Also at:** 643–645 Sydney Rd, Brunswick, 9386 0440.

DANDENONG
201–203 Lonsdale Street
9794 9500
Daily 7am–7pm
Melway 90 D8
Map page 171

Highlight
MIDDLE EASTERN INGREDIENTS

Couscous
This staple of North African cooking comes in different grades. 'Instant' couscous only needs to be soaked in boiling water or stock for five minutes, stirred gently with a little butter and it's ready to use.

Haloumi
Look for ewe's milk haloumi, rather than cow's milk, as it has a better depth of flavour. Haloumi will hold its shape and texture when cooked. Try frying slices in a hot pan or adding to cheese fritters.

Harissa
Harissa is a wonderfully smoky, full-flavoured chilli paste. The most practical way to purchase it is in the small tubes, which will keep refrigerated for weeks. It adds a wonderful chilli kick to soups, marinades, tagines and marinades.

Mograbieh
This is often labelled as Lebanese or giant couscous. It looks like small chickpeas and requires up to thirty minutes' cooking in boiling water. It's wonderful in soups, salads and spicy tagines.

Pomegranate syrup
This superb thick bittersweet fruit syrup is terrific to have in the home pantry. Its sweet and sour flavour is a great addition to barbecue meats, in salad dressings, to glaze ham and drizzle over chicken kebabs.

Rose water
This ancient condiment is made by distilling rose petals and is an essential fragrance and flavouring of Middle Eastern cooking. Add a little to fruit-poaching syrup, panacotta or meringues, or sprinkle over just-roasted fruits.

Balha's Pastry

Walking into Balha's Pastry is like stepping into Arabian Nights. This double-storey, family-run store is a gem on the Middle Eastern food-store scene. The massive semi-circular counter that dominates the store overflows with delectable goodies, while the aroma of spices and syrups waft over you as you open the door. Syrups, nuts and fruits are all blended and baked in traditional Middle Eastern ways. A large menu board is a great start for those new to this style of pastry. Try the syrupy-sweet baklava, filled with a selection of nuts such as pistachio and walnut, or opt for the rolled pistachio-filled and kataifi-wrapped barma. There's also a semolina and coconut slice called namoura, date-filled mamoul biscuits and walnut-filled bird's nests.

BRUNSWICK
761–763 Sydney Road
9383 3944
Daily 9am–11pm
Melway 29 H5
Map page 165

Bas Foods

This enormous new warehouse-sized store offers a good opportunity to stock up on Middle Eastern and other continental foods. The size of the place means you'll be shopping in massive aisles and it may seem a little impersonal, but the value for money and impressive range could balance that out. There are displays of traditional coffee pots, tea cups, saucepans and platters. Aisles are filled with tinned legumes and other vegetables. There are also frozen vegetables, kataifi and filo pastry, feta cheese, olive oil and honey, plus dried fruits of every imaginable kind, from dates, apricots and sultanas to figs and currants. Spices abound here as do pre-packed lentils, chickpeas, kidney beans, split peas and couscous.

BRUNSWICK
419 Victoria Street
9381 1444
Mon–Fri 8am–5.30pm;
Sat 8am–5pm
Melway 29 F7

Cedar Bakery

The name Cedar Bakery may not instantly conjure up images of homemade Lebanese pizzas, olives and nuts, but that is exactly what you get at this Preston retailer. The store offers a front coffee area, bakery at the rear and neatly displayed ingredients in between. There's always a warm welcome here and good advice on ingredients if you need it too. The freshly baked breads and pizzas topped with meats, herbs and haloumi cheese are very popular. There is a great collection of spices, olives and cheese, while the bottles of pomegranate syrup and rose water are a nice buy too. Add to that tetra packs of pomegranate juice, roasted almonds, pumpkin seeds, dried fruit and pulses, and you've got yourself the makings of a one-stop Middle Eastern shop.

PRESTON
33–37 High Street
9484 4999
Daily 8am–10pm
Melway 30 F3
Map page 165

El Fahya Sweets

Stepping into El Fahya Sweets is like being whisked off to a beautiful store in the Middle East. The displays always look so enticing, with their huge trays of freshly baked sweet treats on display. The combination of the enticing aromas of orange-blossom water, rose water and buttery baked pastry make this place very hard to resist. Baklava here comes with fillings of walnuts, pistachio or walnut, which are then cut into diamonds to serve. The great thing here is that the pastries are never too sweet and the nuts still have lots of texture. There are also slices made with semolina and dates, along with deep-fried, custard-filled pastries called ladies' thumbs. The Turkish delight is lovely too. El Fahya Sweets is arguably the finest Middle Eastern pastry shop in town.

BRUNSWICK
648 Sydney Road
9386 6974
Daily 9am–9pm
Melway 29 H6
Map page 165

Marmaris

Melbourne is recognised as a city where interesting food can be found across the length and breadth of the suburbs. Marmaris bakery in suburban Hampton proves that point beautifully. From a space not much bigger than the average café comes some terrific Turkish takeaway food. For many customers the hot item here is the beautiful pide bread. It's made traditionally in a huge oval shape and is topped with sesame and nigella seeds. It has that wonderful oily texture that is essential to good pide bread. If you get beyond the pide bread there's an excellent char-grilled lamb souvlaki on offer, plus dips in flavours such as hummus, eggplant, cucumber, caviar and olive. The Turkish pizzas with spinach and cheese are excellent also.

HAMPTON
537 Hampton Street
9598 0105
Tues–Sun 11.30am–8pm
Melway 76 G4
Map page 169

Middle East Bakeries

Pita bread has become a popular choice for many people, especially for wraps and to make crispy pita chips. Middle East Bakeries is a popular brand around town and here you can visit the source of these breads. Different flavours abound with soy and linseed, herb and garlic, plus sesame pockets. There are bags of souvlaki bread, yeast-free sorj bread (mountain bread) and pitas for souvlaki or as a quick pizza base. The Turkish pide bread is a popular choice too. Middle East Bakeries also offer a good selection of groceries to complement that Middle Eastern meal you have been planning. Browse through the olives, dates, figs, broad beans, haloumi cheese, tahini, canned legumes and pickled vegetables. Dips and pita chips are staples here too.

BRUNSWICK
20–22 Hope Street
9380 2119
Mon–Wed 8am–6pm;
Thurs–Fri 8am–7pm;
Sat–Sun 8am–5pm
Melway 29 G6
Map page 164

Oasis Bakery

This fabulous food store really is an oasis – an oasis of Middle Eastern ingredients for those who love to cook Lebanese, Syrian, Turkish and Egyptian food. Oasis Bakery is a tremendous combination of food store, bakery and café all rolled into one. The shelves here are filled with fragrant spices and spice blends such as zaatar and dukkah. Oasis Bakers even have their own packaging, which holds an incredible selection of dried fruit and nuts – dates, figs, apricots, raisins, pistachios, pine nuts, almonds and numerous others. Keen shoppers can also pick up essentials such as pickled beetroot, tahini, pomegranate syrup, feta, kataifi pastry and couscous. The bakery churns out excellent mixed-meat kebabs, cheese and spinach triangles, and simple pizzas for lunch on the fly.

MURRUMBEENA
Shop 9, 993 North Road
9570 1122
Daily 8am–7pm
Melway 69 A9
Map page 169

Spring Cakes

The food scene of Dandenong offers an incredible mix of different culinary offerings – there are Indian, Sri Lankan, British, Fijian, Italian and Middle Eastern stores and foods to choose from. Spring Cakes fits firmly in the Middle Eastern realm, although it's in the strip known as Little India. It's not a huge store, but the array of ingredients will provide all you'll need to stock up for Middle Eastern cooking. The front window is host to a selection of roasted nuts and snacks, while the front counter is lined with a delicious display of nutty baklava, almond-topped semolina slice and a multitude of different-flavoured Turkish delight. Beyond the sweets and snacks the store offers essentials such as pomegranate syrup, orange-blossom water, dried figs, dates and pistachios, felafel mixes, sheep's milk feta cheese and yoghurt.

DANDENONG
Shop 3, 52D Foster Street
9794 6660
Mon–Sat 9am–6pm
Melway 91A D8
Map page 171

Menu

Breakfast
Ross Stevenson & John Burns — 5.30 am
Neil Mitchell — 8.30 am

Appetiser
Midday news — 12.00 pm

Lunch
Ernie Sigley — 12.10 pm

Entrée
Derryn Hinch — 4.00 pm

Dinner
Gerard Healy & Dwayne Russell — 6.00 pm

Dessert
Bruce Mansfield & Philip Brady — 8.00 pm

Supper
Keith McGowan — Midnight

The interest in organic food is growing at an incredible rate. Stores that were once seen as slightly hippy or alternative are now considered the 'in' places to shop. Devotees of organics claim the food tastes better, lasts longer and is better for human health and the land on which it's produced. Take a wander along the organic aisle at Queen Victoria Market and you'll see hundreds of organic food devotees choosing to buy pesticide-free ingredients. There are also gorgeous retailers such as Dynamic Vegies Organic Food Supply, The Fruit Pedallers Organic Food Store, The Green Grocer, Ripe and so many more, all providing choices for their local communities. Farmers' markets are also terrific spots to get your hands on fresh-from-the-farm organic food.

Dynamic Vegies Organic Food Supply

If we were to nominate the top five organic shops in Melbourne, then this store would be right up there. It's a calm and cool oasis filled with beautiful fresh organic, biodynamic and sometimes conventional ingredients that just makes you want to buy everything and rush home to cook. There's always a stunning range of fruits and vegetables to choose from: beautiful fresh lettuces and salad ingredients over summer, plus stone fruit and berries to enjoy. Cooler weather brings a seasonal change with excellent potato varieties, cabbage, broccoli, silverbeet and beetroot. The beauty of this store is there's so much more besides the fresh things. Choose from organic pasta and sauces, a great range of prepared baby food, spice mixes and blends, chocolate and sweet treats.

ELTHAM
Shop 2–3, cnr Beard Street and Main Road
9439 3462
Mon–Fri 8am–6pm;
Sat 8am–4pm;
Sun 10am–4pm
Melway 22 B2
Map page 171

The Fruit Pedallers Organic Food Store

We've always been impressed with the look and feel of Fruit Pedallers. Step inside the door and you just know there's going to be some excellent organic foods to be found. There's a great range of top-quality organic and biodynamic fruit and vegetables on display. There's a strong seasonal approach, so you'll find beautiful stone fruit, berries and salad ingredients through summer, followed by potatoes, root vegetables, apples and pears into the cooler months. Their range of dairy products is extensive too: organic yoghurts, cheeses, milks and creams. There are also delicious dips, chocolates and crackers, plus pies, pasties and cakes. Essential pantry items such as pasta, nuts, legumes and rice are also on hand.

NORTHCOTE
103 High Street
9489 5824
Mon–Fri 9am–7.30pm;
Sat 9am–6pm;
Sun 10am–6pm
Melway 30 E11
Map page 165

The Green Grocer

With its chocolate-coloured exterior and wide assortment of fresh produce, The Green Grocer is a store that is almost too good to be true. Comprising café, food store and cooking school, The Green Grocer has a friendly environment filled with like-minded people. In the store, choose from fresh seasonal ingredients of exceptional quality that not only look good but taste divine, beautifully displayed in a row of small timber crates. Popular buys are the organic dairy products, including milk, cheeses and ice-cream. There are also pastas, spice mixes and biodynamic meats, Green Grocer preserves and Fairtrade chocolate. The store's ready-made meals are also a winner. Scrumptious breakfasts, coffee, cakes and pies are on offer at the café.

FITZROY NORTH
217 St Georges Road
9489 1747
Mon–Sat 9am–7pm;
Sun 9am–6pm
Melway 30 B12
Map page 164

Leaf

What a delicious combination this store is. A terrific-sized space contains a wide variety of fresh ingredients: everyday fruit and vegetables from apples and pears to potatoes, lettuces and salad ingredients, grapes and much more. Pastries and sourdough bread is brought in daily from Dench Bakers in Fitzroy North. Smallgoods cover the gamut of smoked trout, chicken and bacon, while dairy is well represented with Australian, Italian and French classic cheeses. Meals to go include fresh lasagne, gnocchi and ready-to-top pizza bases. The shelves are lined with excellent-quality preserves and there's French cutlery on hand from Laguiole. The latest release cookbooks are also stocked if you're in need of culinary inspiration. Leaf is a terrific addition to this beachside shopping strip.

ELWOOD
111–113 Ormond Road
9531 6542
Mon–Thurs 7am–8pm;
Fri–Sun 7am–7pm
Melway 67 C4
Map page 170

Macro Wholefoods Market

Macro stores around Melbourne offer a clean and green supermarket approach to food retailing. The shelves here are well stocked with a wide range of ingredients from pasta and pasta sauces to the latest fruit juices, all manner of legumes, flour for home baking, oils, biscuits and baby needs. Snack foods are well covered too with everything from organic corn chips and beetroot chips to tasty carob treats. There are also biodynamic meats, fresh produce, meals, soups and salads to go, plus space to enjoy coffee in store. This approach even extends to the checkout where Macro only uses paper grocery bags. **Also at:** 1068 High Street, Armadale, 9947 1111; 40 Bluff Road, Black Rock, 9914 5111; Shop 2.200, Level 2, Centro, The Glen Shopping Centre, 235 Springvale Road, Glen Waverley, 8804 4688.

RICHMOND
153 Bridge Road
9935 8888
Mon–Fri 8.30am–8pm;
Sat–Sun 9am–7pm
www.macrowhole
foods.com.au
Melway 2G J6
Map page 166

Organic Gertrude

Organic Gertrude is a shining example of the modern organic food store. Its cool interior and smooth lines are softened by planter boxes out front filled with fresh herbs. All of this combines to make it a real drawcard in the Fairfield shopping area. Shelves of breads, organic oils, seeds, nuts and pre-packaged foods sit next to organic jams, chocolates and delicious snacks. There's also an extensive selection of teas, pasta, noodles and Japanese food. Fresh produce shines here too with a selection of the season's best. The pre-packaged meals are fresh and delicious, and include vegetarian soups, curries and quiches. There are non-vegetarian products too with biodynamic meats and organic poultry. And to top it all off a café section at the rear of the store offers healthy meals and good things for lunch on the go.

FAIRFIELD
108 Station Street
9481 4718
Mon–Fri 8.30am–7pm;
Sat 8.30am–5pm;
Sun 9am–4pm
Melway 30 K10
Map page 165

The Organic Union

The Organic Union has always been a beautiful place to shop. The space is colourful and enticing with fresh ingredients displayed in cane baskets and flowers dotted here and there to add a splash of colour and fragrance. As you would imagine the display always takes a seasonal approach – so fresh herbs, lettuces, stone fruit, berries and salad ingredients are available through summer, plums and apples shine in autumn, followed by potatoes, pumpkin and root vegetables in the cooler months. There's a good range of biodynamic milk and dairy products too. A juice bar at the front counter can be accessed from a storefront window. A small selection of sweet treats is usually on offer. If only all greengrocers were this good.

SURREY HILLS
137 Union Road
9890 1292
Mon–Fri 9am–6pm;
Sat 8am–4pm;
Sun 10am–3pm
Melway 46 H11
Map page 167

Organica

There's little doubt of Melburnians' interest in buying and cooking organic food products and ingredients. So much that the original Organica retail store in Prahran has been revamped to allow for more dining space and now been joined by a new outlet in South Melbourne. They offer a terrific range of ready-to-go meals, snacks and drinks all through the day. Soups and sandwiches made with the excellent Baker D. Chirico breads star at lunchtime. Ready-to-eat organic meals range from curries and casseroles to salads, pasta and noodle dishes, plus desserts. The shelves are lined with organic ingredients galore. Browse over pastas, rice, wine and beer, plus health-oriented chocolates and snacks. **Also at:** The Clarendon Centre, 263 Clarendon Street, South Melbourne, 9696 8170.

PRAHRAN
Rear, 546 Malvern Road
(enter via Errol Street)
9510 6787
Mon–Fri 8am–7pm;
Sat 8am–5.30pm;
Sun 10am–5pm
www.organica.com.au
Melway 2M C10
Map page 166

Passionfoods

The name says it all – Passionfoods are passionate about delicious food, healthy living and environmental protection. Walk through the vine-covered doorway to a treasure trove of good things. The shelves at Passionfoods are brimming with breads, pasta, dried fruits, chocolates and cereals. Choose from yoghurts, cheeses, soy sausages, organic wines, desserts and even baby formulas. Passionfoods also offer ready-made meals such as seasonal soups, Moroccan chickpea tagines, innovative seasonal salads, vegetarian lasagnes and delicious desserts. There's also a selection of smoked salmon, organic meats from Belmore Organic and organic poultry. Staff are always on hand for those who want to learn more about the store and products on offer.

SOUTH MELBOURNE
219 Ferrars Street
9690 9339
Mon–Fri 8am–7.30pm;
Sat 8am–7pm;
Sun 9am–6pm
Melway 2K B2
Map page 168

Plump Organic Grocery

The name here really fits as this delightful store is filled with the plumpest, freshest ingredients this side of the Westgate Bridge. Lucky locals can choose from fresh fruit and vegetables that look as if they've just been picked, through to dairy and soy products, organic chicken, pre-packed bacon and ham. The store offers an extensive range of biodynamic and organic products, so it's a terrific opportunity to stock up on dried fruits, eggs, chocolate, juices, bread and cereals, or choose from the sourdough breads. There are organic wines and biodynamic beers on offer too. Plump is part café, and offers a fine selection of Fairtrade coffees and organic teas, plus freshly baked muffins. If you can't make it to the store, take advantage of their home-delivery service, which operates in Yarraville and surrounds.

YARRAVILLE
24 Ballarat Street
9687 6422
Mon–Fri 9am–6.30pm;
Sat 9am–4pm
Melway 42 A9
Map page 163

Ripe the Organic Grocer

A visit to Ripe makes you want to cook up a storm. The philosophy here is to provide top-quality organic produce and to support local growers. Choose from a fantastic selection of seasonal fruit and vegetables, freshly baked breads and stock up on bunches of fresh herbs. Self-serve from tubs of chocolate macadamias, honey apricots, cashews and plump prunes. The grocery selection at Ripe is also extensive – choose from muesli, oils, noodles, pasta and pasta sauces. If you are tempted to sample organic wines, there's a good selection on offer here too. Terrific dairy ranges from milk and cream to beautiful butter. Ripe's Albert Park store offers smoothies and juices from their organic juice bar. **Also at:** 23 Victoria Street, Albert Park, 9699 6405.

SOUTH YARRA
Stall 7–8, Prahran Market,
163–185 Commercial Road
9804 8606
Tues & Sat 6am–5pm;
Thurs–Fri 6am–6pm
Melway 2L H9
Map page 166

Wholefoods Food Store

Wholefoods Food Store has that certain look and feel that only comes when the owners are really into what they do. Here, that's creating a retail space packed with excellent whole foods. There's dried pasta in every style from spelt to rice flour varieties, plus a good selection of dried noodles. There are also lentils, chickpeas, split peas and all the legumes you could wish for. Tea and coffee is well represented with plenty of choices from green to herbal teas. A good selection of fresh produce is on offer to assist with good home cooking. Meat and smallgoods include ham, sausages, porterhouse and rump steak, plus organic chicken in various cuts. Phillippa's bread, slices and biscuits are also on hand. You can even enjoy a coffee and sweet treat after the shopping is done.

BRIGHTON
320 Bay Street
9596 9035
Mon–Sat 8am–7pm;
Sun 9am–5pm
Melway 67 G9
Map page 170

Takeaway/traiteurs

Even the most devoted home cook needs a night off every now and then. This is not to say you'll be happy with a quickly thrown together takeaway meal. No way. What you want is for someone else to prepare something beautiful and handmade, a night for someone else to do the shopping, the chopping and preparing. Melbourne has a number of excellent places dotted around the suburbs that provide just this service. Tartine in Armadale is probably the most famous, and rightly so. The food always looks colourful, fresh and beautifully prepared. Just one bite of their beef and burgundy pie will make you a fan for life. There are also other terrific stores dotted around the suburbs offering an array of beautiful meals – Lafayette Fine Food, Kuche and Replete Providore to name just a few.

Gas Eatery & Supplies

This store has become a much-loved part of the South Melbourne food scene over the past couple of years. This is hardly surprising when you consider the innovative take-home meals they serve. Food here takes its lead from the islands and coast of the Mediterranean – so Spain, Turkey, Greece and Morocco all feature in platters, mezze and picnic boxes. The selection can include spinach, rice and feta croquettes, spicy chipolata sausage rolls, lamb sausages wrapped in vine leaves and their famous Turkish pizzas. There are also flavour-filled house-made dips such as pumpkin and harissa, babaganoush and tzatziki. The keftedes skewers are also excellent. Gas offers the option to eat in, takeaway or come for a beautiful breakfast. Either way you won't leave disappointed.

SOUTH MELBOURNE
253 Coventry Street
9690 0217
Mon–Fri 8am–6pm;
Sat–Sun 8am–5pm
Melway 2K C1
Map page 168

Kuche

Kuche is a delightful new food store in the Beaumaris concourse. The name Kuche means kitchen in German, and visiting this store really is like stepping into a large open kitchen – you can see the food on display and the preparation going on behind the scenes. Delicious take-home meal options include chicken schnitzel and risotto cakes, beef stroganoff and green chicken curry. There's also all the accompaniments you need, from steamed rice and mashed potato to fresh salads. Sweet treats are also prepared daily. This large open-plan kitchen transforms at night to become a local cooking school with a terrific array of classes on offer. Come and learn about barbecuing, Spanish food, vegetarian or send your teens along to learn a few life essentials.

BEAUMARIS
19 South Concourse
9589 0900
Mon–Fri 9am–6pm;
Sat 9am–2pm;
Melway 86 D7
Map page 169

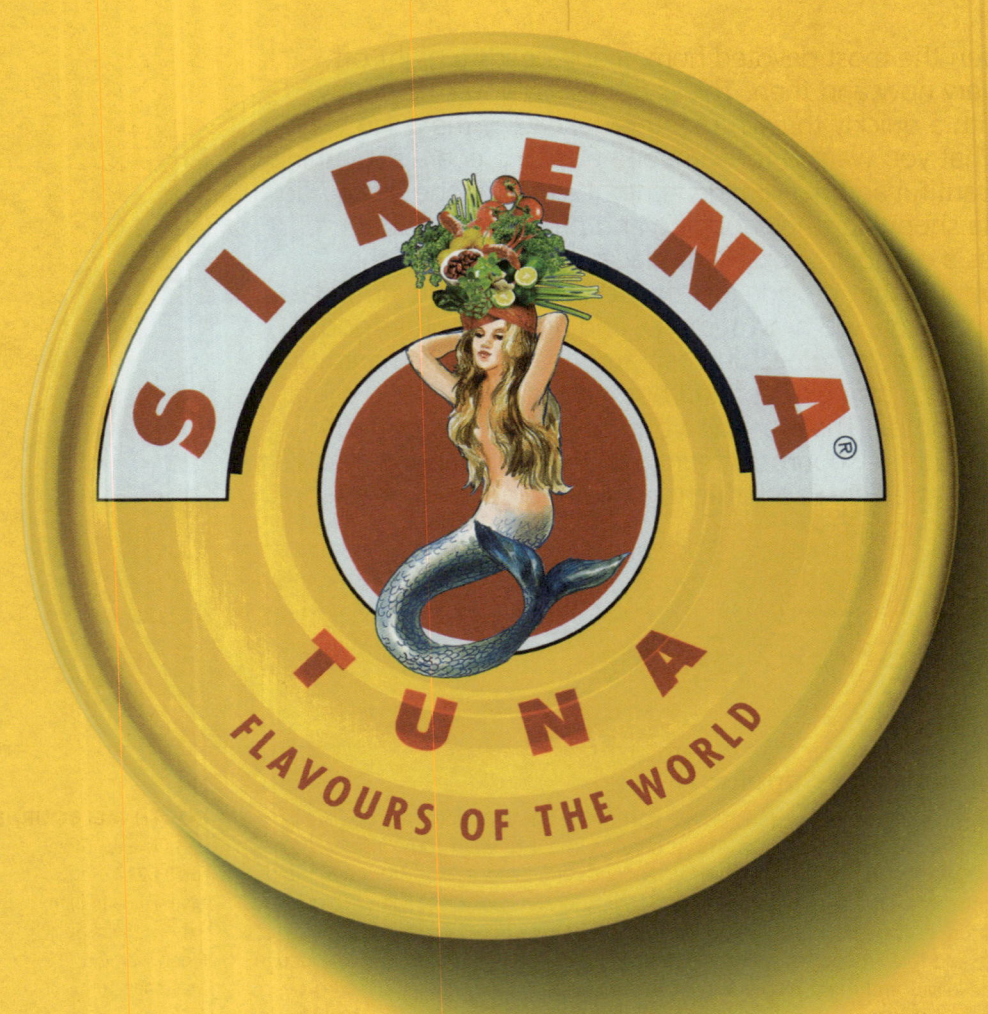

TRY OUR FLAVOURS OF THE WORLD

THAI STYLE, OLIVE TAPENADE, SOY & GINGER AND MORE...

I love my Sirena

Highlight
TAKE-HOME MEALS

Beef and burgundy pie, Tartine, page 122
It's so darned difficult to choose at Tartine because everything looks and tastes so good. On a chilly autumn evening, however, this beautifully rich, puff-pastry-wrapped beef pie will really hit the spot.

Butter chicken, Lafayette Fine Food, page 121
This mild and creamy Indian curry comes as a complete meal with steamed rice. Heat and serve at home for a delicious night of no cooking.

Lemon pepper crumbed chicken schnitzels, Kuche, page 119
Kuche has taken the hassle out of a family favourite meal with these ready-to-heat schnitzels. Heat and serve with mayonnaise and lettuce in a soft roll for the perfect weekend lunch.

Marinated chicken pieces, Tangelo Fine Foods, page 122
Pick up a couple of these plump roasted and glazed chicken pieces for a seriously easy dinner. A few minutes in the oven at home and they're ready to serve.

Lafayette Fine Food

If you ever need to have someone else do your cooking then drop by to see the talented team at Lafayette. Their beautifully presented display of take-home meals has daily specials as well as items that are so popular they are always on. If the orecchietti with broccoli and ricotta is on then it must be Monday; ditto the crispy fried potatoes with garlic and thyme. Tuesday features Thai beef salad and rolled lamb fillet with tomato and rosemary pesto. And so on through the week. Somehow they also find time to whip up meatloaves, terrines, ready-to-barbecue marinated chickens and cooked eye fillet. Beautiful desserts include lemon tart, chocolate mousse and much more. There's also a house-made dressing to brighten up your homemade salads.

BRIGHTON
355 New Street
9596 1867
Mon–Fri 8am–7pm;
Sat 8am–5pm;
Sun 9am–4pm
Melway 76 G3
Map page 170

Provisions Food Store

There are not too many places around town that are a café, a take-home food store and a retailer of cookware and foodies ingredients all rolled into one. Provisions Food Store seems to be able to do just that without missing a beat. Large glass cabinets offer excellent sandwiches, wraps and ready-filled rolls to enjoy in-house or takeaway. The chicken, mayo and lettuce on grain bread is a beauty. There's also a good selection of fresh salads and noodle dishes to try too. The coffee is always spot-on, as is the crispy, dark and delicious chocolate brownie. Shelves near the dining area offer a small selection of cookbooks, platters, glass jugs, bowls and tableware. There are also good-quality spices, mortar and pestles, jams, chutneys and preserves, olive oil and groovy utensils.

CAMBERWELL
250 Camberwell Road
9804 0036
Mon–Fri 8am–5pm;
Sat 8.30am–4pm;
Sun 9am–4pm
Melway 59 J1
Map page 167

Replete Providore

Replete Providore, an essential part of the Hawthorn food scene, is a buzzing space packed with customers throughout the day. Breakfast regulars grab a table and order up big on bircher muesli and ricotta hotcakes. The take-home meal option is huge here too: tomato and chickpea soup, Italian chicken and meatballs, Thai beef curry and beef Provençal all feature strongly. There are also pasta sauces, meat and vegetarian lasagne, quiches and savoury tarts to go. Shelves are laden with great products from Simon Johnson, Tea 2, Grinders and Phillippa's, backed up with their own kitchen-made products and smallgoods from Istra and La Parisienne Pates. Christmas is celebrated in style with puddings, cakes, glazed hams and mince pies to enjoy.

HAWTHORN
302 Barkers Road
9818 4448
Mon–Fri 7.30am–3.30pm;
Sat–Sun 8am–4.30pm
Melway 45 E8
Map page 167

Tangelo Fine Foods

Planning a dinner party but not eager to cook? Head to Tangelo Fine Foods on Malvern Road, where you'll find all sorts of good foods ready and waiting for your hungry guests. From pita chips and petit fours, to more hearty fare such as casseroles and pies, Tangelo has something to please everyone. Popular dishes include chicken schnitzel and chicken strips that are crumbed, cooked and ready to reheat at home. There are also vegetable fritters, and salads to go. Dessert can be covered with classics such as creamed rice pudding, drunken oranges, cupcakes and large decorated cakes. Decorated biscuits such as shortbread and chocolate-dipped meringues are pre-packed and make a terrific afternoon-tea treat. **Also at:** 115 Church Street, Brighton, 9592 1411.

TOORAK
531 Malvern Road
9826 1297
Mon–Fri 7am–5.30pm;
Sat 7am–1.30pm
Melway 2M D10
Map page 166

Tartine

There are many take-home food stores around Melbourne nowadays, but if you want to see and taste where this all began in Melbourne then head for Tartine. Today, Jan Maskiell and her team still rule the roost with beautifully prepared and presented dishes. New things are constantly appearing from the kitchen as the day unfolds and have that take-me-home look. It could be a Moroccan chicken tagine, Catalan chicken or a summer lasagne layered with mushrooms, mint, spinach and feta cheese. Equally good is the oxtail ragu, glazed meatballs, beef and burgundy pies and the stunning-looking tarts. If you need dessert too then check out the cassata cake, napoleon brûlée or a classic passionfruit sponge. With catering available for parties big and small, Tartine really hits all the food-lover buttons.

ARMADALE
1035 High Street
9822 8849
Mon–Fri 8am–6pm;
Sat 9am–4pm;
Sun 10am–4.30pm
Melway 59 A7
Map page 166

Late-night munchies

When most of us are heading for bed, there's a band of food lovers on the prowl for somewhere good to eat. Some work in hospitality and are looking for a bite before heading home, while others need some sustenance after a night on the town. Either way, here are half a dozen diverse options for those with late-night munchies.

Embassy Taxi Cafe
A visit to this Spencer Street institution is like stepping back in time – back to an era when burgers and steak sandwiches were made fresh and with care, when the tables were topped with Formica and service was down to earth. Order one of their beef burgers with the lot (patty, bacon, egg, tomato, onions and shredded lettuce) and you'll soon be a new devotee. You won't have any trouble getting a cab home either!
547 Spencer Street, West Melbourne; 9328 1830; Melway 2A H12; Map page 163

Pellegrini's Espresso Bar
When all you need is a pit stop for a heart-stopping coffee then the famous Pellegrini's will always hit the spot. It's been pumping out authentic Italian style since the 1950s and is still going strong. Order a short black and you'll soon be fuelled with caffeine and ready for the journey home.
66 Bourke Street, City; 9662 1885; Melway 1B T5; Map page 162

Stalactites
This foodie hot spot on the corner of Lonsdale and Russell Streets is a perennial favourite of those who love their souvlaki. It gets absolutely packed some nights, but that's half of the fun. The beautifully cooked lamb wrapped in warm bread with salad and garlic yoghurt sauce is well worth the wait.
177–183 Lonsdale Street, City; 9663 3316; Melway 1B T5; Map page 162

Supper Inn
This legendary Chinese restaurant is tucked away up the cobble-stoned Celestial Avenue. The décor hasn't changed in decades, or the menu really, but that doesn't stop devotees streaming in until 2.30am. Favourites include roast suckling pig and chilli salt quail.
15 Celestial Avenue, City; 9663 4759; Melway 1B P4, Map page 162

Melbourne Kebab Station
Those heading north out of town and looking for more than just a snack should make a beeline for the Melbourne Kebab Station. It's a busy, buzzing sort of place with friendly and speedy service. The classic doner kebab of spit-roast lamb in Turkish bread with salad and garlic sauce is the pick of the place.
Shop 9/10, 451 Sydney Road, Coburg; 9355 7766; Melway 29 H1; Map page 165

Melbourne Supper Club Bar
This has to be one of the most laid-back and relaxing spots to ease an attack of the munchies. Nestled above Spring Street it offers a comprehensive wine list, plenty of beers and a menu that runs from caviar and party pies. It's not easy to get into the place, but it is very easy to stay. Slide on into one of the super-comfy couches and enjoy.
Level 1, 161 Spring Street, City; 9654 6300; Melway 1B V5; Map page 162

After food stores our favourite shops are wine shops. Whether you're picking up much-needed beer on a Friday, a dozen quaffing cleanskins, a special bottle of champagne or some nice wine to stick in the cupboard for dinner on Saturday, these shops are as much a part of our lives as food stores. Many of the wine stores listed here are members of the Alliance of Independent Fine Wine Merchants, a group set up to make a stand against the mediocrity of wines and service offered in chain and some independent stores. Melbourne has been a better place since. All these wine stores offer exceptional wines, backed up with exceptional service, plus regular tastings and formal classes to help you to understand this subject better. You may also like to search out the best glassware or decanter to further enhance your drinking experience.

Armadale Cellars

Owner Phil Hude notched up ten years in 2007; that's a decade of choosing well-known labels such as Grange, Hill of Grace and Mount Mary to sit alongside everyday quaffing bargains and boutique wines from the likes of Giaconda, Paradigm Hill and Shay's Flat. You will have no trouble finding a wine you like here, your only problem may be sticking to the limit of your credit card. There is something for all tastes and budgets. New World and Old World releases add interest and there's always a wine on tasting. You can take part in wine dinners, courtyard tastings over summer, wine-appreciation classes and even master classes on whisky. There are wine glasses and decanters to round out your purchases and wine storage solutions.

ARMADALE
813–817 High Street
9509 3055
Mon–Sat 10am–8pm
www.armadalecellars.com.au
Melway 58 J7
Map page 166

Botanical Wine Store

The Botanical is home to fine food and great wine, and their wine store stocks not only a wide variety of everyday Australian drinking drops, but many imported names, old and rare wines, new releases, and dessert and fortified wines. You can shop one of two ways: come in and wander through the store and parts of the restaurant and pick the brains of the knowledgeable staff or let your fingers do the working via their website. Either way you can still take advantage of the Botanical Dozens deal, which takes all the hard work out of making a decision, offering a great combination of wines, with a great saving. They also stock wine accessories such as glassware, ice buckets and wine guides.

SOUTH YARRA
169 Domain Road
9820 7888
Mon–Fri 7am–11pm;
Sat–Sun 8am–11pm
Melway 2L C2
Map page 168

City Wine Shop

This store is both a retail wine shop and wine bar. You can pursue the shelves looking for new and well-known producers from Victoria, Australia and Europe, or take a seat and indulge in a glass of wine with some of their fine food. They specialise in champagne – what more does anyone need to know? You had best get yourself in there to learn firsthand and check out their range of spirits, liqueurs and boutique beers. You might like to take advantage of their excellent mixed dozens, which typically contain a combination of really interesting wines from Spain, Italy, Portugal, New Zealand and Australia. The upstairs tea room is home to wine classes that cross all boundaries, looking at particular wine varieties, wine regions, and even whisky.

CITY
159 Spring Street
9654 6657
Mon–Thurs 7am–11.30pm;
Fri 7am–1am;
Sat 9am–1am;
Sun 10am–11.30pm
Melway 2F J2
Map page 162

Cloudwine

Stewart, Jacinta and Chris are the clever people behind Cloudwine, who source rare wines and releases from quality, small wineries that are often difficult for the average wine shopper to find. They aim to improve awareness and distribution of quality wines from Australia and New Zealand, as well as micro and handcrafted beers. They are not a group of people to tell you what to do, but are here to educate and sell you quality wine at good prices. Like all good wine shops, there are special offers, particularly on mixed dozens, wine classes and great information from all staff in all stores as they are passionate about what they stock. **Also at:** Shop 10, Dendy Plaza, Church Street, Brighton, 9553 8416; 766 Burke Road, Camberwell, 9882 0954.

SOUTH MELBOURNE
317 Clarendon Street
9699 6700
Mon–Sat 10am–8pm;
Sun midday–7pm
Melway 2K D3
Map page 168

Enoteca Sileno

If the wines of the Old World confuse you with talk of nebbiolo, barbera, sangiovese and dolcetto, then this is the place to head. You will find these grape varieties and much much more. The staff will guide you to a wine that best suits your needs, and maybe even offer the chance to join in at one of their tastings when they explore a particularly grape variety in more detail. Make sure you purchase some moscato, a light, sweet, semi-sparkling dessert wine, and check out the range of grappa, limoncello and the beautifully sweet vin santo; all the best producers are stocked here. Join their wine club for free to obtain special offers and information on new arrivals, dinners and tastings, which are held monthly, and discounts upon presentation of your EnoVita card.

CARLTON NORTH
920 Lygon Street
9389 7000
Mon–Wed 9am–6pm;
Thurs–Sat 9am–9pm;
Sun 10am–4pm
Melway 29 K12
Map page 164

Europa Cellars

As the name suggests, Europa Cellars specialises in the wines of Europe, everything from Austrian rieslings and Italian sangiovese, chianti and pinot grigio. The range of French wines doesn't get better with all regions covered: Bordeaux, Burgundy, the southern and northern Rhône, Alsace and our favourite, Champagne. You will also find wine from the New World: South Africa, North America and Argentina; New Zealand wines feature strongly, plus wines form boutique Australian vineyards. To help you know more about these wines, they hold regular tastings and wine-education classes, plus wine dinners. The real stars of the shop though are the staff. With superb wine knowledge, they will go the extra yards to find the right bottle of wine for you, whatever your budget.

EAST MELBOURNE
Shop G3, 50 Wellington Parade
9417 7220
Mon–Tues 10am–7pm;
Wed–Sat 10am–8pm;
Sun 11am–7pm
Melway 2G E5
Map page 166

Highlight
BEER AND BREWERIES

Emerald Hill Brewery
The roller door goes up on Friday nights, happy hour starts at 5pm, and what more do you need to know? Hand-crafted ales, including pale ale, wheat beer and stout are just some of the options, plus sport on the big screen.
20 Ross Street, South Melbourne; 9696 5491; Melway 2F C12; Map page 168

Mountain Goat Beer
You can indulge in your own personal beer-appreciation night including a tour, tasting and pizza. Wednesday night is the time to head down there, find more out about micro brewing and don't be afraid to ask questions.
Cnr North and Clark Streets, Richmond; 9428 1180; www.goatbeer.com.au; Melway 2H G5; Map page 166

Scruffy Bunch – Microbrewery Tours
The tour starts at Federation Square and heads north to Ravens Brewery for an excursion through this boutique brewery before heading out to the Yarra Valley to explore another three microbreweries, with lunch included to help soak up the alcohol.
9859 4932; www.scruffybunch.com.au

2 Brothers Brewery
Dave and Andrew open the doors to their brewery every Thursday and Friday night. Obviously you come for the beer, but on Thursday night there are German-style hotdogs with all the trimmings and on Friday it's wood-fired pizza and footy.
4 Joyner Street, Moorabbin; 9553 1177; www.2brothers.com.au; Melway 78 A7; Map page 169

Old & Rare Wines Collector House

There are many good bottle shops in Melbourne; each has its own point of difference, whether it's the best of the local stuff or imported wines. This establishment though specialises in old and rare wines. They boast the most comprehensive selection in Australia, with often only one or two bottles of each wine being available. They also stock a full range of commercial wine, beer and spirits, covering all bases. Even if you can't afford some of the price tags, it's nice to dream and you can view the collection of current releases, back vintages and verticals, together with wine from France, Germany, Italy, Spain, the United States and New Zealand. If you're lucky enough to have an established cellar, they will also sell you wine on consignment.

SOUTHBANK
133 Queensbridge Street
9698 8000
Tues–Fri 11am–7pm
Sat 11am–5pm
Melway 2F D9
Map page 168

The Prince Wine Store

This shop has it all: a diverse mix of wines from all over the world, competitive pricing and educated staff. Partners Philip Rich, Michael McNamara and Alex Wilcox showcase their choice of wine in a purpose-built, climate-controlled environment. You will find everything from Craiglee, Clonakilla, Giaconda, Ata Rangi, Giacomo Conterno and Zind-Humbrecht to local options such as Yering Station and Pewsey Vale. Their wine courses offer two streams. One is for customers to become more informed on various topics, from wine basics to French or Italian wines; the other course is for professionals wishing to expand their knowledge. **Also at:** 2A Acland Street, St Kilda, 9536 1155; G22 The Clarendon Centre, South Melbourne, 9645 0178.

SOUTH MELBOURNE
177 Bank Street
9686 3033
Mon–Thurs 10am–8pm;
Fri–Sat 10am–9pm
Melway 2K D2
Map page 168

Randall's

Randall has his finely tuned wine nose in everything, from being a wine merchant (with this store, plus another in Geelong), importer, wine writer and an active wine show judge. He also dabbles in a bit of winemaking on the side, but at his shop he offers a vast range of local and imported wines, including everything from Australia's hottest new wine discoveries to cheap cleanskins. Randall imports wine from Burgundy, Rhône, Chablis, Beaujolais and Champagne, as well as stocking rare wines such as Domaine de la Romanée Conti, Cullen, Moss Wood, Mount Mary, Giaconda, Bindi, Wendouree and Castagna. You will also find releases from New Zealand, the United States and Portugal alongside the vast French range. There are also stunning wine accessories.

ALBERT PARK
186 Bridport Street
9686 4122
Mon–Wed 10am–8pm;
Thurs–Fri 10am–9pm;
Sat 9am–9pm;
Sun 11am–7pm
Melway 2K A6
Map page 168

Rathdowne Cellars

Father and son Eddie and Cameron Kidd have many strings to their bow. In addition to their range of Australian speciality wines including everything from Cullen, Bass Phillip, Clonakilla, Penfolds Grange, Yarra Yering, Charles Melton, Torbreck, Mount Mary and Henschke, they are the Victorian outlet for Rockford Wines. They also cover New Zealand, France, Germany, Italy, Spain and the United States with producers such as Dr Loosen, Armand Rousseau, Guigal, Chateau Margaux, Chateau d'Yquem, Josmeyer and Hugel. Their trump card is the range of wines from Spain, Madeira and Portugal, with over fifty different sherries, ports and madeiras. You will find tastings, masterclasses and dinners around a particular style of wine, plus in-store tastings where you can meet the winemaker.

CARLTON NORTH
348 Rathdowne Street
9349 3366
Mon–Wed 10am–7pm;
Thurs–Sat 10am–9pm;
Sun 11am–7pm
Melway 2B J2
Map page 164

World food

This chapter gathers together a mixed bag of delightful food stores, each with a strong cultural identity. While we've already covered Italian, Asian, Middle Eastern and Indian food stores in separate chapters, these stores fall outside those culinary headings. They provide ingredients for specialised cuisines and are perfect for those hanging for a taste of home or cooks wanting to explore new foods in their kitchen. Aztec Imports for instance is 'the' place in Melbourne to gather ingredients for Mexican cooking with everything from chillies to tortillas, while the new Treats from Home store in the CBD offers homesick Brits all manner of sweets, snacks, biscuits and sauces. The same can be said for The South African Shop, Russian Tidbits and USA Foods. There's a world of food in Melbourne just waiting to be discovered. Go to it!

Aztec Imports

Keen cooks who want to get into authentic Mexican cooking should make the trip to Aztec Imports. It's a bit of trek to the back streets of Tullamarine, but if you're keen it'll be worth the journey. More of a showroom than a food store, the products and ingredients on display are indispensable. One of their specialties is (naturally enough) dried chillies, and with an expansive collection that includes chipotle, habanero, New Mexico, mulato and tepin. There is a chilli heat and flavour to suit every palate, and a great assortment of chilli powders, bean seasonings, chilli pastes and spice blends for every Mexican meal. There's everything you could want, from refried beans and tortillas to drinking chocolate and margarita mixes.

TULLAMARINE
8A Adina Court
9330 1733
Mon–Thurs 8am–4.30pm;
Fri 8am–4pm
Melway 15 H4

Casa Iberica

In a city where Italian and Greek delis rule the roost, Casa Iberica is a rare gem – a delicatessen and food store dedicated to the best Spanish ingredients available. Take the time to browse as there is so much to enjoy. Spanish paprika in different styles from sweet and smoky to hot and smoky are some of the bestsellers here. Tinned tuna, sardines and mackerel also feature. You also find rice for dishes such as paella, plus enormous pans for cooking this classic dish. Terracotta jugs and dishes are excellent too. Have jamon sliced to order, and pick up chorizo (hot or mild), manchego cheese, olives and crusty rolls. Don't leave without stocking up on Portuguese egg tarts for the trip home.

FITZROY
25 Johnston Street
9419 4420
Mon–Fri 8am–5pm;
Sat 8am–2pm
Melway 2C A7
Map page 164

Colossus Supermarket

As the name implies, Colossus is a serious-sized store dedicated to Greek cuisine. Olive oil, for instance, can be purchased in 200 ml bottles or 20 litre tins. The range of dried herbs is abundant, with thyme, oregano and mint being particular favourites. Meze ingredients are a big drawcard, with masses of marinated olives for sale. The deli also boasts a mountain of feta cheese, ham, salami, salted cod, smoked herrings and sardines. The staples are there too, with an assortment of breads and dips on offer. There are also dried broad beans, cannellini beans and chickpeas pre-packaged or self-serve, plus sweet treats such as almond shortbreads and baklava. During Orthodox Easter you can pick up traditional foods such as sweet braided bread with red-dyed egg.

DONCASTER
6–8 Stutt Avenue
9857 9971
Mon–Wed 9am–5.30pm;
Thurs 9am–6pm;
Fri 7am–8pm;
Sat 8.30am–3.30pm
Melway 32 K12
Map page 171

Flavours, Herbs & Spices

This is a beautiful store dedicated to spices and good things for the kitchen. It began in a tiny store just off Greville Street before moving to this more spacious outlet on the Windsor end of Chapel Street. Stock up on everything from Chinese five spice and spearmint to sumac and aniseed. While you're there check out the new range of native herbs and spices from South Australia. There is an extensive range of kitchenware, including tagines and clay pots, along with an eclectic collection of kitchen gadgets. The store offers a great selection of essentials such as oils, vinegars and sauces, plus specialty products such as saffron, orange-blossom water, sea salt and vanilla beans. There are also foodie books to inspire good cooking.

WINDSOR
113 Chapel Street
9521 3288
Mon–Fri 10am–5.30pm;
Sat 10am–5pm
Melway 2P H1
Map page 166

Klein's Kosher Gourmet

This Glen Eira store is a wonderful outlet for those looking for restaurant-quality meals to enjoy at home. As the name suggests the meals here are all prepared in line with kosher practice. Other dietary requirements catered for include vegetarian and vegan, as well as supplying a number of dairy-free and wheat-free products. The selection is really extensive and much of it is frozen when it's prepared. Classic dinners such as chicken cacciatore, beef goulash, chicken and beef curry, and lasagne in regular and family sizes are all available. There are also soups such as lamb shank and barley, Thai vegetable, chicken and corn, and red lentil. Party food is available along with pasta sauces, stocks and desserts. Fresh food to go ranges from salmon patties to fresh baked pastries.

RIPPONLEA
19 Glen Eira Road
9528 1200
Mon–Thurs 9am–6pm;
Fri 8am–3pm
Melway 67 E1
Map page 170

Russian Tidbits

Food from Russia doesn't loom large on the local food scene. Nevertheless, Russian Tidbits is always packed with hungry foodies. Perhaps it is the friendly multilingual staff who are always happy to talk about the different smallgoods and cheeses on offer, or the seemingly never-ending supply of tastings that staff are happy to dish out. More likely it's the dozens of delicious continental smallgoods in the main counter that does the trick with debriciner, kranskys, frankfurts, hams, salamis and kaiserflesh galore. A second chilled display plays host to sauerkraut, smoked salmon, smoked trout, dips, pickled herrings and other goodies. The grocery selection is impressive too with imported gherkins, relishes and jams. Specialty continental cakes are also offered here.

CARNEGIE
113 Koornang Road
9572 3911
Mon–Thurs 9am–6pm;
Fri 9am–7.30pm;
Sat–Sun 9am–5pm
Melway 68 J4
Map page 167

Dining in Melbourne

It's hard to go wrong with dining out in this food-loving city. This is our pick of a few special dining rooms we really like around town. Some are cheap, some are a more expensive 'big night out' and others fall somewhere in between. Regardless of price, they all contribute to create the vibrant food scene we know and love.

Attica
The food and service at Attica continues to gain critical acclaim. With five years under its belt this stylish Ripponlea dining room offers some seriously good dining. Order the tasting menu with matched wines to experience the flavours, textures and excitement of chef Ben Shewery's creative food at its best.
74 Glen Eira Road, Ripponlea; 9530 0111; Melway 67 E1; Map page 170

Bar Lourinha
Chef Matt McConnell offers up an ever-changing menu of delicious Portuguese-inspired food. Dishes to share range from chargrilled quail to smoked eel salad, roast pork, marinated kingfish carpaccio, chargrilled chorizo and a moorish salad of fine cabbage, mint, dill and feta cheese. The wine list is a beauty here too.
37 Little Collins Street, City; 9663 7890; Melway 1B U6, Map page 162

Donovan's
There's no better place to celebrate a special occasion than with a window table at Donovan's restaurant. Enjoy the bay views with stylish food, stylish service and terrific menu options. Start with Tom Cooper's smoked salmon on blinis with a glass of sparkling and you're on your way to pure dining pleasure.
40 Jacka Boulevard, St Kilda; 9534 8221; Melway 2N K9, Map page 170

Gingerboy
Chef Teague Ezard has set up Gingerboy to present his version of hawker food in a contemporary setting. There are small plates to start such as chicken satay dumplings and crispy chilli cuttlefish. Larger dishes such as steamed sea bass with soy, mirin and ginger dressing are excellent. Whatever you do, don't miss the dessert platter.
27–29 Crossley Street, City; 9662 4200; Melway 1B T4; Map page 162

Grossi Florentino Cellar Bar
If you wanted to showcase Melbourne's Italian food heritage then Grossi Florentino is the place. Start with the welcoming Cellar Bar on a Saturday afternoon. Settle in with a glass of sangiovese, a plate of the spaghetti alla bolognese and a serve of sautéed spinach. Then finish with a short black coffee. You won't eat better!
80 Bourke Street, City; 9662 1811; Melway 1B T5; Map page 162

Journal Canteen
Rosa Mitchell is the talented cook behind the flavour-packed food at Journal Canteen. Start with the daily handmade antipasto (the cauliflower polpetti are a must), then perhaps a small soup followed by orecchietti with anchovy and broccoli or sweet and sour braised rabbit. Add a sweet treat, stove top coffee and you'll be hooked too.
Mezzanine, 253 Flinders Lane (CAE Building), City; 9650 4399; Melway 1B M8; Map page 162

MoVida
Ten out of ten to the MoVida crew who night after night pump out full-flavoured, Spanish-inspired dishes. Pop up to the bar, order a glass of grenache, then a selection of small tastes. The Cantabrian artisan anchovy on crouton with smoked tomato sorbet is not to be missed – likewise the acorn-fed Iberico Spanish jamon.
1 Hosier Lane, City; 9663 3038; Melway 1B Q9; Map page 162

Oriental Tea House
The warm welcome at Oriental Tea House is the start of a terrific foodie experience. Try the excellent steamed pork or ginger chicken dumplings with a herbal tea from the extensive list. The more adventurous can experience some excellent barbecue chicken feet. They're some of the best in Melbourne!
455 Chapel Street, South Yarra; 9826 0128; Melway 2L J9, Map page 166

Oyster Little Bourke
Oyster lovers and fans of elegant bistro cooking should make a beeline for Oyster Little Bourke. Settle up to the bar for freshly opened oysters and a glass of something special to accompany. The stylish dining room also makes a perfect spot to enjoy the fantastic daily tasting place, excellent steaks and a bottle or two from the extensive wine list.
35 Little Bourke Street, City; 9650 0988; Melway 1B U4; Map page 162

Pizza & Fichi
Melt-in-the-mouth, thin-based pizzas are all the rage here. We love the bersola pizza in particular. It comes from the oven with wonderful crispy edges before having shaved smoked beef, shaved parmesan and rocket draped on top. If there's room left for dessert, the apple, walnut and cinnamon pizza is a beauty too.
321 High Street, Kew; 9853 5155; Melway 45 D6

The Press Club
George Calombaris has drawn on his Greek food heritage to create a contemporary dining space in the old Herald & Weekly Times building. The Kerasma sharing menus are probably our pick here as they provide a delicious range of amazing dishes to taste and enjoy. This is a great addition to the Melbourne dining scene.
72 Flinders Street, City; 9677 9677; Melway 1B T9; Map page 162

Red Emperor
Yum cha should be enjoyed among masses of hungry people on a Sunday afternoon so that you can try lots and lots of different dishes. Red Emperor offers that very experience every Sunday. Add in some excellent food, speedy service and great views across to the city skyline and you have the complete Chinese package.
Level 3, Southgate; 9699 4170; Melway 1A K12; Map page 168

Rockpool Bar & Grill
Neil Perry's glam restaurant in the Crown Complex is a great addition to the local dining scene. First-timers should start with the four raw tastes of the sea, followed by an aged T-bone steak with a side dish of onion rings. Order up big from the extensive wine list and you'll be in a very happy place.
Shop 1/8 Whiteman Street, Southbank; 8648 1900; Melway 1A E12; Map 168

Vue de Monde
Shannon Bennett's Vue de Monde is without a doubt one of this city's best dining rooms. It begins with style – from the dining room and the décor to the wait staff's uniforms to the cutlery. Then there's the food that has to be tasted to be believed. Come for a special occasion, relax into the experience and forget the budget for one night.
430 Little Collins Street, City; 9691 3888; Melway 1A G6; Map page 162

The South African Shop

Retailers like the South African Shop are essential for those who have left their homeland to live in Melbourne. It's here expats can again get a taste of home and help to keep their homesickness at bay for a while. There's a selection of wines, grape juices and imported liquors. A deli cabinet is lined with specialist ingredients such as fresh boerewors sausages and escort pork sausages, dried biltong and droewors. The shelves are stocked with tomato and chilli sauces, Mrs Ball's chutneys and salad dressings galore. There are tinned and packet soups, plus Safari brand fig, mango, peach and guava fruit rolls. Confectionery is on hand too with imported chocolate bars and snack food brands such as Big Korn, Fritos and Willard's. **Also at:** 461 Hawthorn Road, Caulfield South, 9523 7633.

TEMPLESTOWE
Upper level, rear 112
James Street
9846 8322
Mon–Fri 9.30am–5.30pm;
Sat 9.30am–4pm;
Sun 10.30am–1.30pm
Melway 33 D4
Map page 171

Treats from Home

Expats miss many things when they're living far from home, so being able to source certain foods can be a dream come true. Treats from Home aim to do just that for the large British and Irish population living in Melbourne. Well-known biscuits include Jacobs Club Milk, Fig Rolls, Kimberley's and McVitties Ginger Nuts. Those with a sweet tooth are well looked after with Bassett's Liquorice Allsorts and Jelly Babies, plus Maynard's wine gums. Snacks include Twiglets and McCoy's Salt and Vinegar crisps. Masses of other things are on hand too to provide a taste of home. M&S Gold teabags, Taylors Yorkshire tea, C&B Branston Pickle and Bistro Best Onion Gravy mix. And of course there's the obligatorily HP Brown sauce. A great treat indeed.

CITY
Level 1, 234 Collins Street
9639 2344
Mon–Wed 10am–6pm;
Thurs 10am–7pm;
Fri 10am–8pm;
Sat 10am–5pm;
Sun midday–5pm
Melway 1B M7
Map page 162

USA Foods

A recent move to larger premises has allowed for much more stock at USA Foods. And with the slogan 'The All American Grocery Store' you just know you're in for a treat. Choose from a huge array of classic USA lollies – Hershey bars, Reeses Peanut Butter Cups, even cinnamon Tic-Tacs and York Peppermint Patties. Breakfast cereals are on hand too with famous brand names such as Capt'n Crunch and Cherrynuts, plus Pop Tarts in cherry, berry and cinnamon flavours. The shelves are also filled with popcorn flavouring, tabasco sauce, barbeque rubs, spice blends, chilli sauces (mild to super hot), cake mixes, hot chocolate mixes and chocolate brownie mix. Those missing their Cherry Coke and Dr Pepper soft drinks will find just the thing here. This is a top spot at Halloween too with a great array of special foods.

MOORABBIN
146 Cochranes Road
9555 0288
Mon & Wed–Fri
10am–5pm;
Sat 10am–3pm;
Sun 11am–2pm
Melway 78 C7
Map page 169

Out of town

Leave Melbourne for the day and you will find fresh farm-grown produce, seasonal berries, rare-breeds of pork and cattle, fresh-from-the-sea seafood and dedicated shop owners stocking a variety of good food for the locals to enjoy. Many stores are a local meeting place, stocking not just a loaf of decent bread and the best of the local produce, but also offering a decent coffee, those harder to find items, a good hearty bowl of soup for lunch and informative service on what's best for dinner.

There are some real gems out there – places such as Red Hill Kitchen, Kitchen & Butcher in Healesville, Annie's Providore in Barwon Heads and Cliffy's in Daylesford. We wish they were much closer to home so that they could become our regular shopping spots.

Standouts for the year include Mornington Peninsula Chocolate – we would happily make that drive daily if our waistlines permitted. The new Timboon Railway Shed Distillery is one of the most innovative new stores we have found and McKenzie Ebbels Food Store showcases just what a good food store is all about.

MORNINGTON PENINSULA

The Mornington Peninsula is home to amazing regional produce. Some of these fabulous producers have a shop front, while others sell through various retail outlets and the local farmers' market. There are many farm gates, orchards and seasonal fish sellers to look out for, as well as numerous wineries and the Red Hill brewery to explore. Don't leave without checking out the local cheese makers: Blue Bay in Mornington and Red Hill.

Cornell's Fresh Seafood

This is one of the best fish shops in regional Victoria. Owner Chris Cornell is one of the fishermen that head out into Port Phillip Bay to fish for snapper, flathead and garfish. Other local fishermen help out too, and the range is supplemented by the wholesale market. Locals love the whiting, fresh mussels from the bay and freshly shucked oysters. You will find all the mainstays of your typical fish shop: flake, flathead, prawns, fresh and smoked salmon, snapper and other shellfish. They will happily cut anything to any special requirements and offer advice on the day's best catch and how to cook it, if you're stuck for ideas.

BLAIRGOWRIE
2961 Point Nepean Road
5988 8311
Summer: daily 9am–6pm;
Winter: daily 9am–5pm
(until 6pm on Fri)
Melway 157 G12

Frank's Classic Bakery

This cute small shop is home to some fabulous rustic bread, cakes, tarts and pies. Baker Frank Ammint and his wife Karen are taking care of business nicely with their terrific product and fast, efficient service. Bread comes in all shapes and sizes. They have recently expanded their range of wheat- and gluten-free breads for people with intolerances. The 100 per cent rye is a beauty as is their sourdough in white, wholemeal or multigrain. The German pretzels and the German apple cake are favourites. Other sweet treats include chocolate profiteroles and vanilla slice. Karen can barely grow enough herbs in her garden to keep up with the demand for them in their quiche lorriane, and their flaky hearty pies are as popular as ever.

MORNINGTON
29A Main Street
5975 0205
Mon–Fri 8am–5pm;
Sat 7.30am–4.30pm
Melway 104 D10

Glace Gelato & Juice

Whether it's a hot summer's day and you're hanging out for a scoop of delicious homemade gelati or perhaps a chilly winter's day and it's a serve of their yummy waffles with the aforementioned gelati that takes your fancy, you can be assured of quality all the way. The flavours are seasonal: summer will see mango, passionfruit, berry or pineapple. All-year favourites include chocolate, mubble (marshmallow and bubblegum), yoghurt, dolce latte and choc-orange. The tiramisu on a recent visit was sensational. You can try before you buy, or opt for a cup with one, two, three or four flavours. The gelati makes its way into smoothies, and they also make fruit cocktails and freshly squeezed fruit juices.

SORRENTO
69 Ocean Beach Road
5984 4944
Summer: daily
9.30am–10.30pm;
Winter: daily 10am–6pm
Melway 157 A8

Greg's Gourmet Family Butchers

Greg Goss is pretty proud of himself – he won the best continental sausage at the Victorian Sausage King competition in 2007. That's just one of the many different varieties of sausage you'll find in the cabinet here. There are also new flavours such as sweet chilli and mango chicken, and spicy Italian joining the ranks of honey, lamb and rosemary and the popular pure pork sausage. Alongside the free-range pork, which also gets made into ham, there's the new moisture-infused pork, which is perfect for the barbecue or roasting as it doesn't dry out. The Moroccan lamb steaks and the oven-ready roasts sell well. Precooked dishes include family pies in flavours such as shepherd's, beef and mushroom, and steak and kidney, as well as lasagne, bolognaise sauce and curries.

ROSEBUD
1035 Point Nepean Road
5986 8285
Mon–Fri 6am–6pm;
Sat 6am–2pm;
later in summer
Melway 170 E3

Mornington Peninsula Chocolates

Is it only four years since we became addicted to their Pistachio Royal? Since then, Milton Laycock and Isilda Caldwell have added even more tempting delights: Irish cream heart, chilli and tequila, and strawberry and cream. This immaculate shop is mouth-watering. Friendly staff will greet you, and if you time your visit right you can watch the chocolatiers in action. You may decide to opt for the $2 tasting, three chocolates will give you an idea of the range of their skill, but you are still going to want to eat more. The chocolates are beautifully shiny and glistening. Each mould is hand-polished so the chocolates are at their most tempting. Other favourites include hazelnut praline, Gianduja pyramid and caramel ganache – making this shop our favourite.

MERRICKS
3494 Frankston–Flinders Road
5989 8490
Thurs–Sun midday–5pm
Melway 192 E10

The Red Hill Kitchen

Bernie Furness and Kathy Cook are living the good life. Not only do they grow their own vegetables in their 0.4 hectare market garden, they also transform most of it into wonderful edible treats in the kitchen. Chef Bernie has got it all going on: organic onion sourdough loaves, maybe some brioche or spicy apple buns; open tarts such as caramelised onion and goat's cheese or roast pumpkin and feta. Boxes of produce turn up on the doorstep from local farms and may be turned into seasonal jams such as mulberry or raspberry, or pot-roasted such as quinces. The pies are the real stars of the show though. There's good hearty homemade pastry with fillings (chopped by hand) such as rabbit, prune and bacon, beef and Red Hill ale, braised lamb shank or traditional pasties.

RED HILL
69 Prossers Lane
5931 0186
Fri–Sun 10am–5pm
Melway 190 K6

Scicluna's

This terrific store has quality fruit and vegetables and stocks the best of the fresh produce. With two other stores in bayside Melbourne, they know exactly what they are doing. Service is a large part of their success, and a Saturday morning here is incredible as beachgoers prepare for their weekend feasting. Whether it's spring, summer or winter the very best of the season takes the most prominent position. The pricing is spot-on with plenty of weekly specials, highlighting what's good at the market. The store also stocks dried fruits, nuts, pulses and snack foods such as rice crackers and soy snacks. Dairy is covered with yoghurt, cream and cheeses. Add in juices, dips, pre-cut vegetables, flowers and just about anything else you might want – fresh of course.

SORRENTO
31 Ocean Beach Road
5984 4866
Summer: daily 7am–7pm;
Winter: Mon–Fri 7am–6pm;
Sat–Sun 7am–5pm
Melway 157 A8

Breweries

Country Victoria is scattered with top-class micro breweries. These brewers are passionate, focusing on the quality of their hops, the authenticity of the flavour and dedication to roasting malt. Next time you're out and about indulging in some serious wine tasting, consider a refreshing ale at one of these places. For more information on micro breweries in Melbourne and country Victoria, visit www.pint.com.au.

Bright Brewery
Is it the fresh mountain water, the quality ingredients or the craft brewing techniques that make the beer so good here? Sample their Hellfire Amber Ale, Blowhard Pale Ale, Staircase Porter or Fainters Dubbel. There's also their 'Brewer's Choice', a range of seasonal beers that are only available at the brewery door.
9 Wills Street, Bright; 5755 1301

Grand Ridge Brewery
This old butter factory, now brewery, was one of the first to open, back in the late 1980s. During this time they have perfected their range of beers: Moonlite, Brewers Pilsner, Gippsland Gold, Hatlifter Stout, and Black and Tan. Jokingly referred to as 'The Monastery', because they are so religious about their beer.
Main Street, Mirboo North; 9778 6996

Holgate Bar and Restaurant
Set in the restored nineteenth century Keatings Hotel in Woodend's main street, you can while away an afternoon in front of their open fire sampling their beers, straight from their authentic English beer engines. Sample the bitter pale ale, winter ale, the Mount Macedon Ale and the locally named Woodend Pilsner.
Keatings Hotel, 79 High Street, Woodend; 5427 2510

Mildura Brewery
The old Astor Theatre in Mildura is home to this distinctive brewery. They produce four naturally brewed beers, named after local icons: Mallee Bull, Desert, Honey Wheat and Sun Light. You can watch the whole process while consuming the product. There are specials too, such as the Non-Toxic, so named to commemorate the banning of waste dumping in the Sunraysia region, brewed with local produce such as sultanas and orange to add a zing.
20 Langtree Avenue, Mildura; 5022 2988

Red Hill Brewery
Is it the warm welcome, the great beers, or idyllic setting that makes this brewery such a favourite? It was the beers that drew us here initially (the house Golden Ale, Scotch Ale and Wheat Beer), but we also like the seasonal offerings, such as Belgian Blonde. Come, try, have some fun and enjoy yourself.
88 Red Hill Road, Red Hill South; 5989 2959; Melway 190 K10

Vintara Brewery
Located just a few kilometres out on the Murray Valley Highway, this small boutique brewery offers the chance to sample their beers, which are 100 per cent natural with only grain, malt, hops, yeast and water being used. Expect to see crystal wheat, pale ale or light lager, as well as one-off exclusive beers available seasonally.
Fraser Road, Rutherglen; 0447 327 517

YARRA VALLEY AND THE DANDENONGS

This area makes for the perfect day trip. You can take in a few wineries along the way or just head out for a top pub meal at the Healesville Hotel or a Devonshire tea in the Dandenongs, picking up a few goodies on the way. The Yarra Valley is home to some of the state's top producers of bread, ice-cream, jam, chutney, chocolate and cheese.

The Beef Joint

Where possible, the meat sold here aims to be local (the beef usually is, while the lamb and pork are more seasonal). Luckily, the pork is widely available at Christmas time, and father and son team, Eric and Ben, turn it into their wonderful hams. They are good at making their own smallgoods: bacon, hams, kabana and pastrami. A range of fresh sausages, which tops over thirty varieties, includes bestsellers pork, apple and sage, chorizo, and beef and honey mustard. Look out for the smoked kangaroo fillet and hot oak-smoked lamb. Locally produced Handmade in Healesville products such as duck neck sausages and terrines complement their range and you will also find other local producers such as Cunliffe and Waters relishes, jams and chutneys.

HEALESVILLE
179 Maroondah Highway
5962 4905
Mon–Fri 7.30am–6pm;
Sat 8am–12.30pm
Melway 278 B1

Giant Steps/Innocent Bystander Winery

This impressive venue is primarily a cellar door for the winery, but it is so much more, with its bakery, cheese room, pizzeria and restaurant. They produce the Giant Steps, Innocent Bystander and Sexton wines, and you can try the full range at cellar door, including their wonderful moscato, a light, fruity, slightly sparkling dessert wine. The moscato makes its way into their Turkish delight – be sure to grab a box for the journey home. The bakery has a tempting range of rustic loaves, cakes, pastries and yummy canales encased in bees wax. Bread leads into pizza; watch the chefs at work producing authentic pizza with quality toppings. The cheese room is located at the back of the building and the best is selected for visitors to try each day.

HEALESVILLE
336 Maroondah Highway
1800 661 624 or
5962 6111
Mon–Fri 10am–10pm;
Sat–Sun 8am–10pm
Melway 270 D12

Kitchen & Butcher

This old butcher's store showcases the best of the region in a beautiful setting. They display fresh meat sourced locally where possible, such as the Murrammong lamb. Expect to find Black Angus steaks, Kutabata pork, chicken, duck and veal, but they will also order in specific requirements. Fresh fish, two to three times a week is another feature. The sausages are made on the premises – chorizo, Toulouse, pork and fennel as well as maple breakfast – and end up on the Harvest Café menu. Their own range of products is in high demand; customers get stroppy if there's no tomato and mustard seed relish or olives. Stocks of other local produce – Cunliffe & Waters, Ricci's Bickies, Kennedy & Wilson chocolates and Yarra Valley Pasta – and standard grocery items will save you a trip to the supermarket.

HEALESVILLE
258 Maroondah Highway
5962 2866
Mon–Fri 10am–6pm;
Sat 9am–6pm;
Sun 10am–4pm
Melway 278 C1

Ripe

There has been a change of ownership here, and while it still remains a worthwhile stop for the produce of the area, it's not quiet as brilliant as it once was. Its stars are Yarra Valley produce and Dandenong's queen foodie Ann Creber's Whispers of Provence range of preserves such as elderflower cordial, herb vinegars and jars of quinces. Other well-known names that you will find include Cunliffe & Waters, Kennedy & Wilson chocolates, Yarra Valley Pasta and Yarra Valley cheese. Local wine and beer is also offered for sale and you can enjoy all of the aforementioned items in the jam-packed café. The menu makes the most of seasonal produce teamed with local items.

SASSAFRAS
376–378 Mount Dandenong Tourist Road
9755 2100
Daily 8.30am–6.30pm
Melway 66 F9

Yarra Valley Ice Cream Emporium

Nigel Plowright is the master behind Yarra Valley Ice Cream. He takes the best of the local produce, such as Kennedy & Wilson chocolate, Handmade in Healesville poached fruits or local pinot noir and raspberries, and combines them into frosty delights. This emporium showcases other iced delights such as spiders and the frozen latte, and an arrangement of vanilla ice-cream filled with coffee granita that is proving to be one of the most popular sellers. Yarra Valley hazelnut praline and coffee, vanilla and mascarpone, plus Nigel's exquisite Kennedy & Wilson chocolate mousse ice-cream are joined by his version of rum and raisin, with sultana and spiced red wine. You will also find chocolate fountains, sodas and all manner of ice-cream paraphernalia.

HEALESVILLE
260 Maroondah Highway
5962 6532
Summer:
Daily 11am–6pm;
Winter:
Tues–Sun 11am–5pm
Melway 278 C1

Yarra Valley Pasta

Lisa Colaneri puts her Italian heritage to good use creating some of the finest handmade pasta in the state. Together with her mother Maria, she creates quality pasta using only free-range eggs and Australian durum semolina. This base shop (they have another at Prahran Market, page 105) sells just their pasta and sauces. You will find fresh pasta such as cracked black pepper, or lemon and parsley linguine, fettuccini, spaghettini and organic spelt linguine. The range includes fresh-filled ravioli: beef, chicken or veal; spinach and ricotta; trout and goat's cheese; gorgonzola, prosciutto and dried fig; and roasted fennel, mascarpone and walnut. Cannelloni comes in beef or spinach and ricotta and there's fresh potato gnocchi and beef lasagne too.

HEALESVILLE
325 Maroondah Highway
5962 1888
Mon–Fri 9am–5.30pm
Melway 270 E11

Yering Station Produce Store

This produce store stocks the best of the Yarra Valley, plus imported goodies from the likes of Essential Ingredient, Simon Johnson and Enoteca Sileno. Set in the cellar door, this impressive room showcases the wares beautifully. The local produce is selected from the Yarra Valley Food Group, so you can expect to see such stars as Yarra Valley preserves, Cunliffe and Waters jams and relishes, Kinglake fresh berry sauces, and Yarra Valley cheese, pasta and ice-cream; Ricci's Bickies, Jam Lady Jam's delicious range of jams and the sensational Kennedy & Wilson chocolates are also available. There are one-off homewares such as French market baskets, tea infusers and silicon brushes. You will also find Phillippa's breads on the weekends. The staff are friendly and helpful, too.

YERING
38 Melba Highway
9730 1107
Mon–Fri 10am–5pm;
Sat–Sun 10am–6pm
Melway 275 C6

Dairies

There's something very satisfying about visiting a dairy: seeing the cows, sheep or goats in the paddock, discussing the merits of various cheeses and, of course, sampling them. How else do you get to discover new tastes, or even confirm what you already knew? You'll love 'em all.

Apostle Whey Cheese
This relatively new dairy uses milk from a nearby dairy, some 1600 litres weekly, to produce their range of sixteen soft and semi-hard cheeses. Named after local attractions: Loch Ard Gorgeous (camembert), Southern Breeze (brie) and Apostle Crumble (feta). You can try the entire range in their factory.
9 Gallum Road, Cooriemungle; 5598 7367

De Bortoli Cheese Room
The cheeses showcased here are not necessarily made in the Yarra Valley, but are the best cheeses, sold at the optimum conditions as chosen by *affineur* Richard Thomas. If anybody knows anything about cheese it's him, being an integral part in establishing nearly every dairy in Victoria. Apart from selling the cheeses, they highlight the many attractions of cheese and wine matching.
Pinnacle Lane, Dixons Creek; 5965 2271

Milawa Cheese Factory
Its reputation proceeds this dairy as a 'must do' experience in regional Victoria. David and Anne Brown have brought this dairy to worldwide recognition over the last twenty years with their range of both cow- and goat-milk cheeses. Try the full range, but don't miss their award-winning Milawa blue, King River Gold and Milawa camembert.
Factory Road, Milawa; 5727 3589

Red Hill Cheese
These dedicated folk down south bring us both cow and goat milk cheese to complement the local maritime wines. Enjoy the tastings, meet the cheese maker and enjoy the cheese he has picked as being at the optimum ripeness for today's consumption. Cheeses are named creatively after local towns, such as Merricks Mist, Portsea Picnic and Gunnamatta Gold.
81 William Road, Red Hill; 5989 2035; Melway 190 C2

Timboon Farmhouse Cheese
This organic farm produces its own milk and, in turn, cheeses and has done so for the last fifteen years. Visit 'The Mousetrap' for the complete tasting experience. You can enjoy a platter in their beautiful cottage garden and be seduced by the flavour of organic cheese. The Timboonzola blue when ripe and runny is in a class of its own.
23 Ford and Fells Road, Timboon; 5598 3387

Yarra Valley Dairy
Home to 500 quality cattle, a mixture of Friesians and Jerseys (as they produce extra butterfat), this farmhouse dairy makes a wide range of cheeses including their famous Persian feta, Le Jack (camembert), fresh goat pyramid and their more-ish clotted cream.
70–80 McMeikans Road, Yering; 9739 1222; Melway 275 C10

DAYLESFORD AND SURROUNDS

The Daylesford region is home to excellent pork, trout and smallgoods. In addition, some of the state's best producers are based here: Holy Goat cheeses, Kyneton olive oil and Michel's fine biscuits. The district is renowned for its spring water and bullboar sausages are a regional speciality. There are plenty of farm gate stalls to explore. For more information on the local food and wine producers, visit www.dmproduce.com.au.

The Chocolate Mill

If you are lucky enough to visit at either 11am or 2pm you can join in on their free demonstration and talk – which details the process of tempering and creating chocolates – while watching the chocolatiers whiz up creations before your eyes. All of this information is hunger-inducing stuff, so turn your attention to the edible delights in the counter. Many feature local produce and the range covers some eighty different options. Choices include milk chocolate mice filled with ganache, chocolate echidnas with quince and white chocolate cream, or cardamom spice discs. Owners Jenny Gregory and Chris Weippert created this environmentally friendly straw-bale building. It houses their chocolate shop as well as the chocolate café.

MOUNT FRANKLIN
5451 Midland Highway
5476 4208
Tues–Sun 10am–4.45pm
(closed in February)

Cliffy's Emporium

This rustic building is home to some of the best food in the area. Set among higgledy-piggledy shelving, rustic props and a good dose of country charm you will find goodies such as Country Cuisine preserves, Istra smallgoods, Holy Goat cheeses, and local olive oils, jams and preserves. The only problem you face is deciding whether to fill up your recycled shopping bag and simply take it home to enjoy or whether to settle in and allow the kitchen to showcase this regional food. The menu offering is small, but spot-on. You might get to enjoy a wedge of Puds for all Seasons pudding with fresh cream or local organic vegetable made into a hearty soup. Do both to get a real feel for some excellent country produce!

DAYLESFORD
30 Raglan Street
5348 3279
Sun–Fri 9am–5pm;
Sat 9am–late

Fernleigh Farm's Farm Store

Nicolas and Fiona Chambers cultivate organic produce at their 40-hectare farm in Bullarto, about 10 km from Daylesford. Adjacent to the Wombat State Forest, the area's high rainfall and volcanic soil create a wonderful crop. Depending on the season, you may find carrots, gourmet potatoes, strawberries, herbs, beans, lettuce, corn and fennel, plus greenhouse-grown tomatoes, cucumbers, zucchini and capsicums. Nicolas and Fiona are, however, best known for their pork. They are breeders of Wessex Saddleback pigs, a breed renowned for its fat and therefore flavour – you can pick up a pack of the delicious bacon, ham, spare ribs, leg roasts, sausages, loin or chops. You will also find them at various farmers' markets around the traps. Be warned, the bacon is addictive.

BULLARTO
1070 Trentham Road
5348 5566
Daily 10am–5pm Jan–Sept;
Sat–Sun 10am–5pm
all year

Gourmet Larder

The Gourmet Larder is half food shop, half café, but they always focus on the best produce they can source. The produce is not always regional, after all the locals need to be able to lay their hands on treats such as Maggie Beer pâtés, Milawa cheeses, Cunliffe & Waters preserves and Phillippa's biscuits. The shelves store quality stock, arborio rice and artisan pasta to complement the deli selection of smallgoods. The deli is also home to stuffed figs, apricots with a mascarpone filling, beautiful olives and Tuki's smoked trout pâté and sausages. The café offers breakfast and lunch, focusing on the products sold in the shop.

DAYLESFORD
57A Vincent Street
5348 4700
Daily 9am–5pm

Himalaya Bakery

Joav De Murashkin believes that modern technology has caused a more automated way of producing bread, and that their old-fashioned approach to bread making produces a far superior product. Using only biodynamic wheat or rye flours, unrefined sea salt, purified water and their own natural sourdough leaven, they create breads such as Himalaya, rye, sunflower, walnut, onion and sesame, as well as 100 per cent wholemeal spelt. The range continues into their vegan, sugar-free or gluten-free cakes. Expect to see raspberry cheesecake, apple scrolls and rhubarb tarts. The pies are legendary. They are all vegetarian and the pastry is flaky and delicious. Flavours include potato and spinach, smoked tofu, Mexican bean or samosas.

DAYLESFORD
73 Vincent Street
5348 1267
Mon & Wed–Fri
9.30am–5pm;
Sat–Sun 9am–5pm

Istra Smallgoods

Brothers Sebastian and Bernie Jurcan produce the smallgoods of their Croatian upbringing. With recipes passed down through the generations they recreate, and upgrade where necessary, a genuine range of products all made on the premises. There is everything from mild, hot and Istranian salamis to bacon, prosciutto, capacollo and ham. The range of sausages has expanded to include chorizo and their version of the famed local bullboar. In addition to this, the recently completed larger factory shop sells a range of local products as well as a range of European pantry items to complement their own smallgoods. Easter and Christmas sees swarms of customers descend on the shop to stock up on the European goodies.

MUSK
36 Wheelers Hill Road
5348 3382
Mon–Fri 9am–5pm;
Sat–Sun 9am–2pm

Malmsbury Bakery

There is always a line of parked cars down both sides of the Calder Highway as drivers pop in here to break up their drive time. And why wouldn't you with such a fine array of baked delights? Jan Grant believes in baking as naturally as possible, so it's quality butter, free-range eggs and even locally grown beef in the pies. These pies are probably the number one bestseller. There are flavours such as chunky or minced steak, with or without the addition of onion, mushroom, curry or bacon. The range also extends to sausage rolls, quiches and pasties. Sweet treats cover everything from vanilla slices, eccles cakes, muesli slice, custard tarts and muffins. Travellers often decide to take a well-earned break here and enjoy a hot drink and meal in the tea rooms.

MALMSBURY
73 Mollison Street
5423 2369
Mon–Fri 6am–6pm;
Sat–Sun 7am–6pm

Maloa House Gourmet Delights

Denise Grantham has moved up the street, a couple of doors, but the variety of foods has moved up the scale significantly. The new premises have an on-site kitchen. This allows them to present a wider selection than ever before, and to offer tempting suggestions such as all-day breakfast and a vast array of individual cakes. The premises are also home to tempting homewares and cookbooks, alongside food products sourced from all the big players – Essential Ingredient, Simon Johnson, Enoteca Sileno and cheeses from Calendar Cheese Co. Maloa House's own range of Indian-inspired pickles complements the menu, such as the chilli jelly with the smoked trout and Holy Goat cheese frittata, or tomato kasoundi with their take-home meals such as rogan josh or korma.

WOODEND
95 High Street
5427 1608
Mon–Sat 9am–5.30pm;
Sun 10am–5.30pm

Red Beard Bakery

This is not just a bakery; it's a central hub for the town's folk to gather on any morning and enjoy the open fire, good coffee, warm welcome and light snacks. The bread is extra special though. Brothers Alan and John Reed produce crusty sourdough loaves from the restored 120-year-old wood-fired scotch oven. Watch them in action as you decide what to buy. The breads are named after hair colours: blonde (casalinga), Carmen Miranda (fruit), brunette (wholemeal) and stubble (multigrain). The pizza slabs are awesome and the brothers host pizza nights on Friday where trolleys are wheeled around with various flavours to choose from. There's also some excellent sweet baking here, with choices such as rhubarb cake and an orange and almond cake with a creamy filling.

TRENTHAM
38A High Street
5424 1002
Tues–Sun 8am–5pm

Spa Venison

Set just off the main drag, you may have to look carefully to find this shop, but it's well worth the effort. Farmers Chris Peel and Diane Snell breed venison on their farm north of Ballarat. Here, it's the star, being sold vacuum-packed in cuts such as porterhouse, roast, rump, silverside and topside. There's other game meat too: rabbit, goat, kangaroo and emu. Other venison meat, often mixed with goat, kangaroo or emu, makes it way into their range of sausages: pine nut and spinach, and cranberry and walnut. The alpaca sausages interest most customers as does the venison jerky – one of the top sellers. Tastings are offered of most products, but especially the sausages and their tasty kabana. On top of all this, there are also cheeses and condiments from the local area.

DAYLESFORD
Shop 3/9 Howe Street
5348 3551
Mon & Wed–Fri
10am–5pm;
Sat–Sun 10am–4pm

Sweet Decadence at Locantro

New owners, Richard and Dianne Cody, have bought themselves a piece of Daylesford history. Originally a hotel, it was the first chocolate shop in country Victoria and the first café in Daylesford. Some things haven't changed; you can still pick up old-fashioned treats. More recent additions have been soft caramel, rocky road and Daylesford delights, a mix of white chocolate and tropical fruits covered in milk chocolate. The thirty-two varieties of chocolate are made upstairs: freckles, milkshakes and chocolate caramel macadamia slice to name a few. Leave some room for their mineral-water scones and homemade wild berry jam. The hot chocolates will warm you up if it happens to be one of those cold, windy Daylesford days.

DAYLESFORD
87 Vincent Street
5348 3202
Daily 9.30am–5pm

Farm gates

Grab a plastic bucket, a little enthusiasm for some country air and an appetite for fresh produce such as berries, cherries, olives, chestnuts or vegetables and head out for some fun. Check the seasonal availability of the fruit and vegetables and enjoy the exceptional produce simply, or preserve and turn it into something wonderful to enjoy later.

Adrian & Valda Martin's Biodynamic Fruit
People queue up in December to get the first crop of amazing cherries. The season continues with peaches, plums and apples, and finishes off with quinces. If you're lucky, you may see apricots, but they get snaffled pretty early.
McCleans Lane, Ruffy; 5790 4201

Blue Ox Blueberry Farm
As the name suggests blueberries are the main crop here, but you can also pick up raspberries, boysenberries and blackberries. In season from December to February, they grow eleven different varieties of blueberries so at least one variety is always available. Jams, chutneys and sauces are also on hand.
Lot 16, Smith Street, Oxley; 5727 3397

Deumer's Harcourt Valley Orchard
This family-owned orchard comes up trumps in autumn for their crisp apples and juicy pears. You will find the more common varieties of apples, plus the slightly more unusual mutso and braeburn. Pears include beurre bosc, william, red sensation and packham, and there are famous house-made juices to sample.
3389 Calder Highway, 1.5 km south of Harcourt; 5474 2181

Ellisfield Farm
This farm specialises in offering exceptional produce in the peak of season. It's one of the few places you can buy morello cherries (late December to January), renown for their sour flavour. Normal sweet cherries come in November–December and quinces ripen April through to May. Always ring to check availability.
109 McIlroys Road, Red Hill; 5989 2008

Gentle Annie Berry Gardens
Nestled in the foothills of the Otways, this delightful farm offers pick-your-own options from seasonal berries to heritage apples and pears, plums, apricots, and even rainbow trout. Their delightful tearooms showcase the property's produce.
520 Pennyroyal Valley Road, Deans Marsh; 5236 3391

Gooramadda Olives
Located halfway between Rutherglen and Wodonga, this is of the most beautiful olive tasting rooms. Here you can try their full range of olive oil, table olives, tapenades and dukkah. Great advice is on hand if you want to learn more about the olive oil production, or just enjoy the fruits of somebody else's labour.
1468 Gooramadda Road, Gooramadda via Rutherglen; (02) 6026 5658

Heronswood
Slightly different from your typical farm gate, this National Trust property is home to the Digger's Club, which is all about preserving old-fashioned and heirloom varieties of mostly fruit and vegetables. Wander through the gardens, enjoy lunch in the thatched-roof café and purchase some seeds to bring home to grow your own crop.
105 Latrobe Parade, Dromana; 5987 1877; Melway 159 C9

Lonsdale Hydroponics
Andrew Pearson grows great tomatoes – big, round, juicy red tomatoes full of flavour, as well as cherry toms and ox-heart. Visit their farm gate stall and see for yourself just how good they are. Hydroponic lettuces, such as red and green oak leaf, butter and tatsoi are also available.
21 Yarram Creek Lane, Point Lonsdale; 5258 2665

Maroondah Orchards Fresh Fruit Stall
Open all year round, this orchard produces apples, pears, peaches, nectarines and nashi pears. Just what is available depends on the season, but there are always tempting fruit juices, dried fruit and preserves. Quality and value are both exceptional, as you buy direct from the grower.
719 Maroondah Highway, Coldstream; 9739 1041

Mount Zero Olives
Set up the top end of the Grampians National park, this olive grove is a delight to visit. Their shop and café is set in the old school buildings, lending a countrified air. You will find their olives and oils, all on tasting, plus their other products including chickpeas, lentils, beetroot relish, dukkah and tapenade.
41 Mount Zero Road, Laharum; 5383 8280

Silvan Estate Raspberries
Overlooking the Black Snake ranges, this berry farm enjoys the deep rich red soil of Silvan. Planted over three hectares are summer and autumn raspberries to provide a long crop. You will also find blueberries and brambleberries. The season starts in December and they pride themselves on their gorgeous mixed berry trays for the festive season.
70 Hollis Road, Silvan South; 9737 9415; Melway 123 H6

Sunny Creek Fruit and Berry Farm
Raspberries come in all colours here: red, yellow, purple and black. There are also red, white and black currants and good old plain Jane strawberries. Look out for Cox orange pippins, chestnuts and persimmons in autumn.
69 Tudor Road, Trafalgar; 5634 7526

Sunny Ridge Strawberry Farm
Possibly the largest pick-your-own farm open to the public, it can be quite chaotic in the height of the summer, but it's all worth it for these delicious strawberries. Different varieties take the season from November to April. The café offers Devonshire teas with homemade strawberry jam and their ice-cream is awesome.
Cnr Mornington–Flinders and Shands Roads, Main Ridge; 5989 6273; Melway 255 E1

Weston's Walnuts
There's quite a shop here selling the nuts grown on the property. You will find walnuts, almonds, hazelnuts, pecans and macadamias, plus the jewel in the crown, chestnuts. You will also find local honey, fresh apples and pears in autumn, plus a range of nutty products including panforte, nut cakes and spiced nut mixes.
6261 Great Alpine Road, Eurobin; 5756 2320

GEELONG AND BELLARINE PENINSULA

The Geelong area is known for its fine sourdough bread, with bakers such as Irrewarra and La Madre, and there are great cakes from the likes of Starfish. The local wines feature strongly in all food stores and there are some excellent bottle shops. Fish is another local drawcard. The Bellarine Peninsula is home to numerous small fisheries where you can get the freshest mussels and locally caught fish.

Annie's Provedore

The results of Annie's recent makeover are stunning. The place has a homely modern country feel, and showcases the produce wonderfully. The cake counter is sure to catch your eye; the hedgehog draws people from all over the Bellarine, but the lemon tarts and Mars Bar cupcakes are just as popular. The deli section is home to a full range of cheese and smallgoods such as Istra, John Harbour and the local Birregurra sausages. The shelves are full of necessary staples for dinner, from pasta and sauces, through to rice, pulses and pastes. The take-home meals are very good: Thai chicken curry and pumpkin gnocchi are among the bestsellers, with soup right on their heels in winter. You can enjoy the café or peruse the homewares and goodies on display.

BARWON HEADS
Shop 2, 50 Hitchcock Avenue
5254 3233
Mon–Fri 8am–6pm;
Sat–Sun 7.30am–6pm
Melway 497 B4

Aussie Blue Mussels

This mussel farmer has beds just offshore Portarlington – look out for them as you drive through. At the store you can be assured of finding superbly fresh mussels, and you can pick up some great cooking advice. They also sell a wide range of whole fish such as flounder, trout and snapper, as well as fish fillets, including flathead, gummy shark, leather jackets, Atlantic salmon and the more unusual stargazer fish. Their own marinara mix is pretty good, or the Coffin Bay scallops might be more to your taste. The squid is always as fresh and tender as possible, and there are cooked prawns and freshly shucked oysters to tempt you further.

PORTARLINGTON
42 Geelong Road
5259 3088
Mon–Sat 9am–4pm (closed in winter)
Melway 444 F7

Chas Cole Cellars

Chas Cole does two things exceptionally well. Firstly, it stocks a large variety of premium wines in various vintages such as Moss Wood, Yarra Yering, Bannockburn, Penfolds Grange, Henschke Hill of Grace and Jasper Hill. Secondly, it looks after the more affordable range with exceptional cleanskins, representing great value from some of the area's leading wineries. It has a fine history, being established in one form or another since the late 1850s. The recent move next door presents bigger, brighter premises to explore. Spend some time ogling at their bulk barrels of fortifieds such as Bullers port, plus muscat and tokay. There are plenty of boutique beers to choose from, plus spirits and lots of weekly specials.

BELMONT
Spotlight Shopping Centre, cnr Settlement and Breakwater Roads
5241 1620
Mon–Sat 9am–9pm;
Sun 10am–9pm
Melway 228 A11

Irrewarra Sourdough Bakery

No visit to Geelong or the surrounding area is complete without a loaf of Irrewarra bread. The good news is that their bread is now readily available in Melbourne, Tuesday to Saturday, at various stores and markets. The demand for bread along the Great Ocean Road reaches almost fever pitch during Christmas and early January, but you can always be assured of picking up a loaf of their crusty stuff directly at their shop. All their bread is made from a natural sourdough starter; the range includes casalinga, breakfast seed loaf, sandwich loaf, spicy fruit and nut loaf, and chewy baguettes. They also make delicious hot cross buns at Easter, and at Christmas you will find their mince pies and Christmas fruit loaf. Their panforte and granola are awesome too.

GEELONG
10 James Street
5221 3909
Mon–Fri 9am–3pm
Melway 401 G4

Katos Fish Supply

Founded by Angelo Katos in 1956 and now an icon for fresh fish, the day-to-day business is today overseen by some of his sons, one of whom runs the scallop and squid processing plant in North Geelong. They have also recently opened a retail outlet in Westfield Geelong, where they aim to have the best range of fresh fish to entice us. Obviously, the scallops and squid are well worth a shot, but look out for the local mussels, flake, flathead and mirror dory. House-made bestsellers such as Ed's famous marinara mix and sweet Thai chilli squid are always available with new prepared options appearing. Where possible the fish is local, but backed up by Victorian and Australian varieties from the wholesale market.

GEELONG
Westfield Geelong,
Malop Street
5229 1265
Mon–Thurs 9am–5.30pm;
Fri 9am–9pm;
Sat 9am–5pm;
Sun 10am–5pm
Melway 401 G2

La Madre Bakery

Anna and Tez Kemp have taken Anton Spoljaric's fabulous business from strength to strength over the last two years. By the time this book comes out they will have moved down the road to bigger premises in an attempt to keep up with the demand for the wholesale side of the business. Their aim, though, is to keep the same intimacy of the old shop where you can see the bakers in action and watch the loaves coming straight from the oven. The seed loaf is by far and away the top seller, eclipsing their other casalinga, olive, onion and rye loaves. Easter sees hot cross buns and ginger cookies appear, and at Christmas there are mince pies, cakes and German pfferneuse biscuits. Their bread also makes its way into stores in Geelong and Melbourne; call to find your closest location.

BELL PARK
Shop 1, 29–35 Milton Street
5272 1727
Mon–Fri 7am–8.30pm;
Sat 7am–4pm;
Sun midday–8.30pm
Melway 441 F7

McKenzie Ebbels Food Store

Also known as the Athelstane House food store, this store is owned by the same people and the same care is taken in choosing regional seasonal produce and serving it up to the public with style and service. They make a range of seasonal jams, chutneys, dressings and meals to go such as corned beef with creamy mustard sauce or braised lamb shanks. Local stars include the Drysdale goat's cheese and the feta, which is marinated with Screaming Seeds to create a unique local goodie. The Afghan Azaadi, a local group of refugees, makes authentic tomato or eggplant kasoundi and chutneys. There are local wines and Red Duck beer, a smattering of seasonal produce brought in by local growers, smallgoods from further afield, Istra and John Harbour, and local olive oils and honey.

QUEENSCLIFF
4/44 Hobson Street
5258 4829
Daily 10am–6pm
Melway 499 F10

Newtown Provedore

This great store and small café offers fabulous Genovese coffee, to be taken home or enjoyed in-house alongside their fast and healthy breakfast and lunch options such as filled baguettes, and hearty soups in the cooler months. You will also find a large array of quality antipasto, imported and local cheese, charcuteris, and breads from Phillippa's, Laurent and Irrewarra. Grocery lines cover every cuisine: Stefano de Pieri, Raw materials, Martelli pasta, Agostino Recca Sicilian anchovies, tuna and caperberries, Whisk and Pin muesli and pancake mixes, local Boundary bend olive oil, Simon Johnson, Christine Manfield, Kennedy and Wilson Chocolates, and Barrabool free-range local eggs. Pick up a jar of Newtown Provedore jam made for them by Warren & Hutch Wholesale.

NEWTOWN
317A Pakington Street
5221 5654
Mon–Sat 8.30am–5.30pm
Melway 401 A9

Starfish Bakery

Baker Paul Fox is sticking to his tried and true favourites here, and they are still hitting the right spot. Breads run from high tops, to sourdoughs in normal and rye, and multigrain and wholemeal featuring in breads and rolls. The Squishy is still big news, a fried egg with bacon and herb mayonnaise in a soft roll. You can pop in and grab-and-go, or hang around to enjoy the experience of this busy spot. The coffee is good, the cakes are awesome and the pastries such as croissants are buttery and flaky. The café offers breakfast and lunch, and you can buy take-home meals such as meatballs, curries and pasta dishes to take back to your beach pad.

BARWON HEADS
78 Hitchcock Avenue
5254 2772
Summer:
daily 8.30am–5pm;
Winter:
Wed–Mon 8.30am–5pm
Melway 497 B4

V & R Fruit and Vegetable Market

This store was established by Vince and Rosa Gangemi in 1979 to supply the local European community with quality produce and various ingredients not easily found in Geelong. The variety on offer today has grown enormously and daughter Connie and her husband Joe complete this family-run buisness. They pride themselves on their excellent product, good service and range of ingredients: everything from Irrewarra, La Madre and Zeally Bay. The deli is home to La Parisienne Pates, Holy Goat cheeses, Istra smallgoods and a large range of cheeses. Other local stars include Irrewarra and Timboon ice-cream and Screaming Seeds. To this add Yarra Valley Pasta, olive oils, Gravity coffee, olives, spices, a huge range of salts, chocolates and other sweet treats such as fairy floss and nougat.

GEELONG WEST
5 Pakington Street
5222 2522
Mon–Fri 7.30am–5.30pm;
Sat 7.30am–3pm
Melway 441 K12

Warren & Hutch

This shop specialises in free-range and organic chicken, you will find whole chooks and cuts such as breast, thigh fillets, drumsticks and wings. Game features strongly with rabbit, duck, quail, spatchcock and venison. There are organic smallgoods (hams, salami and other cold meats) and a huge range of sausages, all gluten-free. Other gluten-free specialty items include chicken kievs and schnitzels, pies and sausage rolls, dips and condiments. They keep up with the latest food trends, stocking those harder to find items often featured in magazines. They also make a range of take-home meals: casseroles, tarts, pies and soups. Try one of their freshly baked cakes (such as caramelised apple, lemon curd, and orange and almond) or crumbles for dessert.

GEELONG WEST
156 Pakington Street
5229 7720
Mon–Fri 9am–6pm;
Sat 9am–1.30pm
Melway 451 J2

Fish and chips

There's nothing quite like the sea air to give you an appetite. And everybody loves fish and chips. This pick of Victoria's best will give you some pointers to the best flake, calamari and whiting that the state has to offer.

D'lish Fish
The seagulls don't get much of a look in here; customers are too busy enjoying their fried flake, fat chips and tender calamari to even think about throwing a morsel to the beggars. Care is taken to use quality vegetable oil, you can have your fish flame-grilled and the packs represent excellent value.
43 Ocean Beach Road, Sorrento; 5984 2166; Melway 157 A8

Fish in a Flash
This store is the furthest away from the sea, but it makes the most of the magnificent Murray River and its catch with Murray cod, yellow belly and redfin making their way into the fryer. They are also renowned for their battered Queensland prawns and tasty crisp chips.
602 High Street, Echuca; 5480 0824

Flippin' Fresh Seafoods
A queue is always a good sign that the food is going to be worth the wait. You can eat in or take away; the flake is as fresh as can be and the chips golden and crunchy. As with all good chippers, it's the attention to the quality of the oil that makes all the difference and they are right on to that here.
33 Surfcoast Highway, Torquay; 5261 6146; Melway 237 F6

Port Albert Seafood
Recently renovated and better than ever before, this shop offers a simple but well-executed range of fried fish options. Located just on the wharf, you can enjoy the sea views while scoffing down the wonderful fresh flake and crispy chips.
Wharf Street, Port Albert; 5183 2002

San Remo Fishermen's Co-Op
This place has it all: the best location perched right on the water's edge, a hoard of hungry pelicans to entertain the children and fast, efficient service powering through the orders at a rate of knots. No matter how busy, the produce is always exceptional – fish straight from Bass Strait and crunchy chips.
Marine Parade, San Remo; 5678 5206

Wisharts Seafood at the Wharf
Positioned on the wharf with views out over the heads, this is the most picturesque fish and chippery in Victoria. In summer, the queues will put off most people, but it is well worth the wait for their yummy flake, crisp chips and other marine delights.
Port Fairy Wharf, Port Fairy; 5568 1884

GREAT OCEAN ROAD

Not only is this one of the best scenic drives in Victoria, it's also one of the best food experiences. It starts in Torquay with exceptional fish and chips and extends all the way down to Port Fairy and into the hinterland of the Otway Ranges. You can get it all here: fresh seafood, home-baked cakes, quality meat, local olive oil, fresh berries, organic cheeses and exceptional food stores. There are numerous cafés and fine dining restaurants to experience.

All Fresh Seafoods

This fish shop would rival any of the fish stalls at the markets in Melbourne. Not only is the quality first class, but the service is excellent too. Their nearby processing factory deals directly with trawlers from Portland to ensure the freshest catch. Locally caught Portland Bay bugs, flathead, trevally and sea bream is readily available. Southern rock lobsters are available in season and they are one of the major suppliers to the Melbourne Wholesale Market and overseas, so you know it's going to be good stuff. Back in the shop there's plenty of fresh filleted fish including snapper, ocean perch, dory, flathead and sea bream. Shellfish such as mussels, prawns and oysters are on offer, plus amazingly fresh squid.

WARRNAMBOOL
Shop 11, Norfolk Plaza,
743 Raglan Parade
5562 7653
Mon–Fri 9am– 6pm;
Sat 9am–1pm

Apollo Bay Fishermen's Co-op

It's an essential part of a summer holiday, heading down to the local fisherman's co-op to secure your dinner. Don't leave it till too late though, or all the best stuff will have gone. Like at Lorne, the local crayfish are the stars of the show. You can buy them live out of the tank or opt for the easier option of a precooked one. Locally caught fish might include flathead, sea bream, couta and snapper in season. This array of fish is backed up by the best from the wholesale market, which is a godsend in bad weather when the local fishermen can't get out. There's salmon, oysters, prawns and other white fresh fish fillets to tempt you.

APOLLO BAY
Apollo Bay Wharf,
Breakwater Road
5237 6591
Mon–Thurs 10am–4.30pm;
Fri 10am–5pm;
Sat–Sun 10am–3pm

Cobbs Bakery

Visiting this quaint bakery is like stepping back to yesteryear. Good wholesome bakery items, prepared the good old-fashioned way, and good old-fashioned varieties. You may choose to pick up a loaf of their crusty bread (dark and light rye, sourdough or the popular Scottish malt loaf) or a rich sticky-sweet loaf, which is perfect lathered in butter. Their cakes follow traditional recipes. Vanilla slice is the bestseller, followed hot-on-the-heels by chocolate hedgehog and caramel slices. The giant yoyos filled with a berry cream filling are awesome as are the cupcake-sized sticky date puddings with butterscotch icing. Lastly, but by no means least, the pies. Get one straight from the warmer for lunch: beef and mushroom, beef and kidney, and beef and onion are just the ticket on a cold day.

PORT FAIRY
25 Bank Street
5568 1713
Daily 7am–5.30pm

Farm Foods

The range of meats at these stores is always impressive. Some of it, the Western District beef, lamb and veal, they produce themselves, and they also make their own sausages. Top flavours include Guinness, beef and herb, Old English pork, and veal and herb chipolatas. The steaks are juicy looking, and there's Otway free-range pork, and chicken in all cuts and marinades. Breads come from La Madre and Zen. You will find products from Stefano's, Peter Watson and local olive oils and jams. Each store has a great range of local wines, plus Red Duck beers from Camperdown and a good range of cheese to round out the selection. **Also at:** 1 Symmonds Street, Queenscliff, 5258 4744; 119 Thompson Street, Hamilton, 5572 4040; 4a Gilbert Street, Torquay, 5264 7776.

BIRREGURRA
43 Main Street
5236 2611
Mon 1.30–6pm;
Tues–Sat 9am–6pm;
Sun 10am–6pm

Freshwater Creek Cakes

Some people have been known to purchase one of the gorgeous fresh cream passionfruit sponges and pass it off as their own. Others have also been tempted to eat a whole one all by themselves – no names mentioned. With stories like that, you need to buy one for yourself to see what all the fuss is about. The range of lemon loaves are just perfect for afternoon tea, though you may prefer the chocolate sponges or mud cakes. Fruity options include banana, hummingbird, and carrot and pineapple. Other temptations include packets of classic biscuits such as Anzacs, Florentines and yoyos. You can get a cup of tea and coffee to enjoy them with if you can't wait till you get home, and there's also a range of local jams and local honey.

FRESHWATER CREEK
650 Anglesea Road
5264 5246
Daily 8am–6pm

K. M. Lynch Wine and Spirit Merchants

Peter Lynch has one of the best jobs in the state. This wine shop has existed for over 130 years, during which time various family members have chosen to stock rare and exceptional wines in the underground cellar. Peter chooses wines from the cellar that are 'ready' to come up to the shop for sale; he also gets to choose which current vintages get laid down for future generations. If you purchase wine from them and wish to cellar it in perfectly secure conditions, they will allow you to store your wine downstairs, free of charge. Upstairs, the selection covers Australian cult and classic wines from Rutherglen and Coonawarra to the Hunter Valley and the Barossa. There are also barrels of fortified wines from north-east Victoria, which you can siphon off into your own bottles to take home.

WARRNAMBOOL
116–118 Fairy Street
5562 4939
Mon–Sat 9am–7pm;
Sun 10am–5pm

Lorne Fisheries

Situated right out on the pier at Lorne, time your visit right and you can watch the local fishermen unloading their daily catch – it doesn't get fresher than this. Eighty per cent of the fish sold here has been caught just offshore or along the coast. Snapper, trevally, flathead, blue grenadier, King George whiting and flake might end up in your frying pan. During the summer months, crayfish are the most popular buy for visitors, straight from Bass Strait, cooked fresh and sold to you. Not quite so common, but still amazing, are the velvet crabs caught in the local waters. You will also find South Australian prawns and freshly shucked oysters. You might be attracted to fisherman Christos's poetry, which adorns every available space.

LORNE
Pierhead
5289 1453
Summer: daily 10am–6pm;
Winter: Fri–Mon
10am–5pm

Farmers' markets

To be true and authentic, regional farmers' markets need to source their suppliers from within their local district. The majority comply with this basic requirement, only going outside for produce not grown in the area to balance out their offering.

Ballarat Lakeside Market
This authentic farmers' market is going gangbusters. It has recently become twice monthly and features local producers such as Goldfields honey, Green eggs, Hakubaku (noodles), Goldfields Dairy and Meredith Dairy. Fruit and vegetables will fill up your basket, but leave some space for fresh bread, preserves, nuts and Dana's honey ham.
Lake Wendouree, Ballarat; 0405 193 282; www.inseasonmarkets.com.au; Second and last Saturday of each month 9am–1pm; Second and third Saturday in December.

Castlemaine Farmers' Market
This market has moved over from Harcourt and still maintains a strict charter on local farmers. There's plenty of organics with Fernleigh Farm, Daylesford Organics and Mt Alexander Fruit Garden. Red Beard bread can be found here, plus Goldfield honey, cupcake queen Nadia, Puds for All Seasons, and Coventry Farm cordials, rosemary pesto and yummy Tuscan chickpea dip.
Moyston Street, Castlemaine; 5472 5472; First Sunday of each month 9am–1pm

Central Murray Produce Farmers' Market
During its six years of trading this market hasn't grown much, largely due to their strict enforcement of only having local farmers showcase their wares. The twenty-five stalls might consist of locally farmed barramundi, biscuits and cakes, berries and the amazing stone fruits of the area such as peaches, nectarines and apricots from Cobram and Kyabram.
Alton Reserve, High Street, Echuca; 5480 6343; First, third and fifth Saturdays of each month 8am–1pm

East Gippsland Farmers' Market
At this market it's quality over quantity and the range is strictly regional. You will find Maffra cheese and goat's cheese from Capra, there are avocados grown down near the Mitchell River, smoked meats from Stratford, loads of fruit and vegetables including stone fruit from Johnsonsville, and honey and honeycomb from Raymond Island.
Secondary College Oval, McKeon Street, Bairnsdale; 5156 9342; First Saturday of each month 8am–midday

Hume Murray Farmers' Market
This delightful farmers' market features all the best produce from north-east Victoria and across the border into NSW. You can expect to find the yummy Gundownring ice-cream, Snowline Apples, King Valley free-range pork, asparagus in season, fig preserves, olives, potatoes and a whole host of other seasonal delights.
Gateway Village, Lincoln Causeway between Albury and Wodonga; 0438 582 996 or (02) 6058 2996; Second Saturday of each month 8.30am–midday

Lancefield District Farmers' Market
Of the fifty stalls that turn up regularly at this market, twelve would be selling the best freshest seasonal produce from their paddocks. The rest of the stalls are made up of Holy Goat and Goldfields cheese, Fernleigh Farm, Kyneton olive oil, jams, chutneys and preserves, and local honey producers.
Centre Plantation, High Street, Lancefield; 0407 860 320 or 5429 1214; Fourth Saturday of each month 9am–1pm

Pearcedale Farmers' Market
One of the newest regional farmers' markets and it already is quite a showcase. There's free-range chicken from Somerville, beef, honey from Cockatoo Creek, gluten-free cakes, free-range eggs, jams and chutneys and hydroponic tomatoes. Cheese comes from Blue Bay. Unique pasta sells out each time and there are loads of vegetables, plus a sausage sizzle and a community stall.
Pearcedale Community Centre, 710 Baxter–Tooradin Road, Pearcedale; 5978 6620 or 5989 0335; Third Saturday of each month 8am–1pm

Port Fairy Farmers' Market
This is one of the smallest farmers' markets in the state, but it still follows the creed of primary produce strongly. You are likely to find Portland apples, figs in season, fresh and smoked trout, berries, preserves and vegetables.
Fiddler's Green, cnr Sackville and Bank Streets, Port Fairy; 5568 2421; Third Saturday of the month 8am–1pm

South Gippsland Farmers' Market
This was the second farmers' market to pop up in regional Victoria and it still stays true to its roots of only stocking produce from growers within a local area. You will find Faudel goat's cheese, organic fruit and vegetables, wonderful spuds, some seventeen or eighteen varieties in the full of the season, gorgeous organic blueberries and heritage tomatoes.
Memorial Park, Koala Drive, off South Gippsland Highway, Koonwarra; 5664 0096; First Saturday of each month 8am–12.30pm

Talbot Farmers' Market
One of the largest regional markets with approximately seventy-five stalls, this joins up with the neighbouring Talbot Hall craft market to extend the range further. You will find everything from live chickens and pigs, to an abundance of fruit and vegetables, honey, Holy Goat cheeses, olive and oil, venison, dressings and noodles. BYO wheelbarrow!
Talbot Historic Precinct, Scandinavian Crescent, Talbot; 5463 2001; Third Sunday of each month 9am–2pm

Yarra Valley Farmers' Market
There is a more relaxed feel at this stunning farmers' market. The original in Victoria, it still leads with classy producers such as Cunliffe & Waters, Fruition Breads, Kennedy & Wilson Chocolates and Yarra Valley Ice Cream. Add in berries, stone fruits, potted herbs, buffalo meat, local trout, vegetables of all descriptions and a warm and hearty country welcome, and you have the real deal.
The Barn, Yering Station Winery, Melba Highway, Yering; 9513 0677; Third Sunday of each month 9am–2pm

Lorne Greens

This shop is a small oasis in the middle of the summer chaos. People serious about their food stop off for the fresh salad greens, ripe tomatoes, juicy strawberries and luscious berries. If something good is grown locally it will end up here, such as quinces, cherry tomatoes, nashi pears or organic apples. There's bread from La Madre, the local Old Lorne Road olives and oils, Edmonds honey and Gentle Annie jams. The fridge is home to a compact, but outstanding, range of farmhouse cheeses, including Apostle Whey, Maffra cheddar, plus the best of France and Spain. Other local goodies include wines from Otway Estate, giant yoyos from Colac and that lovely friendly country service.

LORNE
8 Mountjoy Parade
5289 1383
Summer: daily 8am–7pm;
Winter: daily 9am–5pm

Pronto Fine Food Merchants

This delicatessen/food store aims to stock a range of delicious delights for the locals to enjoy. In the deli section you will find smallgoods from the likes of Barossa Fine Foods and Andrew's incorporated into the range of eight different hams, dozen odd salami, sausages and biltong, plus some goodies from the local butcher in Mortlake. Local cheeses include Shaw River buffalo milk cheese and yoghurt, Schultz's Organic, Apostle Whey and Timboon. Shelves are lined with products from Phillippa's, Simon Johnson and Stefano's, plus continental grocery items for the local Dutch and German community. Other gems include local eel pâté, local honey, yoyos by Jo (from Colac) and breads from Zeally Bay and Phillippa's.

WARRNAMBOOL
Shop 12, Norfolk Plaza, 743 Raglan Parade
5561 5424
Mon–Sat 8.30am–6pm;
Sun 10am–6pm

Rebecca's Cafe and Ice Creamery

As much as is possible Rebecca's like to make everything here themselves, using seasonal produce. This is most evident in their rich, luscious ice-creams. Flavours include the standard chocolate, vanilla and berry, and extend to mango, lemon and lime, pina colada and blood orange. Just as much attention is paid to their homemade cakes: cherry ripe hedgehog, lemon tarts, lemon sour cake made with their lemon curd, hummingbird, and pear and walnut. The café side also offers up good home-cooked meals strongly featuring locally caught seafood such as pan-fried calamari with pesto and pasta dishes. This business caters beautifully to everyone from the old to the very young, offering efficient service to complement their good home-cooked meals.

PORT FAIRY
70–72 Sackville Street
5568 2533
Daily 7am–6pm

Timboon Railway Shed Distillery

This amazing new distillery, café and food store is pushing the benchmark for regional food stores. Set up by Caroline Simmons and Tim Marwood with Peter Lynch, this is Victoria's first distillery producing single malt whisky. You can see the distillery in action, learn about the history of illicit distilling in the area, sample the whisky and indulge in their strawberry snaps (made with local strawberries) and coffee cream. The café and food store offers up other regional delights with produce such as Timboon Ice Cream (all their yummy flavours), Gorge Chocolates (try their Loch Ard Liquorice, Bombora Bars and Ocean Allsorts), Apostle Whey cheese, Red Duck beers, Paratte smoked eels, Shultz Organic Produce, Timboon honey and local berries. We're giving ten out of ten to these guys.

TIMBOON
The Railway Yard, Bailey Street
5598 3555
Daily 10am–5pm

FURTHER AFIELD

There's nothing quite like a day trip into country Victoria, exploring some of the state's furthest corners. These shops represent excellent quality and service and, like so many businesses, they are multi-talented, not just selling the best regional produce, but incorporating it into menus and take-home dishes.

Butt's Gourmet Smokehouse

As soon as you step out of your car, the beautiful smoky aromas will entice you in. Set in an old butcher's shop it has traded as a smokehouse for the last thirty years. Attention to detail is obvious. Where possible they source meat locally, everything from whole chickens and breast fillets, duck breast, racks of lamb, beef and turkey breast. Fish such as trout and salmon are exquisitely cooked, and if you are lucky enough to visit when smoked eels are around do yourself a favour and grab one or two – they're amazing. The real star of the show is the ham, in all types of varieties, including on the bone and boneless. The choices are just so difficult.

ALBURY
417 Tribune Street
(02) 6021 3987
Mon–Fri 8.30am–5.30pm;
Sat 8.30am–midday

Darriwill Farm

The home of Darriwill Farm is located just outside of Geelong. This 340-hectare property has extensive plantings of vines and olives, which are transformed and turn up as wine and oils in the shop. Dougal and Nellie Ramsay's idea is to create preserves that capture the season and much of the original produce comes from this property. There are eleven shops in Melbourne and regional Victoria, all replicating a traditional country store – decked out in duck-egg blue, and rustic country furnishings. They also stock fresh bread, fresh cheeses, food as gift items, homewares and kitchen utensils, and lots of beautiful things you just can't live without. The original Hamilton store also houses a restaurant.

HAMILTON
169 Gray Street
5571 2088
www.darriwillfarm.com.au
Mon–Thurs
9.45am–5.30pm;
Fri 9.45am–6pm;
Sat 9.30am–3pm

Food Wine Friends

Doing all that a good regional food store should do, this treasure specialises in the food and wine of the area, and then encourages you to enjoy it with friends. You will find Milawa Cheese and Milawa Mustards, Walkabout Apiaries scented honeys and the Beechworth preserves range, which utilise local stuff such as muscat in their chocolate butter and the wine in the raspberry shiraz conserve. Olives and olive oils are big business in the north and you will find the major players such as Kiewa Estate, EV, Lyric and Osborne's range of extra virgin oils and table olives here. There is a selection of homewares and hampers available, plus wines from well-known names including Chrismont, Pizzini, Gapsted and others.

BRIGHT
2/6 Ireland Street
5750 1312
Daily 9am–5pm

Koonwarra Fine Food & Wine Store

Sometimes it seems so easy; you take the best seasonal food, source the finest regional produce, cook with some of it, and showcase the rest along with local wines and beers in a nice country setting. It's not always that easy, but they make it seem so here. Whether you're grabbing produce or a good cup of coffee on your way through, or stopping off for a delightful lunch in their gorgeous cottage garden, you can be assured of quality all the way. They also aim to be as sustainable as possible, supporting organic, low-impact suppliers, practices and products. They handmake their own produce, cakes, desserts, condiments and bottled fruits, which star on the menu. It's a real gem.

KOONWARRA
South Gippsland Highway
5664 2285
Daily 9am–5pm

Lakes Entrance Fisherman's Co-op

This Co-op is one of the largest in Victoria with a fleet of vessels that fish for orange roughy, squid, scallops, prawns, rock lobster and barracouta. They are a major supplier to the Victorian fresh fish market and also have a direct-to-the-public outlet, guaranteeing you fresh fish, whether you live here or are holidaying. The entrance to the ocean can be treacherous, particularly in bad weather and this plays a big part in just what the daily catch will be. You may find flathead, snapper, flake, whiting, gemfish, rockling, blue-eye and trevally. Other seafood is sourced from elsewhere (for example, the Tasmanian salmon and Sydney rock oysters) to ensure an extensive range.

LAKES ENTRANCE
Bullock Island
5155 1688
Daily 9am–5pm

Mansfield Regional Produce Store

Dean and Gillian Belle took over this place in 2007 and have made it as popular as a hot water bottle on a cold night. It's like a little piece of Melbourne's food scene tucked away in the main street, with a strong focus on regional produce. You will find products such as King Valley dips, Milawa cheese, Ruffy preserves, and Mt Buffalo hazelnuts that make their way into extraordinary flourless chocolate and hazelnut cake. Chef Gillian also whips up the best brownies the area has seen, plus her outstanding rhubarb cakes and muffins in all flavours. The wine room is home to an excellent range of local wines, perfect to complement their Friday night dinners and monthly 'Bracket & Jam' sessions. Organic sourdough bread, great coffee and good country cooking are the other drawcards.

MANSFIELD
68 High Street
5779 1404
Tues–Sun 9am–5pm

Milawa Mustards

Anna and David Bienvenu started making mustard in 1982. The mustard plants are grown on their own property, along with herbs and the other ingredients that make their way into their products. Originally, David handmade five mustards; there are now eighteen in the range. They are grouped from mild to moderate, hot and extremely hot to help you choose the perfect mustard. Flavours include mild or hot honey, rosemary, dill and lemon, bourbon, horseradish, balsamic or spicy oriental. You can get the mustard of your choice in a pottery jar as a keepsake or gift. They also make mustard pickles, chilli paste, quince jelly and tomato chilli jam. Their dressings, all based around their mustards, include mild honey, spicy oriental or balsamic mustard dressing.

MILAWA
The Old Emu Inn,
The Cross Roads
5727 3202
Daily 10am–5pm
www.milawamustard.com.au

Plump Harvest Produce

They are particularly proud of their slow-fermented organic sourdough bread here. All up they make a dozen different varieties that vary daily, so make sure you leave with at least one loaf tucked under your arm. A more indulgent way to enjoy Plump Harvest is to eat in their café; the bread gets transformed into their toasted sandwiches or served alongside hearty soups. They also offer a range of take-home meals and fresh salads. You will find delicate tarts such as raspberry and almond, lemon, and chocolate and hazelnut, next to muffins, slices and cakes. They use only seasonal local produce. This business has over 200 local suppliers and you can buy from a range that includes nuts in season, nougat, preserves (including their own label), local beers and wines.

MYRTLEFORD
72 Great Alpine Road
5752 2257
Wed–Sun 8am–4pm

Q Foods

Noelle Quinn was the champion for sourcing regional produce for the local Hume–Murray Food Bowl for several years. She took all she discovered and learned and brought it to this bright and cheerful regional shop and café. You will find produce including Blue Ox jams, Formici smallgoods, Milawa cheese and bakery, Osborne olives, Snowline fruits and Ramelton free-range eggs. Much of this makes its way into their breakfast and sandwiches and seasonal fruit goes into their freshly squeezed juices. Coffee comes from Zo'i and tea from T2. Sandwiches and salads are on offer for lunches during the warmer weather, moving onto soups and braises in the cooler weather. House-baked cakes and cupcakes such as rhubarb and spice complete the picture.

ALBURY
Shop 1/555 Dean Street
(02) 6021 1994
Mon–Fri 7am–5pm;
Sat–Sun 7am–2pm

Ruffy Produce Store

Just five years ago Helen McDougall and Doug Maclean created Ruffy Produce Store, a perfect model of regional food showcased simply through local produce, simple cooking, seasonality and a warm country welcome. You can pop by and pick up a jar of their preserves including cucumber pickles, beetroot chutney, rhubarb chutney and our favourite, the brilliant crunchy fennel pickles. These appear on the menu next to things such as Smithy's smoked meats, Yea cheddar and Donnybrook blue and brie, alongside other simple dishes such as baguettes and salads. It's the perfect place to unwind, whether inside by the open fire in winter, or outside under one of the shady oak trees in summer. Great coffee and a range of local produce completes the picture.

RUFFY
26 Nolans Road
5790 4387
Sat, Sun & public holidays
8am–6pm

Stefano's Good Food Store Cafe & Bakery

Stefano is one busy man, he has a finger in just about every pie and the fruition of all these dealings can be found under this roof. Lyndall Vandenberg and Stefano together create a range of seasonal preserves, using local produce. Depending on the time of year you may find pickled green tomatoes, pickled asparagus, blood orange marmalade or apricot jam. There are also pasta sauces, dried pasta and preserved quinces in season. On top of this, Stefano helps to make Victorian Olive Grove oils – a wide range of different olive oils, including flavoured oils such as lemon and mandarin, as well as table olives. You will find books by Stefano and about him, aprons, plus his T-shirts and hats. You can eat in or order a picnic hamper.

MILDURA
27 Deakin Avenue
5021 3627
Mon–Sat 7.30am–2.30pm;
Sun 8.30am–1.30pm

Pies

There's nothing like an open road to work up an appetite. Out there in country Victoria, pies are a great way to battle hunger pangs, and the pie makers of this state take their work seriously. The best beef is cooked long and slow with just the right amount of gravy and the best pastry to complement the filling. Go hit the road!

Conway's Pies
Whether it's a regular meat pie, one with the addition of onion, mushroom, curry or bacon, or a slightly more exotic option such as pizza pie or chicken and leek, you are in for a treat. You'll find juicy meat encased in flaky pastry. Choose from three sizes: individual, family or party.
51 Pynsent Street, Horsham; 5382 0847

Gillies Pie Shop
This pie shop opened in 1951 and is a true icon of Bendigo. Lunchtime can see customers fanaticlly queuing for their hot juicy pies. Beef pies are the main go, in all flavours and sizes, but there are also pasties, sausage rolls and other savoury pastries.
Hargraves Mall, Bendigo; 5443 4965

Hearty Pies & Cakes
Master pie maker Robert Gravenstock cooks his beef filling for 2½ hours to ensure it is tender and flavoursome. Buy a hot one to go, or grab a family one to take home. More adventurous options include Madras curry, chunky vegetable and cauliflower cup with cheese sauce.
Shop 2, 115 Pakington Street, Geelong West; 5222 1239

Heiner's Bakery
This classic Australian bakery serves up the best meat pies in the north-east – tender beef in a rich gravy in the most perfect of pastries. The base is firm enough to hold the filling, the top flaky and buttery. A triumph. There's a café and a full range of bakery items such as doughnuts, slices, tarts and lamingtons.
87 Standish Street, Myrtleford; 5752 1430

Parkers Pies
Although your classic meat pie can be found here, it's the gourmet flavours that are a drawcard. They use local wines for extra flavour and regional produce wherever possible. Lamb and rosemary, Indian curry or steak, mushroom and red wine are all awesome. This bakery also makes cakes, so you can have dessert too.
86–88 Main Street, Rutherglen; (02) 6032 9605

Pyrenees Pies & Takeaway
This store has possibly the biggest variety of pies anywhere! If it moves, it will more than likely end up as a filling here: buffalo, venison, camel, emu and even crocodile and prawn. There are beef options for the less adventurous and good homemade cakes such as bee stings and vanilla slices.
120 High Street, Avoca; 5465 3280

Maps

CITY

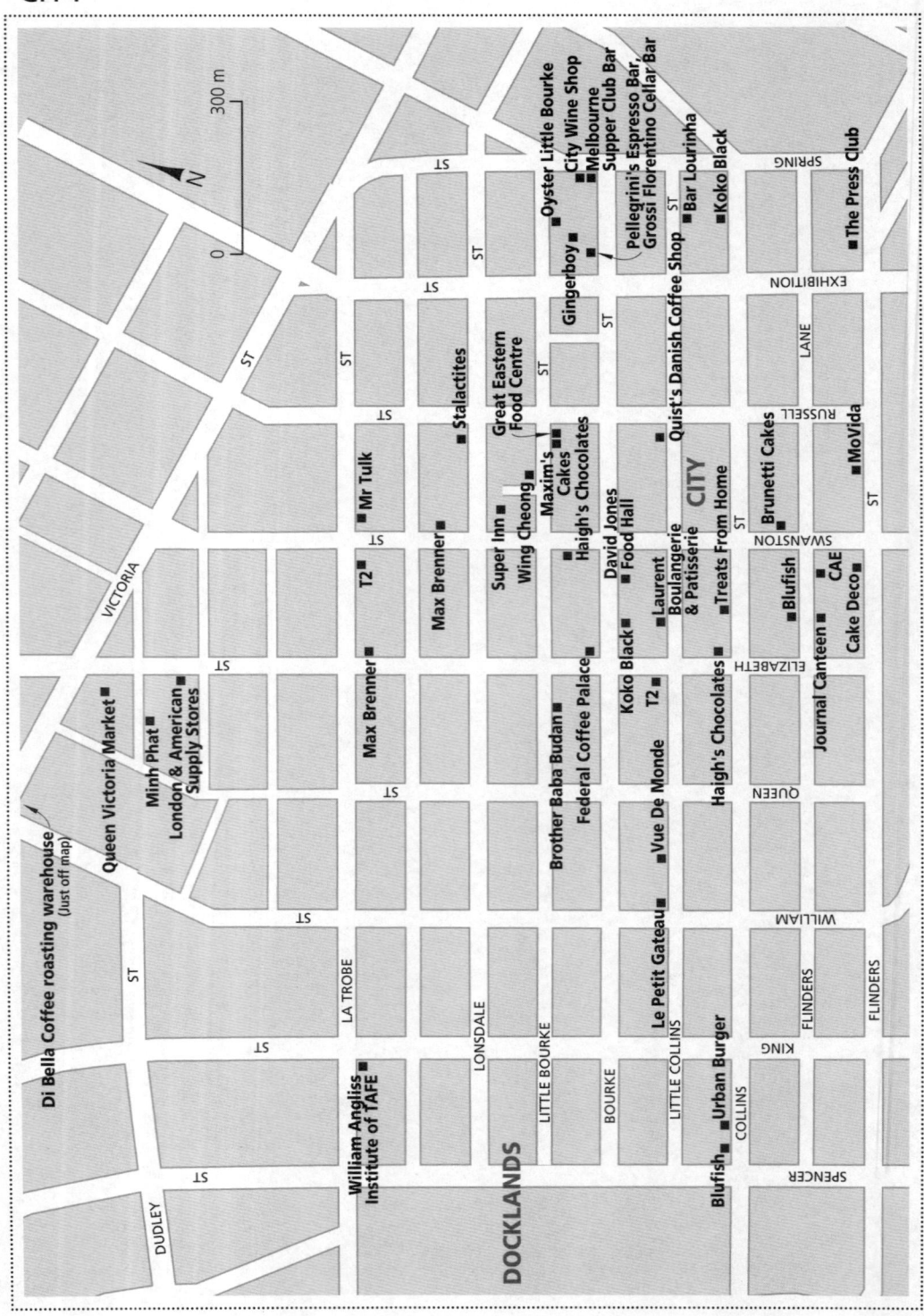

WESTERN SUBURBS

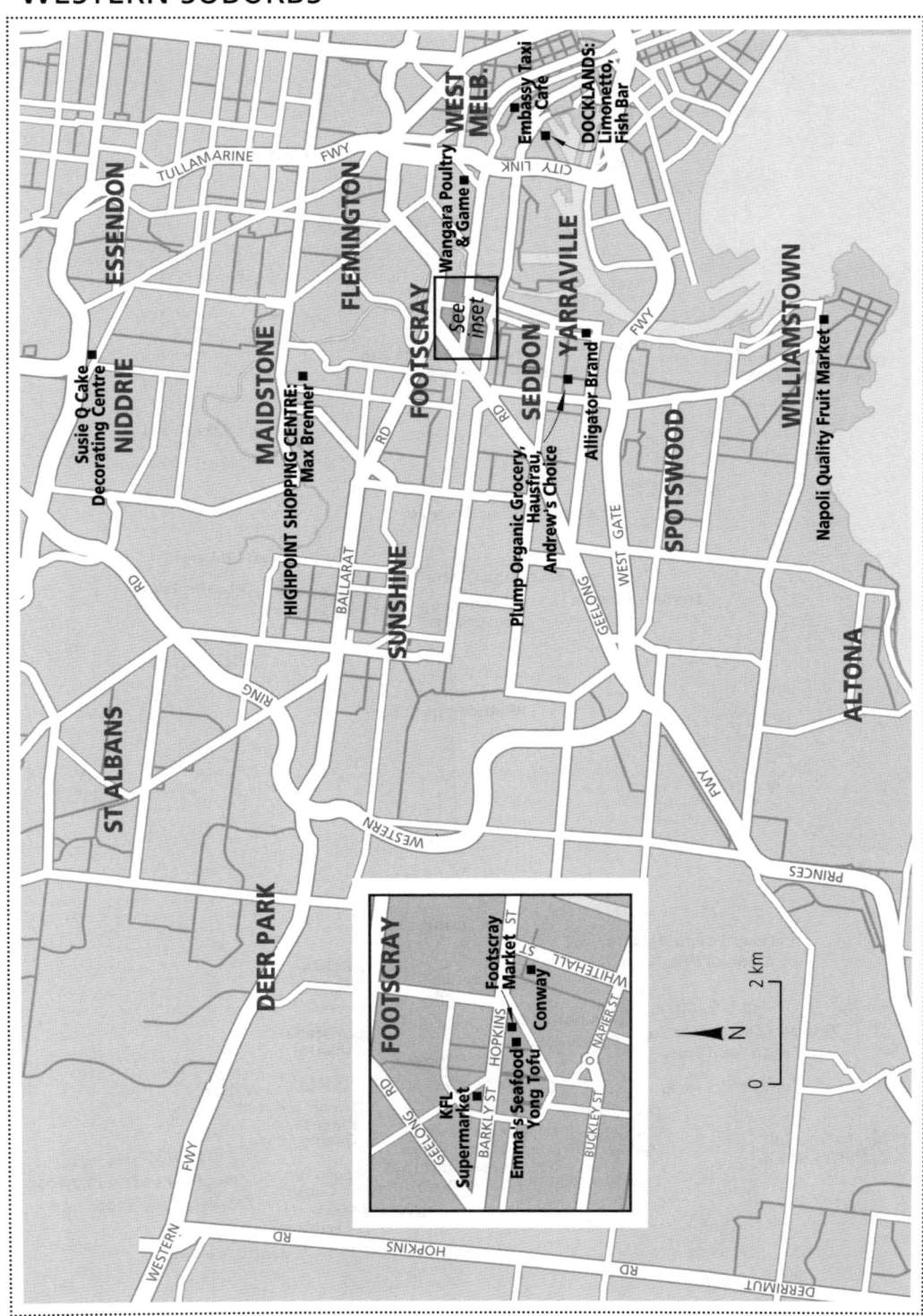

INNER NORTH

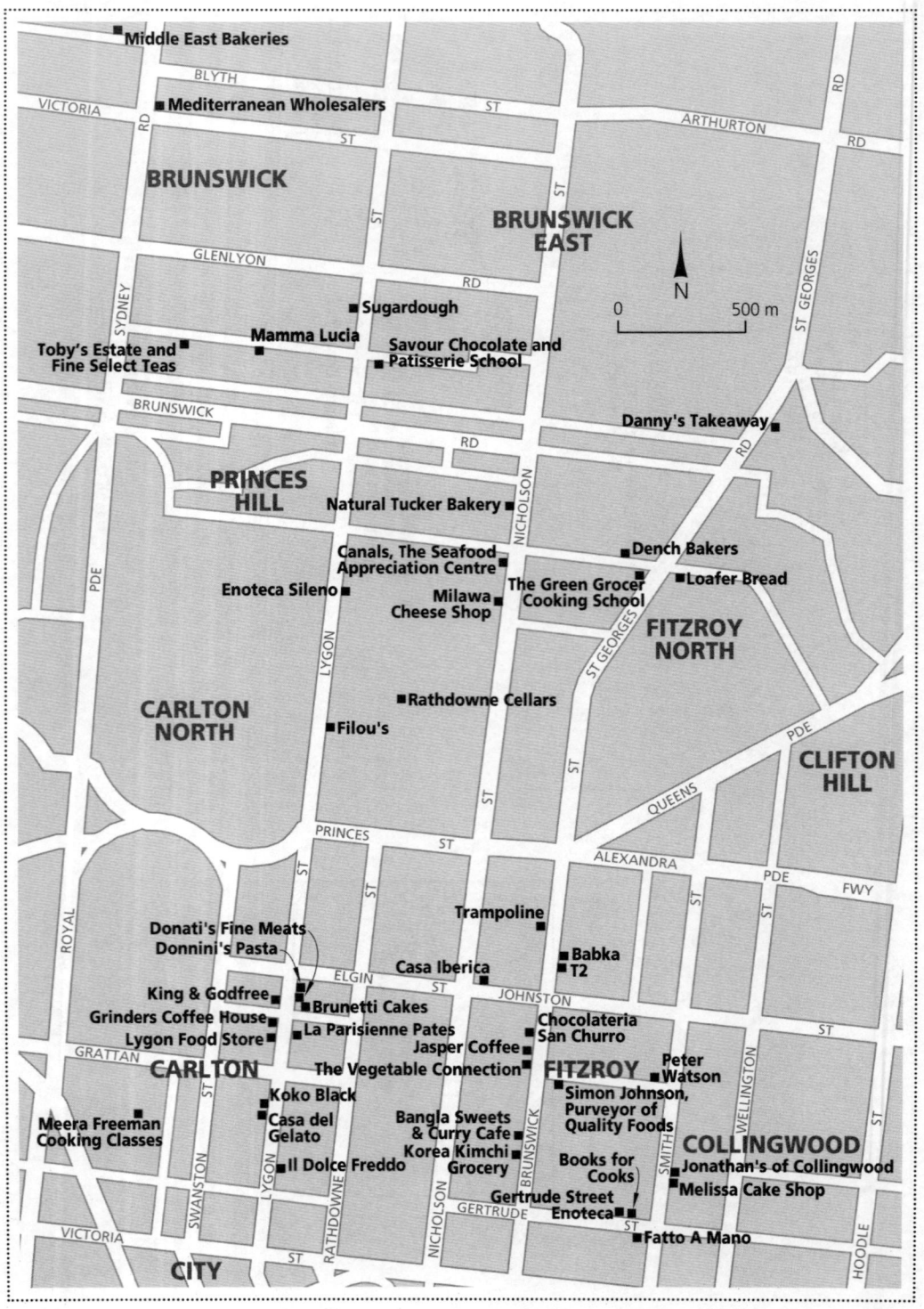

NORTHERN SUBURBS

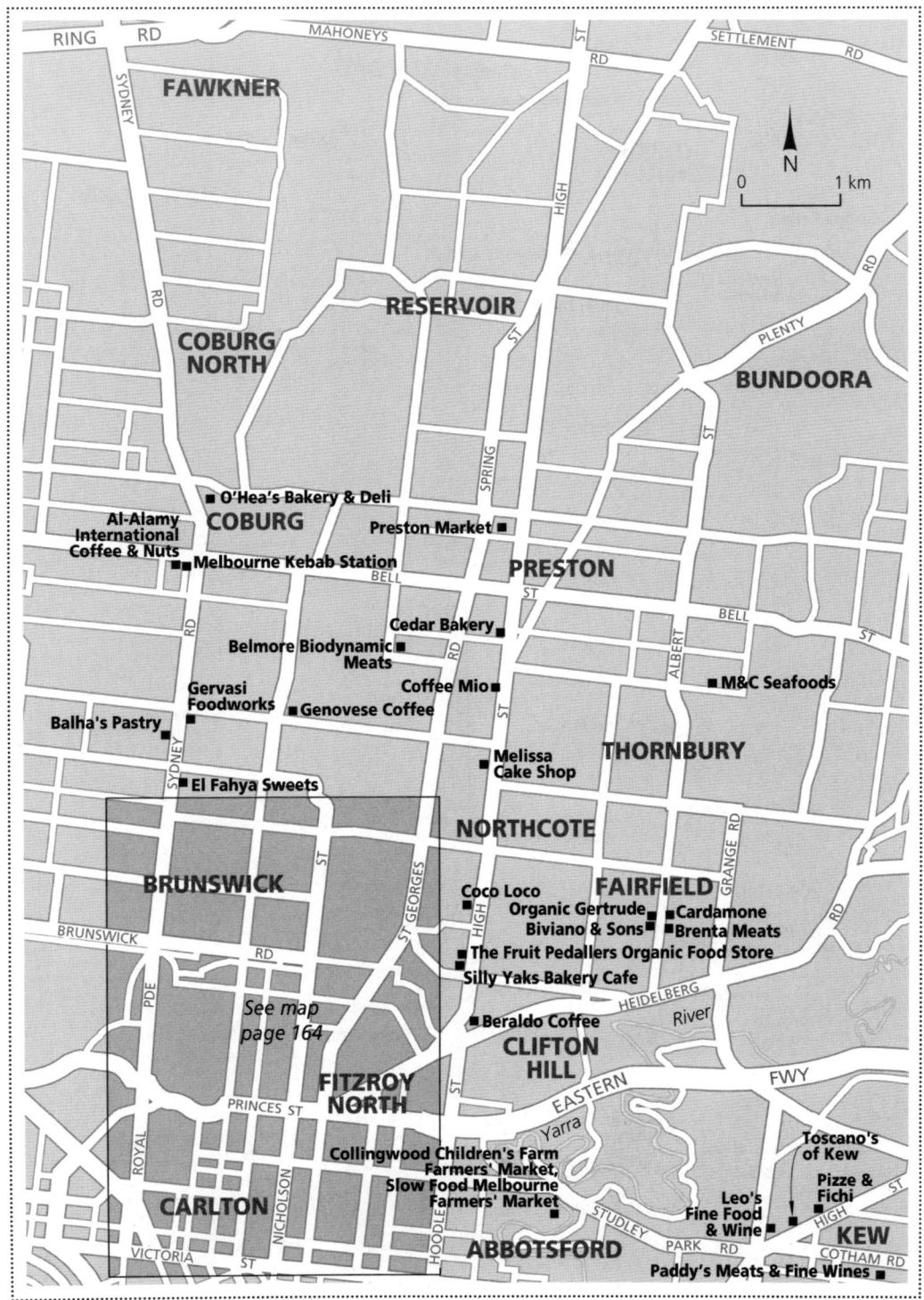

INNER EAST

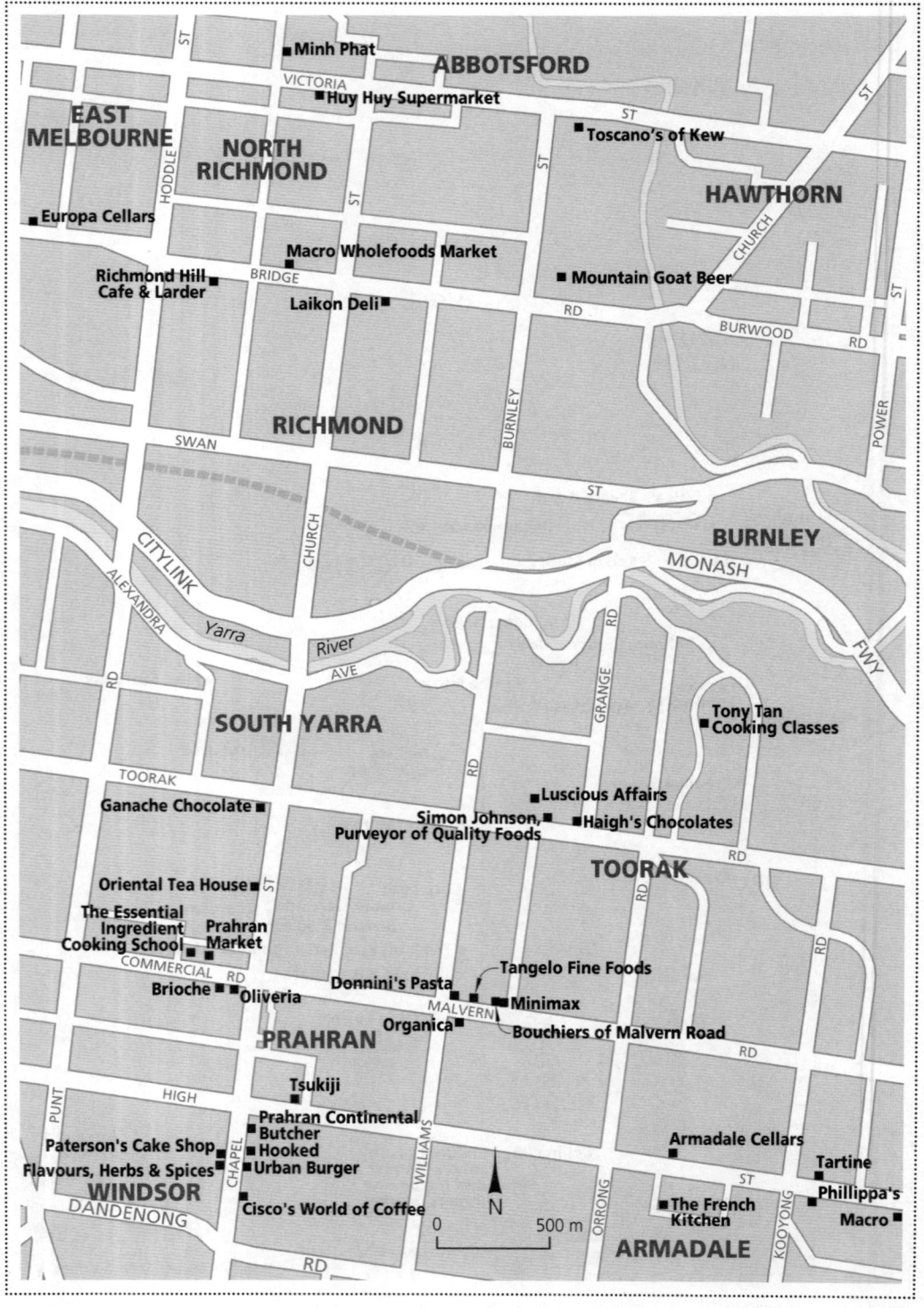

HAWTHORN TO MURRUMBEENA

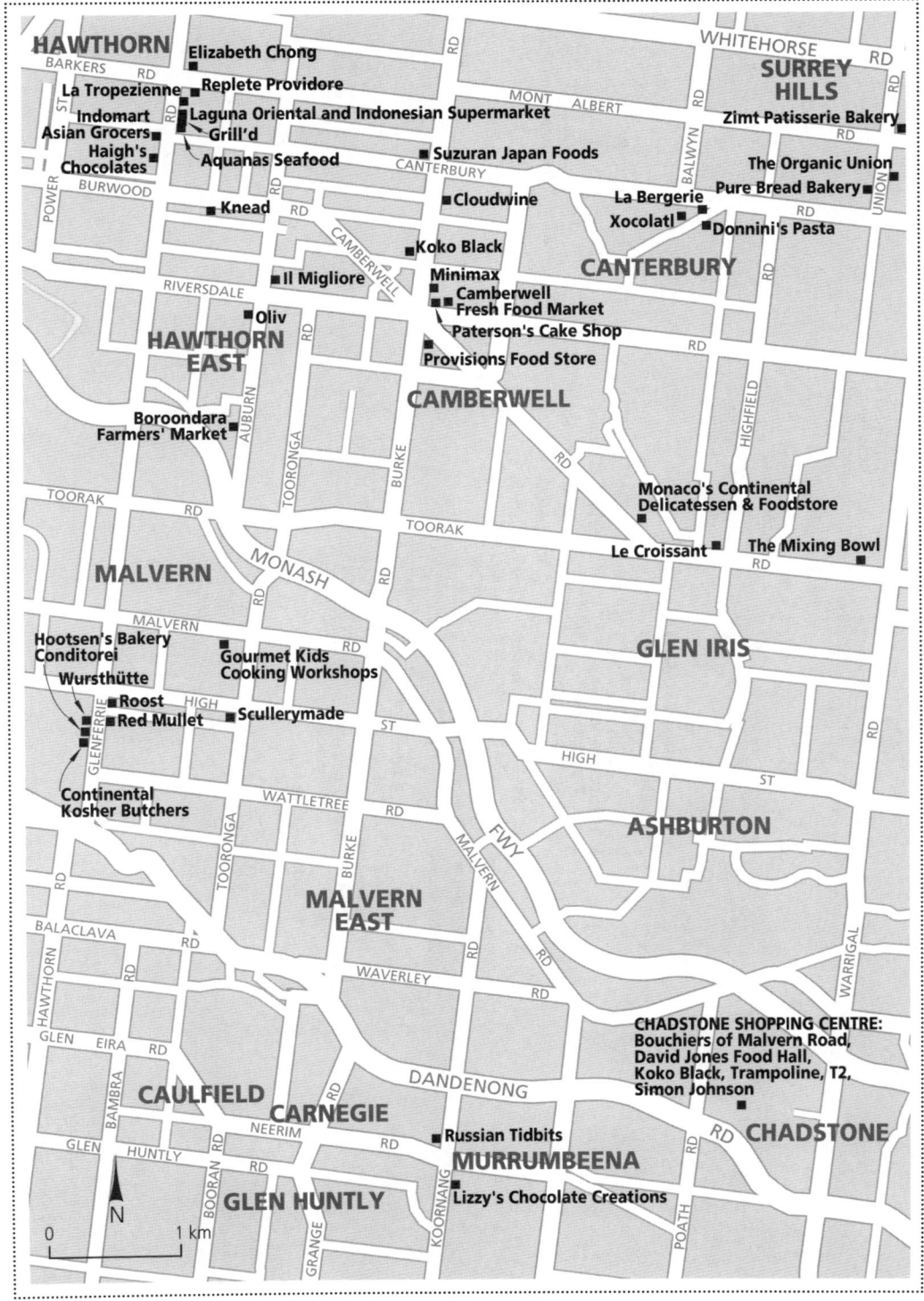

INNER SOUTH

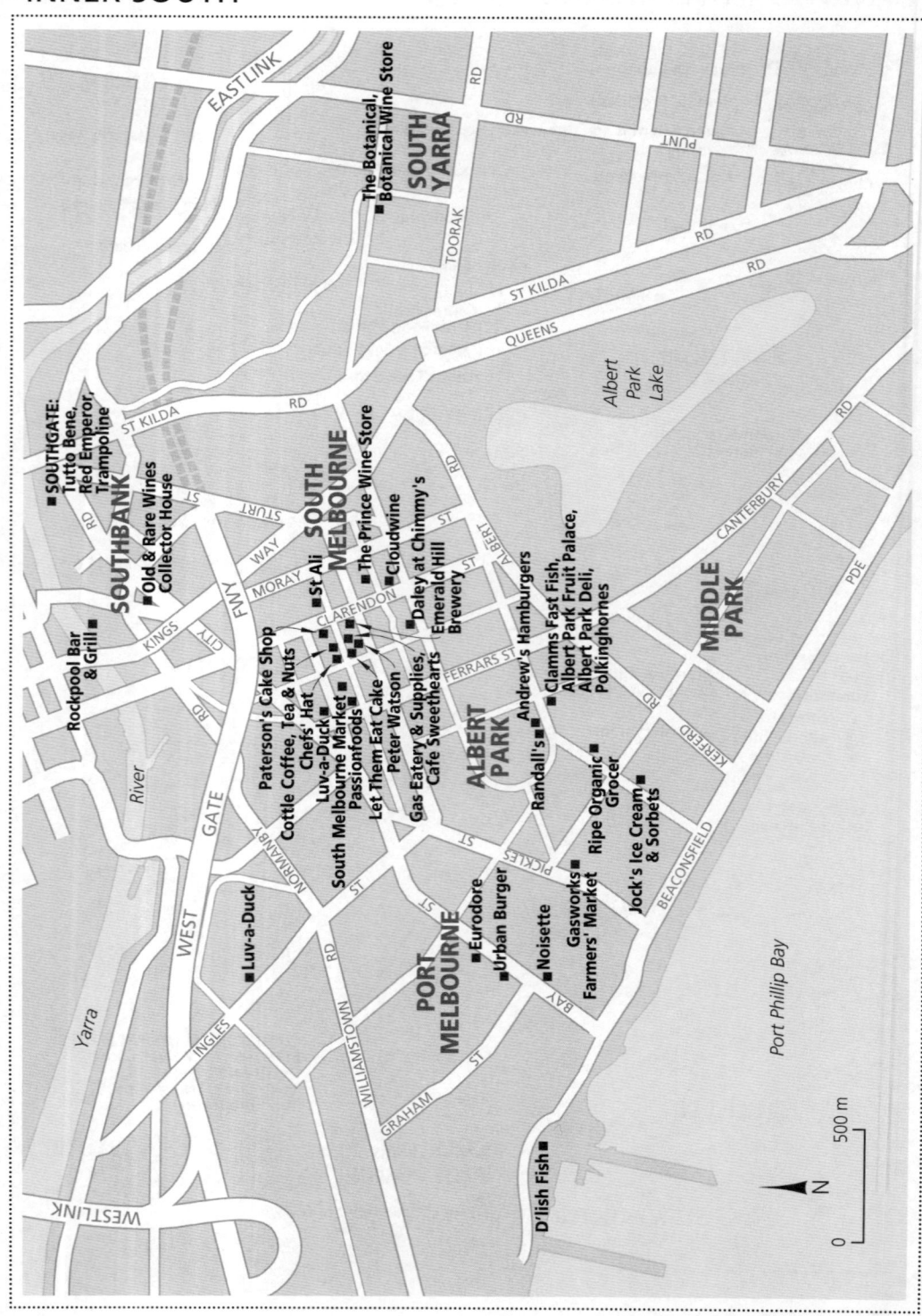

HAMPTON TO SPRINGVALE

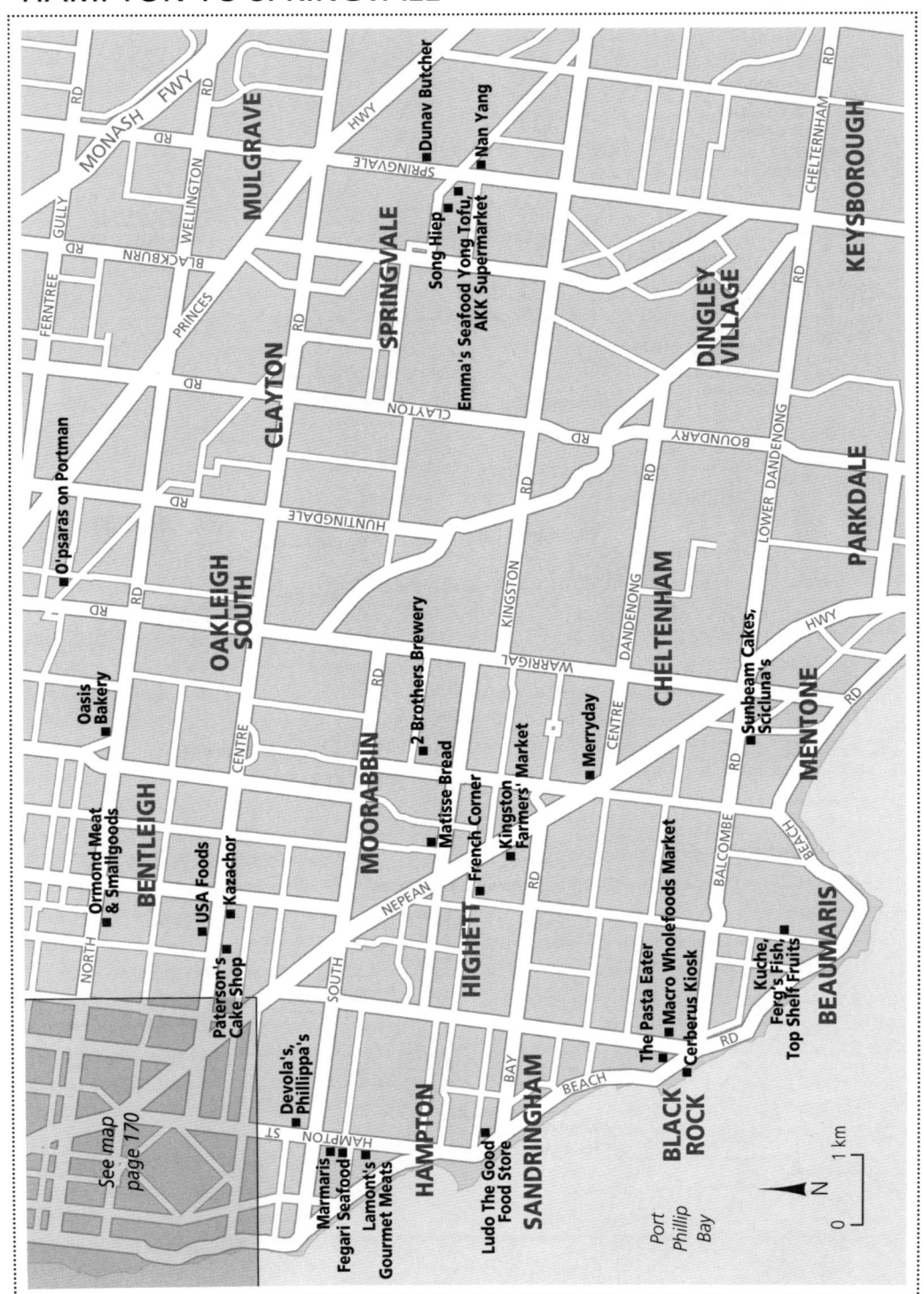

ST KILDA TO BRIGHTON

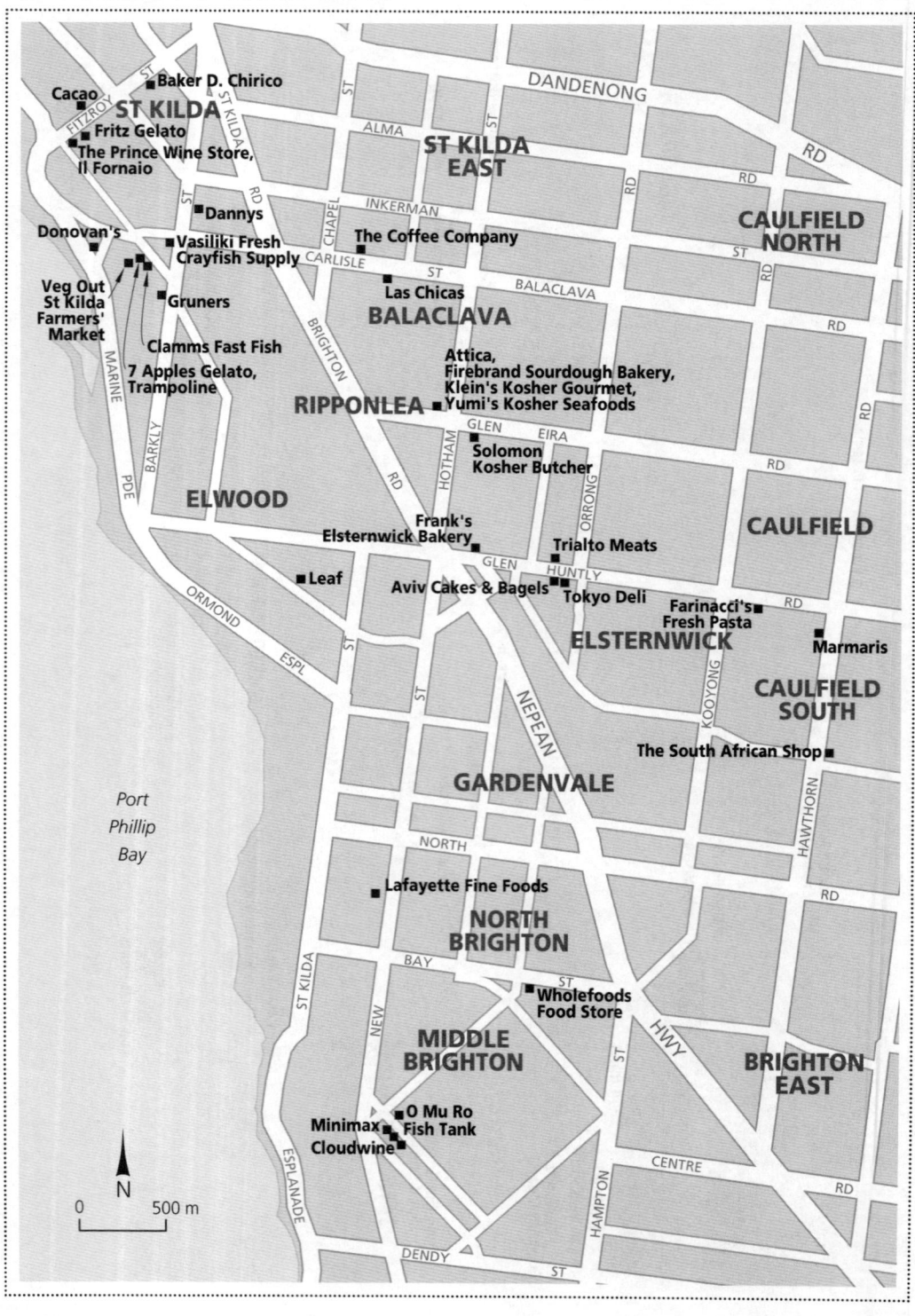

EASTERN SUBURBS

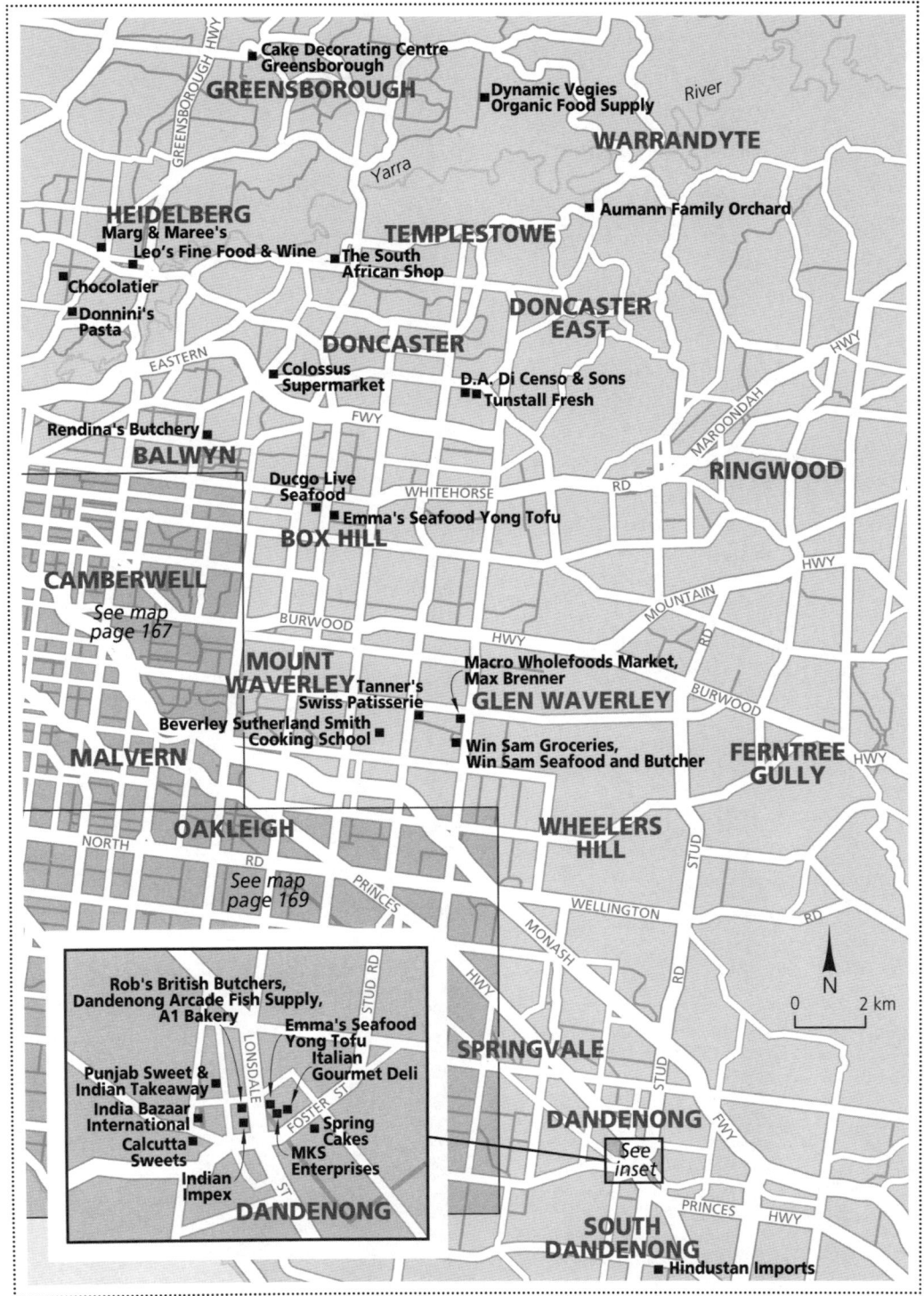

Indexes

Store index

A

A1 Bakery (Dandenong) 108
Adrian & Valda Martin's Biodynamic Fruit (Ruffy) 146
AKK Supermarket (Springvale) 3
Al-Alamy International Coffee & Nuts (Coburg) 108
Albert Park Deli (Albert Park) 52
Albert Park Fruit Palace (Albert Park) 74
All Fresh Seafoods (Warrnambool) 152
Alligator Brand (Yarraville) 89
Andrew's Choice (Yarraville) 24
Andrew's Hamburgers (Albert Park) 32
Annie's Provedore (Barwon Heads) viii, 148
Apollo Bay Fishermen's Co-op (Apollo Bay) 152
Apostle Whey Cheese (Cooriemungle) 142
Aptus Seafoods (South Melbourne) 102
Aquanas Seafood (Hawthorn) 67
Armadale Cellars (Armadale) 125
Attica (Ripponlea) 132
Aumann Family Orchard (Warrandyte) 74
Aussie Blue Mussels (Portarlington) 148
Aviv Cakes & Bagels (Elsternwick) 10
Aztec Imports (Tullamarine) 130

B

Babka Bakery Cafe (Fitzroy) 10
Baker D. Chirico (St Kilda) 11, 12, 19
Balha's Pastry (Brunswick) 109
Ballarat Lakeside Market (Ballarat) 154
Bangla Sweets & Curry Café (Fitzroy) 84
Bar Lourinha (City) 132
Bas Foods (Brunswick) 110
Beef Joint, The (Healesville) 140
Bella Vedere (Coldstream) 40
Belmore Biodynamic Meats (Thornbury) 24
Beraldo Coffee (Northcote) 44

Beverley Sutherland Smith Cooking School (Mount Waverley) 40
Bill's Farm (City) 52, 56
Biviano & Sons (Fairfield) 75
Blue Ox Blueberry Farm (Oxley) 146
Blufish (City) 70
Books for Cooks (Fitzroy) 96
Borek Shop, The (City) 102
Boroondara Farmers' Market (Hawthorn East) 59, 60
Botanical Hotel, The (South Yarra) 20
Botanical Wine Store (South Yarra) 125
Bouchiers of Malvern Road (Chadstone/City/Hawksburn) 25, 26
Brenta Meats (Fairfield) 25
Bright Brewery (Bright) 139
Brioche (Prahran) 11
Brother Baba Budan (City) 46
Brunetti Cakes (Camberwell/Carlton/City) 11
Butt's Gourmet Smokehouse (Albury) 157

C

Cacao Fine Chocolates (City/St Kilda) 35, 39
CAE Cooking School (City) 40
Café Sweethearts (South Melbourne) 20
Cake Deco (City) 16
Calcutta Sweets (Dandenong) 84
Camberwell Fresh Food Market (Camberwell) 101
Canals, The Seafood Appreciation Centre (Carlton North) 67
Cardamone (Fairfield) 89
Cardinia Ranges Farmers' Market (Pakenham) 59
Casa del Gelato (Carlton) 79
Casa Iberica (Fitzroy) 130
Castlemaine Farmers' Market (Castlemaine) 154

Cedar Bakery (Preston) 110
Central Murray Produce Farmers' Market (Echuca) 154
Cerberus Kiosk (Black Rock) 70
Chas Cole Cellars (Belmont) 148
Chef's Hat (South Melbourne) 96
Chicken Pantry, The (City) 25, 26
Chocoholic Tours (City) 103
Chocolateria San Churro (Fitzroy) 37
Chocolatier (Hampton/Ivanhoe) 37
Chocolate Lover, The (South Melbourne) 35
Chocolate Mill, The (Mount Franklin) 143
Cisco's World of Coffee (Windsor) 44
City Wine Shop (City) 126
Clamms Fast Fish (St Kilda/Albert Park) 68, 70
Claringbold's Seafoods (South Yarra) 68
Cliffy's Emporium (Daylesford) 143
Cloudwine (Brighton/Camberwell/South Melbourne) 126
Cobbs Bakery (Port Fairy) 152
Coco Loco (Northcote) 37
Coffea Café (City) 102
Coffee Company, The (Balaclava) 45
Coffee Mio (Thornbury) 45
Collingwood Children's Farm Farmers' Market (Abbotsford) 60
Colossus Supermarket (Doncaster) 131
Continental Kosher Butchers (Malvern) 25
Conway (Footscray) 68
Conway's Pies (Horsham) 160
Cornell's Fresh Seafood (Blairgowrie) 137
Cottle Coffee, Tea and Nuts (South Melbourne) 45
Curds and Whey (City) 53
Curry Creations (South Yarra) 85

D

D. A. Di Censo & Sons (Doncaster East) 26
Daley at Chimmy's (South Melbourne) 11
Damian Pike, Wild Mushroom Specialist (South Yarra) viii, 75
Dandenong Arcade Fish Supply (Dandenong) 68
Danny's Takeaway (Fitzroy North) 32
Darriwill Farm (Hamilton) 157

David Jones Food Hall (Chadstone/City) 63
De Bortoli Cheese Room (Dixons Creek) 142
Delicatess (South Yarra) 26, 53, 56
Dench Bakers (Fitzroy North) 12
Deumer's Harcourt Valley Orchard (Harcourt) 146
Devola's (Brighton) 75
Di Bella Coffee Roasting Warehouse (North Melbourne) 45
Diana Marsland Cooking (Woodend) 40
D'lish Fish (Port Melbourne) 70
D'lish Fish (Sorrento) 151
Donati's Fine Meats (Carlton) 26
Donnini's Pasta (Canterbury/Carlton/Hawksburn/Ivanhoe) 90
Donovan's (St Kilda) 132
Ducgo Live Seafood (Box Hill) 69
Dunav Butcher (Springvale) 28
Dynamic Vegies Organic Food Supply (Eltham) 114

E

East Gippsland Farmers' Market (Bairnsdale) 154
El Fahya Sweets (Brunswick) 110
Elizabeth Chong (Kew) 40
Ellisfield Farm (Red Hill) 146
Embassy Taxi Cafe (West Melbourne) 123
Emerald Hill Brewery (South Melbourne) 127
Emma's Seafood Yong Tofu (Box Hill/Footscray/Springvale) 3
Enoteca Sileno (Carlton North) 63, 64, 126
Essence Food Studio (Werribee) 41
Essential Ingredient, The (South Yarra) 41, 64, 98
Eurodore (Port Melbourne) 53
Europa Cellars (East Melbourne) 126

F

Farinacci's Fresh Pasta (Caulfield) 90
Farm Foods (Birregurra/Queenscliff/Hamilton/Torquay) 153
Fatto A Mano (Fitzroy) 12, 15
Federal Coffee Palace (City) 46
Fegari Seafood (Hampton) 69

Ferg's Fish (Beaumaris/Hampton) 69
Fernleigh Farm's Farm Store (Bullarto) 143
Filou's (Carlton North) 13, 19
Firebrand Sourdough Bakery (Ripponlea) 13
Fish Bar (Docklands) 70
Fish in a Flash (Echuca) 151
Fish Tank (Brighton) 70
Flavours, Herbs & Spices (Windsor) 131
Flippin' Fresh Seafoods (Torquay) 151
Food Wine Friends (Bright) 157
Foodies' Tours of Melbourne (City) 103
Footscray Market (Footscray) 102
Frank's Classic Bakery (Mornington) 137
Frank's Elsternwick Bakery (Elsternwick) 13
French Kitchen, The (Armadale) 41
French Shop, The (City) 53
Fresh Generation (City) 75
Freshwater Creek Cakes (Freshwater Creek) 153
Fritz Gelato (Richmond/St Kilda/South Melbourne/South Yarra) 79, 81
Fruit Pedallers Organic Food Store, The (Northcote) 114

G

Ganache Chocolate (South Yarra) viii, 37, 39
Gas Eatery & Supplies (South Melbourne) 20, 119
Gasworks Farmers' Market (Albert Park) 60
Genovese Coffee (Coburg East) 46
Gentle Annie Berry Gardens (Deans Marsh) 146
Gervasi Foodworks (Brunswick) 90
Giant Steps/Innocent Bystander Winery (Healesville) 140
Gillies Pie Shop (Bendigo) 160
Gingerboy (City) 132
Glace Gelato & Juice (Sorrento) 137
Glenora Heritage (Kyneton) 60
Gooramadda Olives (Gooramadda) 146
Gourmet Kids Cooking Workshops (Malvern) 41
Gourmet Larder (Daylesford) 144
Grand Ridge Brewery (Mirboo North) 139
Great Eastern Food Centre (City) 4
Green Grocer, The (Fitzroy North) 41, 115
Greensborough Cake Decorating Centre (Greensborough) 16
Greg's Gourmet Family Butchers (Rosebud) 138
Grill'd (Hawthorn) 32
Grinders Coffee House (Carlton) 48
Grossi Florentino Cellar Bar (City) 132
Gruners (St Kilda) 28

H

Hagen's Organic & Biodynamic Meats (City/South Yarra) 28
Haigh's Chocolates (City/Hawthorn/Toorak) 38, 39
Hausfrau (Yarraville) viii, 13, 19
Hearty Pies & Cakes (Geelong West) 160
Heiner's Bakery (Myrtleford) 160
Heronswood (Dromana) 147
Himalaya Bakery (Daylesford) 144
Hindustan Imports (Dandenong) 85
Holgate Bar and Restaurant (Woodend) 139
Hooked (Windsor) 70
Hootsen's Bakery Conditorei (Malvern) 14
Hume Murray Farmers' Market (Lincoln Causeway) 154
Huy Huy Supermarket (Richmond) 4

I

Il Dolce Freddo (Carlton) viii, 80, 81
Il Fornaio (Toorak/St Kilda) 14
Il Migliore (Hawthorn) 14
India Bazaar International (Dandenong) 85
Indian Impex (Dandenong) 85
Indomart Asian Grocers (Hawthorn) 4
Irrewarra Sourdough Bakery (Geelong) 12, 149
Istra Smallgoods (Musk) 144
Italian Gourmet Deli (Dandenong) 90

J

Jasper Coffee (Fitzroy/South Yarra) 48
Jock's Ice Cream & Sorbets (Albert Park) 80, 81
John Cester Poultry & Game (South Yarra) viii, 28
Jonathan's of Collingwood (Collingwood) 29
Journal Canteen (City) 132

K

K. M. Lynch Wine and Spirit Merchants (Warrnambool) 153
Katos Fish Supply (Geelong) 149
Kazachor (Bentleigh) 54
KFL Supermarket (Footscray) 4
King & Godfree (Carlton) 91
Kingfisher Seafoods (Camberwell) 69
Kingston Farmers' Market (Highett) 60, 61
Kitchen & Butcher (Healesville) 140
Klein's Kosher Gourmet (Ripponlea) 131
Knead (Hawthorn) 14
Koko Black (Camberwell/Carlton/Chadstone/City) 38, 39
Koonwarra Fine Food & Wine Store (Koonwarra) 158
Korea Kimchi Grocery (Fitzroy) 5
Kuche (Beaumaris) 98, 119, 121

L

La Bergerie (Canterbury) 54
La Madre Bakery (Bell Park) 149
La Parisienne Pates (Carlton) 26, 29
La Tropezienne (Hawthorn) 15
Lafayette Fine Food (Brighton) 121
Laguna Oriental and Indonesian Supermarket (Hawthorn) 5
Laikon Deli (Richmond) 54
Lakes Entrance Fisherman's Co-op (Lakes Entrance) 158
Lamont's Gourmet Meats (Hampton) 29
Lancefield District Farmers' Market (Lancefield) 154
Las Chicas (Balaclava) 20
Laurent Boulangerie Patisserie (City) 15
Le Croissant (Burwood) 17, 19
Le Petit Gateau (City) viii, 17, 19
Leaf (Elwood) 115
Leo's Fine Food & Wine (Heidelberg/Kew) 64
Let Them Eat Cake (South Melbourne) 17
Limonetto (Docklands) 80
Lizzy's Chocolate Creations (Carnegie) 38
Loafer Bread (Fitzroy North) 17
London & American Supply Stores (City) 99
Lonsdale Hydroponics (Point Lonsdale) 147

Lorne Fisheries (Lorne) 153
Lorne Greens (Lorne) 156
Ludo The Good Food Store (Sandringham) 54
Luscious Affairs (Toorak) 41
Luv-a-Duck (Port Melbourne/South Melbourne) 29
Lygon Food Store (Carlton) 93

M

M & C Seafoods (Preston) 71
McKenzie Ebbels Food Store (Queenscliff) 149
Macro Wholefoods Market (Armadale/Black Rock/Glen Waverley/Richmond) 115
Malmsbury Bakery (Malmsbury) 144
Maloa House Gourmet Delights (Woodend) 145
Mamma Lucia (Brunswick) 56
Mansfield Regional Produce Store (Mansfield) 158
Marg & Maree's (Heidelberg Heights) 16
Marmaris (Hampton) 110
Maroondah Orchards Fresh Fruit Stall (Coldstream) 147
Matisse Bread (Moorabbin) 18
Max Brenner (City/Glen Waverley/Maribyrnong/South Melbourne) 38
Maxim's Cakes (City) 5
Mediterranean Wholesalers (Brunswick) 64, 65
Meera Freeman Cooking Classes (Carlton) 41
Melbourne Kebab Station (Coburg) 123
Melbourne's Chinatown with Elizabeth Chong (City) 103
Melbourne Supper Club Bar (City) 123
Melissa Cake Shop (Collingwood/Thornbury) 18
Merryday (Cheltenham) 16
Middle East Bakeries (Brunswick) 111
Milawa Cheese Factory (Milawa) 142
Milawa Cheese Shop (Carlton North) 56
Milawa Mustards (Milawa) 158
Mildura Brewery (Mildura) 139
Minh Phat (City/Abbotsford) 5
Minimax (Brighton/Camberwell/Hawksburn) 99
Mixing Bowl, The (Burwood) 16
MKS Enterprises (Dandenong) 86

Monaco's Continental Delicatessen & Foodstore (Camberwell) 93
Monsieur Truffe (South Yarra) 39
Mornington Peninsula Chocolates (Merricks) 138
Mountain Goat Beer (Richmond) 127
Mount Zero Olives (Laharum) 147
MoVida (City) 133
Mr Tulk (City) 20
Mushroom Hunts in May (Main Ridge) 103

N
Nan Yang (Springvale) 6
Napoli Quality Fruit Market (Williamstown) 76
Natural Tucker Bakery (Carlton North) 18
Newtown Provedore (Newtown) 150
Nick and Sue's Gourmet Deli (Camberwell) 56
Noisette (Port Melbourne) 18

O
O Mu Ro (Brighton) 6
Oasis Bakery (Murrumbeena) 111
O'Heas Bakery & Deli (Coburg) 93
Old & Rare Wines Collector House (Southbank) 127
Oliv (Hawthorn) 93
Oliveria (Prahran) 94
O'psaras on Portman (Oakleigh) 71
Organic Gertrude (Fairfield) 115
Organic Union, The (Surrey Hills) 116
Organica (Prahran/South Melbourne) 116
Oriental Tea House (South Yarra/ City) 48, 133
Ormond Meat & Smallgoods (Ormond) 30
Oyster Little Bourke (City) 133

P
Paddy's Meats and Fine Wines (Kew) 30
Parkers Pies (Rutherglen) 160
Passionfoods (South Melbourne) 116
Pasta Eater, The (Black Rock) 94
Paterson's Cake Shop (Bentleigh/Camberwell/South Melbourne/Windsor) 19
Pearcedale Farmers' Market (Pearcedale) 155
Pellegrini's Espresso Bar (City) 46, 123

Pete 'n' Rosies (South Yarra) 57
Peter Watson (Fitzroy/South Melbourne) 65
Phillippa's (Armadale/Brighton) 12, 15, 19, 21
Pickadeli (South Melbourne) 57
Pizza & Fichi (Kew) 133
Plump Harvest Produce (Myrtleford) 159
Plump Organic Grocery (Yarraville) 116
Polish Deli (City) 57
Polkinghornes (Albert Park) 30
Port Albert Seafood (Port Albert) 151
Port Fairy Farmers' Market (Port Fairy) 155
Prahran Continental Butcher (Prahran) 30
Prahran Market (South Yarra) 105
Press Club, The (City) 133
Preston Market (Preston) 105
Prince Wine Store, The (St Kilda/South Melbourne) 128
Pronto Fine Food Merchants (Warrnambool) 156
Prosser's (City) 71
Provisions Food Store (Camberwell) 121
Punjab Sweet & Indian Takeaway (Dandenong) 87
Pure Bread Bakery (Surrey Hills) 21
Pyrenees Pies & Takeaway (Avoca) 160

Q
Q Foods (Albury) 159
Queen Victoria Market (City) 106
Queen Victoria Market Cooking School, The (City) 41
Queen Victoria Market Foodies' Tour (City) 103
Quist's Coffee (City) 46, 48

R
Randall's (Albert Park) 128
Rathdowne Cellars (Carlton North) 128
Rebecca's Cafe and Ice Creamery (Port Fairy) 156
Red Beard Bakery (Trentham) 145
Red Emperor (Southgate) 133
Red Hill Brewery (Red Hill South) 139
Red Hill Cheese (Red Hill) 142
Red Hill Kitchen, The (Red Hill) 138
Red Mullet (Malvern) 70

Rendina's Butchery (Balwyn North) 31
Replete Providore (Hawthorn) 15, 122
Richmond Hill Cafe & Larder (Richmond) 15, 56, 57
Ripe (Sassafras) 141
Ripe the Organic Grocer (Albert Park/South Yarra) 117
Rob's British Butchers (Dandenong) 31
Rockpool Bar & Grill (Southbank) 133
Roost (Malvern) 99
Ruffy Produce Store (Ruffy) 159
Russian Tidbits (Carnegie) 131

S

St Ali (South Melbourne) 20, 49
San Remo Fishermen's Co-Op (San Remo) 151
Savour Chocolate and Patisserie School (Brunswick East) 42
Scicluna's (Frankston/Mentone/Sorrento) 76, 138
Scruffy Bunch – Microbrewery Tours (City) 127
Scullerymade (Malvern) 99
Secrets of Sydney Road (Brunswick) 103
7 Apples Gelato (St Kilda) 80, 81
Silly Yaks Bakery Café (Northcote) 21
Silvan Estate Raspberries (Silvan South) 147
Simon Johnson, Purveyor of Quality Foods (Chadstone/Fitzroy/Toorak) 64, 65
Slow Food Melbourne Farmers' Market (Abbotsford) 60, 61
Solomon Kosher Butcher (Elsternwick) 31
Song Hiep (Springvale) 31
South African Shop, The (Templestowe) 134
South Gippsland Farmers' Market (Koonwarra) 155
South Melbourne Market (South Melbourne) 106
Spa Venison (Daylesford) 145
Spring Cakes (Dandenong) 111
Stalactites (City) 123
Starfish Bakery (Barwon Heads) 150
Sugardough Panificio and Patisserie (East Brunswick) 21
Sunbeam Cakes (Mentone) 22
Sunny Creek Fruit and Berry Farm (Trafalgar) 147
Sunny Ridge Strawberry Farm (Main Ridge) 147
Sunnybrae Cooking School (Birregurra) 42
Supper Inn (City) 123
Susie Q Cake Decorating Centre (Nidree) 16
Suzuran Japan Foods (Camberwell/South Yarra) 6
Sweet Decadence at Locantro (Daylesford) 145

T

T2 (Chadstone/City/Fitzroy) 49
Talbot Farmers' Market (Talbot) 155
Tangelo Fine Foods (Toorak/Brighton) 121, 122
Tanner's Swiss Patisserie (Syndal) 22
Tartine (Armadale) viii, 121, 122
Theo's & Sons Fresh Seafood (South Yarra) 71
Timboon Farmhouse Cheese (Timboon) 142
Timboon Railway Shed Distillery (Timboon) 156
Toby's Estate Coffee and Fine Select Teas (Brunswick) 49
Tokyo Deli (Elsternwick) 6
Tony Tan Cooking Classes (Toorak) 42
Top Shelf Fruits (Beaumaris) 76
Toscano's of Kew (Kew/Richmond) 76
Traditional Pasta Shop (City) 94
Trampoline (Chadstone/City/Doncaster/Fitzroy/Malvern/St Kilda/Southbank) 81
Treats from Home (City) 134
Trialto Meats (Elsternwick) 32
Tsukiji (Prahran) 7
Tunstall Fresh (Doncaster East) 77
Tutto Bene (Southbank) 81, 82
27 Deakin, Stefano's Good Food Store Cafe & Bakery (Mildura) 159
2 Brothers Brewery (Moorabbin) 127

U

Urban Burger (Port Melbourne) 32
USA Foods (Moorabbin) 134

V

V & R Fruit and Vegetable Market (Geelong West) 150
Vasiliki Fresh Crayfish Supply (St Kilda) 72

Veg Out St Kilda Farmers' Market (St Kilda) 60, 61
Vegetable Connection (Fitzroy) 77
Vintara Brewery (Rutherglen) 139
Vue de Monde (City) 133

W

Wangara Poultry & Game (Kensington) 33
Warren & Hutch (Geelong West) 150
Weston's Walnuts (Eurobin) 147
Wholefoods Food Store (Brighton) 117
William Angliss Institute of TAFE (City) 42
Win Sam Groceries (Glen Waverley) 8
Win Sam Seafood and Butcher (Glen Waverley) 72
Wing Cheong (City) 8
Wisharts Seafood at the Wharf (Port Fairy) 151
Wursthütte (Malvern) 33

X

Xocolatl (Canterbury/Kew East) 39

Y

Yarra Valley Dairy (Yering) 142
Yarra Valley Farmers' Market (Yering) 142
Yarra Valley Ice Cream Emporium (Healesville) 141
Yarra Valley Pasta (Healesville) 141
Yarra Valley Pasta (South Yarra) 94
Yering Station Produce Store (Yering) 141
Yoyo Sushi (Camberwell) 102
Yumi's Kosher Seafoods (Ripponlea) 72

Z

Zimt Patisserie Bakery Café (Mont Albert) 22

Locality index

A

ABBOTSFORD
Collingwood Children's Farm Farmers' Market 60
Minh Phat 5
Slow Food Melbourne Farmers' Market 60, 61

ALBERT PARK
Albert Park Deli 52
Albert Park Fruit Palace 74
Andrew's Hamburgers 32
Clamms Fast Fish 68, 70
Gasworks Farmers' Market 60
Jock's Ice Cream & Sorbets 80, 81
Polkinghornes 30
Randall's 128
Ripe the Organic Grocer 117

ALBURY
Butt's Gourmet Smokehouse 157
Q Foods 159

APOLLO BAY
Apollo Bay Fishermen's Co-op 152

ARMADALE
Armadale Cellars 125
French Kitchen, The 41
Macro Wholefoods Market 115
Phillippa's 12, 15, 19, 21
Tartine viii, 121, 122

AVOCA
Pyrenees Pies & Takeaway 160

B

BAIRNSDALE
East Gippsland Farmers' Market 154

BALACLAVA
Coffee Company, The 45
Las Chicas 20

BALLARAT
Ballarat Lakeside Market 154

BALWYN NORTH
Rendina's Butchery 31

BARWON HEADS
Annie's Provedore viii, 148
Starfish Bakery 150

BEAUMARIS
Ferg's Fish 69
Kuche 98, 119, 121
Top Shelf Fruits 76

BELL PARK
La Madre Bakery 149

BELMONT
Chas Cole Cellars 148

BENDIGO
Gillies Pie Shop 160

BENTLEIGH
Kazachor 54
Paterson's Cake Shop 19

locality index

BIRREGURRA
Farm Foods 153
Sunnybrae Cooking School 42

BLACK ROCK
Cerberus Kiosk 70
Macro Wholefoods Market 115
Pasta Eater, The 94

BLAIRGOWRIE
Cornell's Fresh Seafood 137

BOX HILL
Ducgo Live Seafood 69
Emma's Seafood Yong Tofu 3

BRIGHT
Bright Brewery 139
Food Wine Friends 157

BRIGHTON
Cloudwine 126
Devola's 75
Fish Tank 70
Lafayette Fine Food 121
Minimax 99
O Mu Ro 6
Phillippa's 12, 15, 19, 21
Tangelo Fine Foods 121, 122
Wholefoods Food Store 117

BRUNSWICK
Balha's Pastry 109
Bas Foods 110
El Fahya Sweets 110
Gervasi Foodworks 90
Mamma Lucia 56
Mediterranean Wholesalers 64, 65
Middle East Bakeries 111
Secrets of Sydney Road 103
Toby's Estate Coffee and Fine Select Teas 49

BRUNSWICK EAST
Savour Chocolate and Patisserie School 42

BULLARTO
Fernleigh Farm's Farm Store 143

BURWOOD
Le Croissant 17, 19
Mixing Bowl, The 16

C

CAMBERWELL
Brunetti Cakes 11
Camberwell Fresh Food Market 101
Cloudwine 126
Kingfisher Seafoods 69
Koko Black 38, 39
Minimax 99
Monaco's Continental Delicatessen & Foodstore 93
Nick and Sue's Gourmet Deli 56
Paterson's Cake Shop 19
Provisions Food Store 121
Suzuran Japan Foods 6
Yoyo Sushi 102

CANTERBURY
Donnini's Pasta 90
La Bergerie 54
Xocolatl 39

CARLTON
Brunetti Cakes 11
Casa del Gelato 79
Donati's Fine Meats 26
Donnini's Pasta 90
Grinders Coffee House 48
Il Dolce Freddo viii, 80, 81
King & Godfree 91
Koko Black 38, 39
La Parisienne Pates 26, 29
Lygon Food Store 93
Meera Freeman Cooking Classes 41

CARLTON NORTH
Canals, The Seafood Appreciation Centre 67
Enoteca Sileno 63, 64, 126

Filou's 13, 19
Milawa Cheese Shop 56
Natural Tucker Bakery 18
Rathdowne Cellars 128

CARNEGIE
Lizzy's Chocolate Creations 38
Russian Tidbits 131

CASTLEMAINE
Castlemaine Farmers' Market 154

CAULFIELD
Farinacci's Fresh Pasta 90

CHADSTONE
Bouchiers of Malvern Road 25, 26
David Jones Food Hall 63
Koko Black 38, 39
Simon Johnson, Purveyor of Quality Foods 64, 65
T2 49
Trampoline 81

CHELTENHAM
Merryday 16

CITY
Bar Lourinha 132
Bill's Farm 52, 56
Blufish 70
Borek Shop, The 102
Bouchiers of Malvern Road 25, 26
Brother Baba Budan 46
Brunetti Cakes 11
Cacao Fine Chocolates 35, 39
CAE Cooking School 40
Cake Deco 16
Chicken Pantry, The 25, 26
Chocoholic Tours 103
City Wine Shop 126
Coffea Café 102
Curds and Whey 53
David Jones Food Hall 63
Federal Coffee Palace 46
Foodies' Tours of Melbourne 103

French Shop, The 53
Fresh Generation 75
Gingerboy 132
Great Eastern Food Centre 4
Grossi Florentino Cellar Bar 132
Hagen's Organic & Biodynamic Meats 28
Haigh's Chocolates 38, 39
Journal Canteen 132
Koko Black 38, 39
Laurent Boulangerie Patisserie 15
Le Petit Gateau viii, 17, 19
London & American Supply Stores 99
Max Brenner 38
Maxim's Cakes 5
Melbourne Supper Club Bar 123
Melbourne's Chinatown with Elizabeth Chong 103
Minh Phat 5
MoVida 133
Mr Tulk 20
Oriental Tea House 48, 133
Oyster Little Bourke 133
Pellegrini's Espresso Bar 46, 123
Polish Deli 57
Press Club, The 133
Prosser's 71
Queen Victoria Market Cooking School, The 41
Queen Victoria Market Foodies' Tour 103
Queen Victoria Market 106
Quist's Coffee 46, 48
Scruffy Bunch – Microbrewery Tours 127
Stalactites 123
Supper Inn 123
T2 49
Traditional Pasta Shop 94
Trampoline 81
Treats from Home 134
Vue de Monde 133
William Angliss Institute of TAFE 42
Wing Cheong 8
Genovese Coffee 46

COBURG
Al-Alamy International Coffee & Nuts 108
Melbourne Kebab Station 123
O'Heas Bakery & Deli 93

locality index

COLDSTREAM
Bella Vedere 40
Maroondah Orchards Fresh Fruit Stall 147

COLLINGWOOD
Jonathan's of Collingwood 29
Melissa Cake Shop 18

COORIEMUNGLE
Apostle Whey Cheese 142

D

DANDENONG
A1 Bakery 108
Calcutta Sweets 84
Dandenong Arcade Fish Supply 68
Hindustan Imports 85
India Bazaar International 85
Indian Impex 85
Italian Gourmet Deli 90
MKS Enterprises 86
Punjab Sweet & Indian Takeaway 87
Rob's British Butchers 31
Spring Cakes 111

DAYLESFORD
Cliffy's Emporium 143
Gourmet Larder 144
Himalaya Bakery 144
Spa Venison 145
Sweet Decadence at Locantro 145

DEANS MARSH
Gentle Annie Berry Gardens 146

DIXONS CREEK
De Bortoli Cheese Room 142

DOCKLANDS
Fish Bar 70
Limonetto 80

DONCASTER
Colossus Supermarket 131
Trampoline 81

DONCASTER EAST
D. A. Di Censo & Sons 26
Tunstall Fresh 77

DROMANA
Heronswood 147

E

EAST BRUNSWICK
Sugardough Panificio and Patisserie 21

EAST MELBOURNE
Europa Cellars 126

ECHUCA
Central Murray Produce Farmers' Market 154
Fish in a Flash 151

ELSTERNWICK
Aviv Cakes & Bagels 10
Frank's Elsternwick Bakery 13
Solomon Kosher Butcher 31
Tokyo Deli 6
Trialto Meats 32

ELTHAM
Dynamic Vegies Organic Food Supply 114

ELWOOD
Leaf 115

EUROBIN
Weston's Walnuts 147

F

FAIRFIELD
Biviano & Sons 75
Brenta Meats 25
Cardamone 89
Organic Gertrude 115

FITZROY
Babka Bakery Cafe 10
Bangla Sweets & Curry Café 84

locality index

MERRICKS
Mornington Peninsula Chocolates 138

MILAWA
Milawa Cheese Factory 142
Milawa Mustards 158

MILDURA
Mildura Brewery 139
27 Deakin, Stefano's Good Food Store Cafe & Bakery 159

MIRBOO NORTH
Grand Ridge Brewery 139

MONT ALBERT
Zimt Patisserie Bakery Café 22

MOORABBIN
2 Brothers Brewery 127
Matisse Bread 18
USA Foods 134

MORNINGTON
Frank's Classic Bakery 137

MOUNT FRANKLIN
Chocolate Mill, The 143

MOUNT WAVERLEY
Beverley Sutherland Smith Cooking School 40

MURRUMBEENA
Oasis Bakery 111

MUSK
Istra Smallgoods 144

MYRTLEFORD
Heiner's Bakery 160
Plump Harvest Produce 159

N

NEWTOWN
Newtown Provedore 150

NIDREE
Susie Q Cake Decorating Centre 16

NORTH MELBOURNE
Di Bella Coffee Roasting Warehouse 45

NORTHCOTE
Beraldo Coffee 44
Coco Loco 37
Fruit Pedallers Organic Food Store, The 114
Silly Yaks Bakery Café 21

O

OAKLEIGH
O'psaras on Portman 71

ORMOND
Ormond Meat & Smallgoods 30

OXLEY
Blue Ox Blueberry Farm 146

P

PAKENHAM
Cardinia Ranges Farmers' Market 59

PEARCEDALE
Pearcedale Farmers' Market 155

POINT LONSDALE
Lonsdale Hydroponics 147

PORT ALBERT
Port Albert Seafood 151

PORT FAIRY
Cobbs Bakery 152
Port Fairy Farmers' Market 155
Rebecca's Cafe and Ice Creamery 156
Wisharts Seafood at the Wharf 151

locality index

COLDSTREAM
Bella Vedere 40
Maroondah Orchards Fresh Fruit Stall 147

COLLINGWOOD
Jonathan's of Collingwood 29
Melissa Cake Shop 18

COORIEMUNGLE
Apostle Whey Cheese 142

D

DANDENONG
A1 Bakery 108
Calcutta Sweets 84
Dandenong Arcade Fish Supply 68
Hindustan Imports 85
India Bazaar International 85
Indian Impex 85
Italian Gourmet Deli 90
MKS Enterprises 86
Punjab Sweet & Indian Takeaway 87
Rob's British Butchers 31
Spring Cakes 111

DAYLESFORD
Cliffy's Emporium 143
Gourmet Larder 144
Himalaya Bakery 144
Spa Venison 145
Sweet Decadence at Locantro 145

DEANS MARSH
Gentle Annie Berry Gardens 146

DIXONS CREEK
De Bortoli Cheese Room 142

DOCKLANDS
Fish Bar 70
Limonetto 80

DONCASTER
Colossus Supermarket 131
Trampoline 81

DONCASTER EAST
D. A. Di Censo & Sons 26
Tunstall Fresh 77

DROMANA
Heronswood 147

E

EAST BRUNSWICK
Sugardough Panificio and Patisserie 21

EAST MELBOURNE
Europa Cellars 126

ECHUCA
Central Murray Produce Farmers' Market 154
Fish in a Flash 151

ELSTERNWICK
Aviv Cakes & Bagels 10
Frank's Elsternwick Bakery 13
Solomon Kosher Butcher 31
Tokyo Deli 6
Trialto Meats 32

ELTHAM
Dynamic Vegies Organic Food Supply 114

ELWOOD
Leaf 115

EUROBIN
Weston's Walnuts 147

F

FAIRFIELD
Biviano & Sons 75
Brenta Meats 25
Cardamone 89
Organic Gertrude 115

FITZROY
Babka Bakery Cafe 10
Bangla Sweets & Curry Café 84

Books for Cooks 96
Casa Iberica 130
Chocolateria San Churro 37
Fatto A Mano 12, 15
Jasper Coffee 48
Korea Kimchi Grocery 5
Peter Watson 65
Simon Johnson, Purveyor of Quality Foods 64, 65
T2 49
Trampoline 81
Vegetable Connection 77

FITZROY NORTH
Danny's Takeaway 32
Dench Bakers 12
Green Grocer, The 41, 115
Loafer Bread 17

FOOTSCRAY
Conway 68
Emma's Seafood Yong Tofu 3
Footscray Market 102
KFL Supermarket 4

FRANKSTON
Scicluna's 76, 138

FRESHWATER CREEK
Freshwater Creek Cakes 153

G

GEELONG
Irrewarra Sourdough Bakery 12, 149
Katos Fish Supply 149

GEELONG WEST
Hearty Pies & Cakes 160
V & R Fruit and Vegetable Market 150
Warren & Hutch 150

GLEN WAVERLEY
Macro Wholefoods Market 115
Max Brenner 38

Win Sam Groceries 8
Win Sam Seafood and Butcher 72

GOORAMADDA
Gooramadda Olives 146

GREENSBOROUGH
Greensborough Cake Decorating Centre 16

H

HAMILTON
Darriwill Farm 157
Farm Foods 153

HAMPTON
Chocolatier 37
Fegari Seafood 69
Ferg's Fish 69
Lamont's Gourmet Meats 29
Marmaris 110

HARCOURT
Deumer's Harcourt Valley Orchard 146

HAWKSBURN
Bouchiers of Malvern Road 25, 26
Donnini's Pasta 90
Minimax 99

HAWTHORN
Aquanas Seafood 67
Grill'd 32
Haigh's Chocolates 38, 39
Il Migliore 14
Indomart Asian Grocers 4
Knead 14
La Tropezienne 15
Laguna Oriental and Indonesian Supermarket 5
Oliv 93
Replete Providore 15, 122

HAWTHORN EAST
Boroondara Farmers' Market 59, 60

locality index **185**

HEALESVILLE
Beef Joint, The 140
Giant Steps/Innocent Bystander Winery 140
Kitchen & Butcher 140
Yarra Valley Ice Cream Emporium 141
Yarra Valley Pasta 141

HEIDELBERG
Leo's Fine Food & Wine 64

HEIDELBERG HEIGHTS
Marg & Maree's 16

HIGHETT
Kingston Farmers' Market 60, 61

HORSHAM
Conway's Pies 160

I

IVANHOE
Chocolatier 37
Donnini's Pasta 90

K

KENSINGTON
Wangara Poultry & Game 33

KEW
Elizabeth Chong 40
Leo's Fine Food & Wine 64
Paddy's Meats and Fine Wines 30
Pizza & Fichi 133
Toscano's of Kew 76

KEW EAST
Xocolatl 39

KOONWARRA
Koonwarra Fine Food & Wine Store 158
South Gippsland Farmers' Market 155

KYNETON
Glenora Heritage 60

L

LAHARUM
Mount Zero Olives 147

LAKES ENTRANCE
Lakes Entrance Fisherman's Co-op 158

LANCEFIELD
Lancefield District Farmers' Market 154

LINCOLN CAUSEWAY
Hume Murray Farmers' Market 154

LORNE
Lorne Fisheries 153
Lorne Greens 156

M

MAIN RIDGE
Mushroom Hunts in May 103
Sunny Ridge Strawberry Farm 147

MALMSBURY
Malmsbury Bakery 144

MALVERN
Continental Kosher Butchers 25
Gourmet Kids Cooking Workshops 41
Hootsen's Bakery Conditorei 14
Red Mullet 70
Roost 99
Scullerymade 99
Trampoline 81
Wursthütte 33

MANSFIELD
Mansfield Regional Produce Store 158

MARIBYRNONG
Max Brenner 38

MENTONE
Scicluna's 76, 138
Sunbeam Cakes 22

MERRICKS
Mornington Peninsula Chocolates 138

MILAWA
Milawa Cheese Factory 142
Milawa Mustards 158

MILDURA
Mildura Brewery 139
27 Deakin, Stefano's Good Food Store Cafe &
   Bakery 159

MIRBOO NORTH
Grand Ridge Brewery 139

MONT ALBERT
Zimt Patisserie Bakery Café 22

MOORABBIN
2 Brothers Brewery 127
Matisse Bread 18
USA Foods 134

MORNINGTON
Frank's Classic Bakery 137

MOUNT FRANKLIN
Chocolate Mill, The 143

MOUNT WAVERLEY
Beverley Sutherland Smith Cooking School 40

MURRUMBEENA
Oasis Bakery 111

MUSK
Istra Smallgoods 144

MYRTLEFORD
Heiner's Bakery 160
Plump Harvest Produce 159

N

NEWTOWN
Newtown Provedore 150

NIDREE
Susie Q Cake Decorating Centre 16

NORTH MELBOURNE
Di Bella Coffee Roasting Warehouse 45

NORTHCOTE
Beraldo Coffee 44
Coco Loco 37
Fruit Pedallers Organic Food Store, The 114
Silly Yaks Bakery Café 21

O

OAKLEIGH
O'psaras on Portman 71

ORMOND
Ormond Meat & Smallgoods 30

OXLEY
Blue Ox Blueberry Farm 146

P

PAKENHAM
Cardinia Ranges Farmers' Market 59

PEARCEDALE
Pearcedale Farmers' Market 155

POINT LONSDALE
Lonsdale Hydroponics 147

PORT ALBERT
Port Albert Seafood 151

PORT FAIRY
Cobbs Bakery 152
Port Fairy Farmers' Market 155
Rebecca's Cafe and Ice Creamery 156
Wisharts Seafood at the Wharf 151

locality index

PORT MELBOURNE
D'lish Fish 70
Eurodore 53
Luv-a-Duck 29
Noisette 18
Urban Burger 32

PORTARLINGTON
Aussie Blue Mussels 148

PRAHRAN
Brioche 11
Oliveria 94
Organica 116
Prahran Continental Butcher 30
Tsukiji 7

PRESTON
Cedar Bakery 110
M & C Seafoods 71
Preston Market 105

Q

QUEENSCLIFF
Farm Foods 153
McKenzie Ebbels Food Store 149

R

RED HILL
Ellisfield Farm 146
Red Hill Cheese 142
Red Hill Kitchen, The 138

RED HILL SOUTH
Red Hill Brewery 139

RICHMOND
Fritz Gelato 79, 81
Huy Huy Supermarket 4
Laikon Deli 54
Macro Wholefoods Market 115
Mountain Goat Beer 127
Richmond Hill Cafe & Larder 15, 56, 57
Toscano's of Kew 76

RIPPONLEA
Attica 132
Firebrand Sourdough Bakery 13
Klein's Kosher Gourmet 131
Yumi's Kosher Seafoods 72

ROSEBUD
Greg's Gourmet Family Butchers 138

RUFFY
Adrian & Valda Martin's Biodynamic Fruit 146
Ruffy Produce Store 159

RUTHERGLEN
Parkers Pies 160
Vintara Brewery 139

S

ST KILDA
Baker D. Chirico 11, 12, 19
Cacao Fine Chocolates 35, 39
Clamms Fast Fish 68, 70
Donovan's 132
Fritz Gelato 79, 81
Gruners 28
Il Fornaio 14
Prince Wine Store, The 128
7 Apples Gelato 80, 81
Trampoline 81
Vasiliki Fresh Crayfish Supply 72
Veg Out St Kilda Farmers' Market 60, 61

SAN REMO
San Remo Fishermen's Co-Op 151

SANDRINGHAM
Ludo The Good Food Store 54

SASSAFRAS
Ripe 141

SILVAN SOUTH
Silvan Estate Raspberries 147

SORRENTO
D'lish Fish 151
Glace Gelato & Juice 137
Scicluna's 76, 138

SOUTH MELBOURNE
Aptus Seafoods 102
Café Sweethearts 20
Chef's Hat 96
Chocolate Lover, The 35
Cloudwine 126
Cottle Coffee, Tea and Nuts 45
Daley at Chimmy's 11
Emerald Hill Brewery 127
Fritz Gelato 79, 81
Gas Eatery & Supplies 20, 119
Let Them Eat Cake 17
Luv-a-Duck 29
Max Brenner 38
Organica 116
Passionfoods 116
Paterson's Cake Shop 19
Peter Watson 65
Pickadeli 57
Prince Wine Store, The 128
South Melbourne Market 106
St Ali 20, 49

SOUTH YARRA
Botanical Hotel, The 20
Botanical Wine Store 125
Claringbold's Seafoods 68
Curry Creations 85
Damian Pike, Wild Mushroom Specialist viii, 75
Delicatess 26, 53, 56
Essential Ingredient, The 41, 64, 98
Fritz Gelato 79, 81
Ganache Chocolate vii, 37, 39
Hagen's Organic & Biodynamic Meats 28
Jasper Coffee 48
John Cester Poultry & Game viii, 28
Monsieur Truffe 39
Oriental Tea House 48, 133
Pete 'n' Rosies 57
Prahran Market 105

Ripe the Organic Grocer 117
Suzuran Japan Foods 6
Theo's & Sons Fresh Seafood 71
Yarra Valley Pasta 94

SOUTHBANK
Old & Rare Wines Collector House 127
Rockpool Bar & Grill 133
Trampoline 81
Tutto Bene 81, 82

SOUTHGATE
Red Emperor 133

SPRINGVALE
AKK Supermarket 3
Dunav Butcher 28
Emma's Seafood Yong Tofu 3
Nan Yang 6
Song Hiep 31

SURREY HILLS
Organic Union, The 116
Pure Bread Bakery 21

SYNDAL
Tanner's Swiss Patisserie 22

T

TALBOT
Talbot Farmers' Market 155

TEMPLESTOWE
South African Shop, The 134

THORNBURY
Belmore Biodynamic Meats 24
Coffee Mio 45
Melissa Cake Shop 18

TIMBOON
Timboon Farmhouse Cheese 142
Timboon Railway Shed Distillery 156

TOORAK
Haigh's Chocolates 38, 39
Il Fornaio 14
Luscious Affairs 41
Simon Johnson, Purveyor of Quality Foods 64, 65
Tangelo Fine Foods 121, 122
Tony Tan Cooking Classes 42

TORQUAY
Farm Foods 153
Flippin' Fresh Seafoods 151

TRAFALGAR
Sunny Creek Fruit and Berry Farm 147

TRENTHAM
Red Beard Bakery 145

TULLAMARINE
Aztec Imports 130

W

WARRANDYTE
Aumann Family Orchard 74

WARRNAMBOOL
All Fresh Seafoods 152
K. M. Lynch Wine and Spirit Merchants 153
Pronto Fine Food Merchants 156

WERRIBEE
Essence Food Studio 41

WEST MELBOURNE
Embassy Taxi Cafe 123

WILLIAMSTOWN
Napoli Quality Fruit Market 76

WINDSOR
Cisco's World of Coffee 44
Flavours, Herbs & Spices 131
Hooked 70
Paterson's Cake Shop 19

WOODEND
Diana Marsland Cooking 40
Holgate Bar and Restaurant 139
Maloa House Gourmet Delights 145

Y

YARRAVILLE
Alligator Brand 89
Andrew's Choice 24
Hausfrau viii, 13, 19
Plump Organic Grocery 116

YERING
Yarra Valley Dairy 142
Yarra Valley Farmers' Market 142
Yering Station Produce Store 141

Published in 2008 by
Hardie Grant Books
85 High Street
Prahran, Victoria 3181, Australia
www.hardiegrant.com.au

All rights reserved. No part of this publication may be reproduced, stored in a retrieval system or transmitted in any form by any means, electronic, mechanical, photocopying, recording or otherwise, without the prior written permission of the publishers and copyright holders.

The moral rights of the authors have been asserted.

Copyright text © 2008 Allan Campion and Michele Curtis

ISBN 978 1 74066 634 3

Text design by Sharyn Raggett
Cover design by Greendot Design
Cover photography by Tim James
Cover food styling and propping by Deborah Kaloper
Typesetting by Kirby Jones
Maps by Country Cartographics
Printed and bound in Australia by BPA Print Group

Internal photographs courtesy iStockphoto and Shutterstock (23, 58, 62, 113)

The Age is a registered trademark of the Age Company Limited

Any and all advertising space sold in connection with this publication is totally independent of and unconnected to the editorial content and opinions of the editors, contributors and authors expressed therein.

10 9 8 7 6 5 4 3 2 1

'The selection of recipes is outstanding ...'
STEPHANIE ALEXANDER

IN THE KITCHEN

ALLAN CAMPION AND MICHELE CURTIS

$69.95 hardback

more than **1000** recipes for every day

Ease into your kitchen today with Australia's new bible of home cooking.

More than 1000 recipes for every day

Hardie Grant Books

$29.95 paperback

2009

The Foodies' Diary

Seasonal produce, recipes, festivals and farmers' markets

Allan Campion   Michele Curtis

epicure   good living

Inspiration for every foodie on what to eat and cook based on the best fresh produce available each month of the year.

Includes more than 60 delicious recipes with stunning colour photography throughout

Hardie Grant Books